LABOUR OF LOVE IN LIVERPOOL

A HISTORY OF BETHEL CHAPEL, HEATHFIELD ROAD LIVERPOOL

D. BEN REES

Modern Welsh Publications Ltd

The History of Bethel, Heathfield Road Chapel, Liverpool 15 and the experiences of the members of Smithdown Place Schoolroom, Webster Road Chapel, Ramilies Road schoolroom, Heathfield Road and Bethel chapels. The story from Smithdown Lane to Smithdown Place, by Penny Lane (1864-2008).

D. Ben Rees

Published by Modern Welsh Publications Ltd., Allerton, Liverpool 18 for the Presbyterian Church of Wales, Bethel, Heathfield Road, Liverpool 15.

Modern Welsh Publications
2008

The publishers would like to acknowledge the assistance and guidance of every member of the Consultative Committee of Bethel Presbyterian Church of Wales in producing this book.

Hardback ISBN 978-0-901332-89-9
Paperback ISBN 978-0-901332-90-5

This beautiful volume is published with the financial support of the Liverpool Presbytery of the Presbyterian Church of Wales, Bethel Sunday School as well as Modern Welsh Publications and other individuals who are named in the Welsh version of this remarkable story of the Welsh in the city of Liverpool.

Published by Modern Welsh Publications Ltd, Allerton, Liverpool. Designed by Siôn Morris of Cinnamon Design, Liverpool and printed and bound by Gomer Press, Llandysul, Ceredigion, Wales.

Cyflwynedig i Dafydd a Hefin, Tomos a Joshua,
ffrindiau da i'w tad a'u tad-cu.
(Dedicated to Dafydd and Hefin, Tomos
and Joshua, loyal friends to their father and
grandfather, D. Ben Rees).

Members of the Consultative Committee for the Two Volumes:

Reverend Dr D. Ben Rees (Chairman)
Gareth James,
Humphrey Wyn Jones,
Roderick Owen,
Siôn Wyn Morris (Designer)
Dr Patricia Williams (Secretary).

CONTENTS

CHAPTERS **Page.**

INTRODUCTION

At a meeting of the Publications Consultative Committee of our church on 26 March 2007 we all agreed that an English version of the history of the Welsh language churches of Smithdown Lane, Webster Road, Heathfield Road and Bethel should be published in English. I had completed the first draft of the Welsh language version called *Codi Stêm a Hwyl yn Lerpwl* and was encouraged by Dr Pat Williams, Gareth James, and Siôn Wyn Morris to consider preparing this volume. I began immediately that very week and I am grateful that, within six weeks, I had completed the first draft. I am grateful to Dr W T Rees Pryce, Dr J. Gwynfor Jones and Dr Pat Williams for reading this version and making important suggestions as well as the input of the committee to the eventual appearance of a volume that will serve as a comprehensive record of the Welsh contribution to their city of adoption. It makes sense that this volume was written in the year we celebrated eight hundred years of Liverpool history, a world heritage city. The photographs add greatly to this book. The same material, most of it in the Welsh language, which has been inaccessible to our English friends and neighbours in Liverpool, can now be read. Most of the people commemorated in this book could say with John Elias, the gifted popular preacher from Anglesey, who loved Liverpool:

> If any good has been done by my imperfect labour, God in his grace performed it. To him belongs the glory; I was as nothing.

The Strategy and Stewardship Committee, as well as the Elders of Bethel, have been very supportive of this project. I hope readers will enjoy reading the historical account of the Welsh people in one specific area of Liverpool.

D. BEN REES
1 February 2008

Chapter 1

THE LEGACY OF SMITHDOWN LANE

The story of Bethel Chapel, Heathfield Road, Liverpool 15 is an account of the courage of the Welsh in Liverpool. An alternative title of this book could easily be 'From Smithdown Lane to Smithdown Place', for the move from their former chapel in Smithdown Road, as we shall see in this chapter, took fifty years to complete. The Welsh came in their hundreds from 1770 onwards, attracted by the growing affluence of Liverpool in its heyday as an important centre for the slave trade. Many of the Welsh sailors were employed on the slave ships, not as captains but as sailors. The majority made Liverpool their base, in the area around Pall Mall and Tithebarn Street. It was in Pall Mall that they built their first chapel in 1787, and from then until the 1920s of the twentieth century they built at least 70 chapels, churches, mission halls in Liverpool and Bootle.

There were a number of reasons for this decision. Worshipping in English churches and chapels in Liverpool did not satisfy their spiritual hunger for God's Word to be proclaimed in the language of their own upbringing. Worshipping in rented buildings made them feel like lodgers; consequently they desired to purchase their own centres and to be completely independent. The services in the Anglican churches and Nonconformist chapels were conducted through the medium of English, whereas the worshippers had been brought up in the rural areas of Wales as monoglot Welsh speakers, and the majority had suffered economic hardship through religious persecution at the hands of Anglican clergymen and the landowners, who supported the parish church structure. These young Welsh men and women did not desire a building that would cater for their spiritual needs for an hour or two on a Sunday but a building that would be open to them every night of the week, a home from home. They longed for home, and the chapel was the pivot of their spiritual lives, as well as their social centre. They wanted to preserve the symbol of their strong Nonconformist faith, and this is why they opened the first Welsh chapel in Pall Mall Liverpool in 1787.

Secondly, the Welsh who flocked to Liverpool would have failed to survive in Liverpool without the assistance of the chapels. They did not

The Welsh came in their hundreds to Liverpool

Smithdown Lane today

build secular or even inter-denominational centres, but established churches with allegiance to the various religious denominations, which existed in Wales at that time. In 1787 the Welsh of Pall Mall built a Welsh Calvinistic Methodist chapel, as it was easier to get support from the Calvinistic Methodist Presbyteries, though officially they were within the Anglican Church. The Baptists and the Independents were fully fledged denominations, so it was natural for them to establish their denominational chapels. Every denomination wanted to be represented in the growing town of Liverpool, to wave its badges of office and to attract as many Welsh people as possible to join their community.

Calvinistic Methodism which until 1811 was a movement within the Anglican Church, insisted on being a thriving movement that had its own symbols of power, such as a chapel that they had themselves planned and built. They built their second chapel in Bedford Street in 1806, and in Rose Place in 1826 and in Burlington Street, near the Docks, in 1829. In reality Pall Mall was very close to the Liverpool to Leeds Canal; Bedford Street was in an area where the Welsh had settled, while Rose Place and Burlington Street were in a bustling part of Liverpool. But between Rose Place and Bedford Street, the Welsh Calvinistic Methodists were without a Welsh religious centre. The Welsh Anglicans had established an extremely flourishing community in Russell Street (just behind the modern day Adelphi Hotel complex), and the Welsh Independents (Annibynwyr) had established centres in Great Crosshall Street and later Brownlow Hill. There was a large number of streets in the vicinity of London Road,

Brownlow Hill, Mount Pleasant, where there were Welsh people who were not Anglicans or Independents, and the Calvinistic Methodists saw their opportunity.

The Welsh needed another centre. By 1839 the Calvinistic Methodists were ready to extend their influence and they found a room in Great Oxford Street, near Brownlow Hill, where they held a Sunday School. They did not stay long. They found a more accessible room in Pembroke Street. This street was close to Brownlow Hill but also within striking distance of Pembroke Place, an area which became very familiar to Welsh medical men and women. Thousands of patients from north Wales, attended the Royal Liverpool Hospital, when it was situated in this locality. By 1841 they had moved again, this time towards Mount Pleasant. They bought land in Mulberry Street, a road which today links Mount Pleasant with Myrtle Street and Catharine Street, to build a large chapel to hold a congregation of five hundred. This chapel was first opened on 21 March 1841 and then, on 27 September, they arranged to elect elders from the membership. Only one elder was chosen, namely David Davies, Mount Gardens, a kind-hearted businessman who cared deeply for the cause in Mulberry Street chapel. They were fortunate in persuading the Reverend Henry Rees, a native of Llansannan and a brother of the Welsh Independent minister, the Reverend William Rees (Gwilym Hiraethog) to settle in Liverpool. Both proved themselves to be outstanding men of faith in Victorian Liverpool. Henry Rees came to live near the chapel in 1834. In that same year, his brother moved to minister to the Welsh Independents on Brownlow Hill and later at Grove Street Chapel.

The Lane where it all started

Reverend William Rees
(Gwilym Hiraethog: 1802-83)

Mulberry Street succeeded in gaining members, 107 in 1841, 242 in 1847: then, in 1850, there were 257 and by 1853 the total was 321. The number of members increased to 368, and in 1859 it reached a total of 409. In addition to those committed as members there were hundreds who were listeners without committing themselves to membership. The building was too small, so they decided to move. Some in the congregation wanted to relocate in Myrtle Street, others in Grove Street, but in the end they bought a piece of land from the Liverpool Corporation in Chatham Street. This building became one of the finest chapels in the city. The University of Liverpool bought the chapel in 1949, and in 2002 the Merseyside Welsh Heritage Society placed a plaque on its frontage to commemorate Henry Rees.

In the period 1840 to 1860 a new settlement appeared on the south side of Liverpool. The name for this neighbourhood is Windsor. This was to the south of Crown Street and towards Smithdown Lane, and further up to Upper Parliament Street and Lodge Lane. A large number of Welsh-speaking families had moved into the Windsor Ward, and since Chatham Street Chapel, guided by the Reverend Henry Rees, had a genuine concern for them, they arranged a Sunday School to be held in a rented room in Holden Street, a road from Crown Street towards Upper Parliament Street. There were 130 attending this Sunday School in 1864, and a year later their numbers had increased to 154. Out of the 154 there were 60 children who needed basic grounding in the Christian faith. They soon experienced the same situation as their predecessors: lack of accommodation, because the rented room had become too small. Chatham Street decided to build a new schoolroom in Smithdown Lane, nearly opposite Chatsworth Street, and the new building was opened on 10 April 1864. The building costs came to £1,100. Soon the number attended increased from 170 in 1864 to 278 in 1865, including 108 children. The adults were members of either Chatham Street or Bedford Street Welsh Presbyterian Chapels. Unfortunately a disagreement arose between the trustees of the two chapels and the leaders of Smithdown Lane Sunday School concerning extending their activities. The local leaders wanted to hold a service on Sunday evenings and weekly meetings as there was a substantial number of Welsh speakers in the vicinity who were not members of either Chatham Street or Bedford Street Chapels. Soon they had arranged morning and evening services, with Sunday School in the afternoon, until the officers of the Liverpool Presbytery claimed the key to the building. The local leaders relented but the need and the desire remained. The Presbytery as well as the two chapels had to reconsider their position and in 1866 they conceived an interesting plan. It was the appointment of a Chaplain in the area, and they eventually appointed a young man, Daniel David Jones, from Adwy'r Clawdd near Coedpoeth, Wrexham who later was to minister at Bangor. Chatham Street Chapel paid his salary and expenses.

These two chapels attracted exceptional ministers. The Reverend Dr David Saunders took care of Bedford Street and later took the initiative in persuading his flock to build a new large chapel in Princes Road in 1865. In Chatham Street, the Reverend Henry Rees had built a church of compassion with active missionary outreach. When he first came to Liverpool the Reverend John Elias of Anglesey wrote to him on 2 March 1838 on the need for enthusiasm as a Christian minister. John Elias told his younger friend:

> Therefore, my dear friend, take courage and be strong: draw near to the throne of grace, for 'grace and mercy in the time of need.' Commit the cause of the church in all its dangers to him, that he may govern the minds and tongues of all. Do not cherish the wavering that is in your mind respecting your stay in Liverpool. The field, it is true, is very extensive for you to cultivate, and you also feeble; but you are in an advantageous position to seek to do good: and though you cannot of yourself do anything, yet thy Lord can make use of you as an instrument.

This was an honest piece of advice and Henry Rees was used extensively by the Lord in his Liverpool pastorate. The success of Welsh Presbyterianism in Liverpool between 1836 and 1869 was largely due to the brilliance and the godliness of Henry Rees and his co-worker, the Reverend John Hughes, who wrote the three volumes *Hanes Methodistiaeth Cymru* (The History of Welsh Methodism) between 1853 and 1856.

Henry Rees had extensive gifts, a remarkable memory, a wonderful voice, a striking personality who could enthraul his large congregation with his *hwyl*. Henry Rees's voice would gradually rise into a crescendo of eloquence, his brow covered with beads of sweat, his face indicating his intense conviction, an astounding revelation of God's message. His sermons were a public revelation of his own inner Godliness.

Reverend Henry Rees (1798-1869)

We cannot express fully the grief that came to the Welsh Presbyterians in Liverpool on 18 February 1869 when the Reverend Henry Rees died at the home of his daughter, Mrs Annie Davies at Benarth, near Conwy. His doctor, Dr Robert Gee, (the brother of the Denbigh based publisher Thomas Gee) had travelled from Liverpool to Conwy. He realised that he could not help his beloved minister and he returned to inform the members of Chatham Street and Smithdown Lane of his serious illness. The *Seiat* [Society] was turned into a prayer meeting.

The following year Daniel David Jones, the young chaplain mentioned earlier, moved. He had done a good day's work to keep the Missionary Church at Smithdown Lane in a flourishing state. They continued without any assistance for nearly two decades. By 1882 there were at least 300 Welsh people frequenting the Smithdown Lane Schoolroom. In fact, on Sundays the schoolroom was so well attended, that they considered building a new centre. They also felt that they should move closer to Lodge Lane, and after years of considering the situation they decided to move to the area where there was extensive building taking place, around Earle Road and the southern part of Smithdown Road. There was a large area to the north of Smithdown Cemetery and the Workhouse Hospital. Here they bought land in Webster Road and that was to become the new centre.

A schoolroom which catered for the Welsh Anglicans of Smithdown Road area.

Princes Road Church which needs renovation

Areas of importance in the saga of the Liverpool Welsh.

Welsh countryside

Typical Welsh homestead at the end of the Victorian era.

Beauty of Wales.

A home of an immigrant from Anglesey.

Watching for ships in distress on their way past Anglesey and Moelfre to Liverpool.

Chapter 2

EARLY EFFORTS IN WEBSTER ROAD
(1889-1896)

The efforts and initiative of those in Smithdown Lane to move to a new building in Webster Road is a story worth recording. It shows the determination of those Welshmen and women to exert their presence in the religious life of Liverpool. It reminds one of similar efforts in other parts of Britain, such as the determination of William Bray, a Methodist preacher in Cornwall, who built three chapels with his own hands. Some of his contemporaries regarded him as out of his mind. Billy Bray would answer them: 'Wise men could not have preached in the Chapel if Silly Billy had not built it.' It was the similar sense of courage, endeavour and commitment amongst the Calvinistic Methodists of Smithdown Place at the end of the nineteenth century as was experienced by Billy Bray and his followers in Cornwall earlier in the century.

In Liverpool as in Cornwall there were critics of the Welsh building decision. The main concern in Liverpool was that the new chapel in Webster Road was so far from the bulk of the population. It is true there were new streets being laid out below the Workhouse Hospital (where the large Asda store is located today) and Smithdown Road Hospital where at the time there were open fields. From there up to Penny Lane and Calderstones there were only green fields. The critics would remind everyone that 'Liverpool would never extend its boundaries as far as Calderstones'. It was deemed impossible for people to go to their work in Liverpool from such a distance, and they were afraid that the site of the new chapel would be too inaccessible to those who had been involved in Smithdown Lane. The same fear was expressed in 1926 when they built Heathfield Road Chapel, and also when the Webster Road congregation moved to another new home.

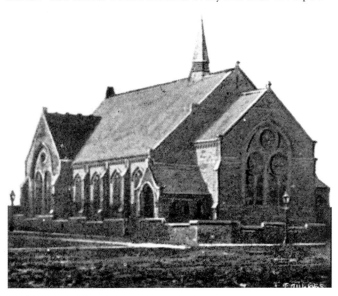

Webster Road in 1889

The officers of the Building Committee of Webster Road, three men who had been the leading lights in Smithdown

Place, namely William Parry, Parliament Street (Chairman), John Jones, Tennyson Street (Treasurer) and Robert T. Jones (Secretary) were quietly confident that they had made the correct decision. The designer and architect of the chapel were C. O. Ellison and Sons, while the builders were Bootle-based Samuel Webster. The foundation stone was laid on 20 November 1886 by Samuel Smith, MP for Flint Boroughs and a generous Liverpool Scottish merchant. They built a chapel for a congregation of 300, and behind it stood a small schoolroom. The land was bought for £805, and they paid £1,766 to the builders, and another £250 was spent on small items. According to the records published in March 1889 there remained a debt of £1,460 to clear.

The first elders of the chapel were elected in October 1889, namely John Jones, Salisbury Road; John Jones, Tennyson Street and Robert E. Jones, Beaumont St. Robert E. Jones only served as elder for a year and resigned before the end of 1892, as did John Jones, Tennyson Street. It was then that they elected as a congregation another leader in the person of Hugh Hughes, Heathcote Street. They made another effort in May 1893 to have an extra leader, but only Edward Owen, Smithdown Road was chosen. All this indicates that the situation was fragile, and there was a great deal of disagreement amongst the membership. In September 1894 two more elders were elected, Hugh Griffiths, Ash Grove, and also Owen Hughes, Carrick Street, who became one of the stalwarts of Webster Road, and later Heathfield Road. Again, in December 1895, they gave members another opportunity to elect

Webster Road Welsh Chapel

elders and this time they elected John Jones, Barrington Road (Mayfield, Dudlow Lane from 1904 till his death in 1935).

The Church was visited in the middle of 1893 by a deputation from the Presbytery to persuade them to consider extending a call to a Minister, but they were unable to accept the challenge. However, two years later they extended a call to the Reverend William Owen, of Tŷ'n Llain, in the parish of Bodfari, then in Flintshire. He began his ministry on 1 October 1896. It had been a church without a minister from 1889 to 1896, and this period can be divided into four sections.

1.   Facing the financial burden

In his first report in March 1889 William Parry, Upper Parliament Street mentioned that they had a 'great burden' in the form of £1,460 worth of debts that depressed them as a community. Many of the leaders responded generously. William Parry himself donated the sum of fifty pounds, as did the Treasurer, John Jones. The politician Samuel Smith MP gave £10, and fifty shillings came from one of the most popular preachers of his day, the Reverend John Williams, Brynsiencyn, Anglesey, and for a time minister of Princes Road Welsh Chapel in Liverpool. A donation was made in the name of the Reverend Evan Rees,

Webster Road Chapel in its days as the Cameo Cinema.

The site of Webster Road Chapel in 2005

known by his bardic name of Dyfed, who came from Cardiff to Liverpool occasionally to preach and to adjudicate in the *eisteddfodau*. Two guineas came from the missionary, the Reverend T. Jerman Jones. He had decided to leave North-East India for Wales to recover his health, but died on 14 April 1890 on board his ship not far from Dungeness. He was buried in Smithdown Road Cemetery on 18 April 1890.

In their address to the young church in 1891 John Jones, Albert Park and John Jones, Hartingdon Road were very concerned about those members who were apathetic towards the Debt Fund. They both stressed that it was the 'duty of every member of the Church to feel that the whole work was blessed by God and dependent on their own efforts, and nobody else could do the work that the Lord has given to them to fulfil'.

Another list of named subscribers appeared in 1892, and among those who contributed were the Liverpool-based William Rathbone the Sixth and Member of Parliament for the Caernarfon constituency. His contribution was one guinea, while an individual calling himself 'Unworthy' gave five shillings. However there were some members who did not respond at all. In 1893, the elders mentioned that there were 350 members who had not contributed a penny to the Ministry during 1892. The following year it was the same story. But as the years went by it all changed, and in his first address to the church, the Reverend William Owen congratulated the members for the condition of the building and its upkeep. They were also concerned in that period with the practice of 'many of the members to pay for their pews at the end of the year rather that at the beginning of the year'. Ideally, payment should have been made every week if possible.

A view of Smithdown Road today

2.   Winning and Losing Ground

The number of communicants at the end of the first year came to 124 (the majority had been members of Chatham Street Chapel), and at the end of 1889 they had 203 members in Webster Road. In 1890 there were 33 new members, but as John Jones Albert Park admitted, they were mostly members from other Welsh chapels in Liverpool. Only two came from the community without a previous chapel allegiance. The following year twenty members were lost, three through death, six left without their membership card, a decline of eleven. It was noted that no one had joined from the surrounding community or from the chapel's young people. The same story appeared the following year. They had to excommunicate one member in 1894, and this, as well as the loss of nine members who did not ask for their membership, was a matter of great concern.

A confident note is found in the 1896 Annual Report, when the minister was pleased to announce that 22 new members had joined the fellowship during the year. He was full of optimism as to the eventual growth of this community. The Sunday School is often mentioned, and it was regarded as an extremely important institution within the chapel. These are the statistics for 1889:

Male Teachers (including officers of the Sunday School)	19
Female Teachers	8
Adult members	92
Children under 15 years of age	88
TOTAL	**207**

In their comments John Jones and Hugh Hughes were often very negative, and this was particularly true of their attitude to the Sunday School: 'We would like to see the Sunday School growing and more enthusiasm for this institution. Brothers, pray for us, so that the Word of God might run and gain adherents, so that the Church will have more and more people who have been saved.' This hope is expressed in the following year; with the sincere hope that the Sunday School becomes a nursery for the Church. At the beginning of 1895 they were more positive and the young people were praised for their contribution.

3.   The Meetings of the Church

In 1889 a pattern was emerging, that reflected a great deal of activity. On Sunday at ten o'clock a service was held, then a Sunday School at 2.15 and evening service at six o'clock. On Tuesday the Church Meeting was held at 7.30pm, then on Wednesdays, the Children's Meeting and on Thursdays, a Prayer Meeting. During the winter months the Literary Society, as well as the Reading Group, met. By 1891 they had added a Tonic Sol-fa Class on Monday and a permanent Reading Group on Friday night. In 1894 they formed a Society for the Promotion of Religion, and the officers congratulated the young people that were enthusiastic on its behalf as well as the Sunday School. By 1895 there was a great deal of activity in Webster Road on behalf of the Missionary Society, the Home Missionary Society, the Temperance organisation, a Library Committee and the Literary Society. The minister could report in his first written address to the chapel the 'excellent work done in the reading group, Literary Society, and the Society for Promotion of Religion, by enlarging the attitude of the young people towards the challenge of the Gospel to life in a city.'

4.   Values

Temperance was an important issue widely held amongst the membership of the Webster Road Chapel community of the 1890's. Indeed, the Calvinistic Methodists had been in the vanguard of the temperance witness. In Liverpool two Ministers in particular, namely the Reverend Griffith Ellis of Bootle and the Reverend Owen Owens of Anfield Road Chapel were extremely vocal in their condemnation of public houses and the widespread availability of alcohol in a city like Liverpool.

Another important matter was the missionary witness. As far as missionary work in North-East India was concerned it began in Liverpool when the first missionary, Thomas Jones, was sent out with his wife Anne in 1840. One feels the positive atmosphere towards missionary work quite clearly in the archives of Webster Road chapel in the 1890's.

The members had a clear conception of their roles as Christians in the world. There are plenty of examples of their concern for people in distress and difficult circumstances. In 1890 £3-17-1½ were collected towards a colliery disaster in Glamorgan and a sum of £1 to the poor. The following year they mentioned that they had sent 18 shillings to assist the miners, £1-18-7 towards medical institutions belonging to the Armenians, and £2-4-8 to a colliery disaster at Tylorstown in the Rhondda Valley. However, it was the spiritual needs that appear most consistently in the chapel reports. They insisted that members should not consider self-pride as a justification for believing in Christ. The true God is revealed in his Son as the Saviour of mankind, for he came to seek and to save the lost, dying for the helpless, the ungodly, yes, even for enemies. This was the crux of their Calvinist theology.

Reverend Owen Jones, minister of Chatham Street Chapel between 1872 and 1892.

John Hughes, Moneivion, builder and an elder

Reverend Lodwig Lewis, Seacombe.

Reverend Owen J. Owens (1851-1925) who ministered at Rock Ferry Welsh Chapel for 41 years (1884-1925)

Reverend Griffith Ellis (1844-1913), minister of Stanley Road Welsh Chapel, Bootle from 1876 to 1911.

A building of importance and with a Liverpool Welsh connection at Cemaes, Anglesey.

The fishing village of Cemaes.

Welsh Bay.

Snowdonia in its glory.

Mynydd Paris in Anglesey.

Gorslwyd Calvinistic Methodist Chapel, Rhosybol, Anglesey, the spiritual home of a number of Webster Road members.

A chapel in the village of Fourcrosses, on the border of Lleyn and Eifionydd districts of Gwynedd .

The square at Llanerch-y-medd, Anglesey.

An Anglesey cottage which was the home of a Liverpool Welsh person.

The grandeur of Pwllheli.

Chapter 3

THE FLOURISHING MINISTRY OF THE REVEREND WILLIAM OWEN (1896-1906)

After a period of seven years without a full time minister of the Gospel the community at Webster Road needed a pastor. They were able to persuade the son of a minister to accept the call. The Reverend William Owen had inherited many of the characteristics of his well-known father, the Reverend Robert Owen, Tŷ Draw, Mold. The family had moved from Bodfari at the beginning of October 1896 and had settled at 11 Rossett Avenue, near Sefton Park. The Reverend Owen and his wife Ann had three children, a daughter called Mary, and two sons, Gwilym and Robert Tudor Owen. It was not easy in the beginning but William Owen, through his personality, changed the situation. The historian, the Reverend John Hughes Morris said of him: 'Through the strength of his character, his kindness and patience, he succeeded in regaining full and happy co-operation in the church'. He became a hero to his people. William Owen showed a great deal of kindness. One of those who remembered him, Miss Laura Jones (then at 33 Scholar Street), used to remind me in her old age of his support to the children and young people, particularly those who were accepted as students at colleges and universities. Within the Liverpool Presbytery he was regarded as a dependable person, a first class administrator and leader.

Reverend William Owen, first minister of Webster Road

In addition to his personality and his caring ministry a number of other factors contributed to William Owen's success. The growth of the community around him offered opportunities for enlarging his sphere of influence. The electric trains which had been introduced in Liverpool made travelling easier: it meant that the Welsh could live in any of the streets built off Smithdown Road. Street after street of terraced houses appeared and their close-knit atmosphere endeared them to the Welsh, who had migrated to Liverpool from similarly built houses in the small villages of Gwynedd. Many of those bred in these streets remembered with nostalgia the closely knit community where Welsh was the dominant language of conversation. They met in the streets and in Webster Road Chapel. A large number of the officers lived within 300 yards of Webster Road Chapel, though an increasing number of Welsh families had found houses in the area around Deepfield and Fallowfield Road. The Sunday School Superintendent, John Hughes, lived in 15 Ramilies Road while his namesake, who was Superintendent of the Children's Sunday School, lived at 22 Ramilies Road. This road is near to Penny Lane and very near to the present Welsh Chapel at the bottom end of Heathfield Road. It is no surprise that the Building Committee of Webster Road Chapel built a schoolroom in zinc in Ramilies Road for those families who had settled in the upper reaches of Smithdown Road and around Penny Lane. This was to be a Sunday School in Ramilies Road Chapel catering mostly for children. By 1903 there were two Sunday Schools, one in Webster Road and the other in Ramilies Road. The building in Ramilies Road still remains but is now used as a chapel for an evangelical Protestant group of Christians. The end result of building this schoolroom at Ramilies Road was to divide the congregation into two groups, and in a short period of time, the children of Ramilies Road became strangers to those who attended

Samuel Smith, MP. who laid the foundation stone of Webster Road Chapel.

the Webster Road schoolroom. Also it was evident that the standard of living of the two groups was very different. Those Welsh people who lived around Penny Lane were more affluent than those who lived in the streets around Webster Road. Those in the lower end of Smithdown Road aspired to move to the upper part of the road. An excellent example of this is John Jones, 29 Barrington Road, who was elected an elder in 1895. He was born in 1853 in Carreglefn, Anglesey, the oldest of nine children. He left the local primary school when he was 13 to work as a farm labourer. John Jones soon realised that labouring on a farm meant hard, heavy work; and at the same time he noticed men from the parish who had migrated to Liverpool returning well dressed and looking extremely prosperous. He then realised that they were joiners and carpenters, who, like himself, had been poor and without many prospects in life. He was determined to improve his lot and soon made plans to be trained as a carpenter with an expert craftsman in the neighbouring village of Rhosybol. Within a few weeks he had gained enough confidence to trek to Liverpool where he found work with an Anglesey born Liverpool-Welsh builder, who operated from Anfield. Jones spent his leisure time mastering the English language in an evening class. He joined the Netherfield Road Welsh Chapel, then the impressive Princes Road Chapel, and he was amongst the fifty who established a new chapel in David Street in the Dingle. Then because of his ambition to succeed in business he moved to Smithdown Road, and he became one of the pioneers of Webster Road Chapel. In 1880 Jones married Catherine Parry, a Welsh speaking girl from Gorslwyd, Anglesey, and they moved to 29 Barrington Road. Two sons, John Richard Jones

John Jones, Barrington Road, later Dudlow Drive, an influential elder.

and W. H. Jones, were born to them. His wife died in 1887 but he brought up his sons to follow in his own footsteps. He did not re-marry but ventured to build new houses on a large scale between Earle Road and Penny Lane.

John Jones moved to 9 Crawford Avenue in 1901 but, by 1906, he had built for his family a beautiful mansion in Dudlow Lane, Calderstones, calling it Mayfield. A hundred years later this house is still an impressive building, just as it was in the lifetime of John Jones, between 1906 and 1936. One cannot praise him enough for his activities, his support for his Minister, and also as a catalyst for the growth of Liverpool.

Another builder, with the same motivation and dynamism, was John Hughes, Moneivion. Wherever he lived he called his home Moneivion, with the result that we have Moneivion, Heathfield Road; Moneivion, Allerton Road; Moneivion, Green Lane. By 1900 he was also an elder in Webster Road.

A native of Llanrhyddlad, Anglesey, he became one of the most influential and important builders, not only in Liverpool but in Britain. He was for a time in partnership with John Jones, but later with his brother, Thomas Hughes he bought land in Birkenhead, Wallasey, Newton-le-Willows, Birmingham, Liverpool and London where he built large housing estates. As his son-in-law, J. R. Jones, said in an entry on him, with regards to an estate called Kenton in London: 'In short, one of the satellite towns of London has been brought into existence through the enterprise and determination of a Welsh builder born of humble circumstances in Anglesey.' He died in 1936, a flourishing businessman. He gave up the eldership in Webster Road after the religious revival of 1904-5. Through the drive and determination of people like John Jones and John Hughes the chapel was enlarged in 1899, by extending the schoolroom and building a small gallery within the chapel, opposite the pulpit. They also built a large schoolroom on the plot of land behind the chapel, which they had bought ten years earlier. They organised a bazaar at St George's Hall in the centre of the city, and through the co-operation of Welsh people in Liverpool, a profit of £2,164-1s-1d was made in November 1899.

There were plenty of working men available for John Jones and John Hughes – all members of Webster Road Chapel. When Welsh men folk arrived from Anglesey and Caernarfonshire in boats they would ask for a specific chapel – Princes Road or Webster Road or Stanley Road or one of scores of others – and would attend on the following Sunday with their membership document, which opened doors to them for employment. The main builders of Wavertree were all members at Webster Road chapel, as elders or as members of the Finance Committee (most of those who did well in this organisation would be voted in later as a leader) or as officers in the Sunday School or one of the other organisations, such as the Foreign Mission Committee, the Loan Fund Committee or the Library Committee. Men and women from Wales would ask for these leaders and would be introduced to them in the fellowship after the services. This pool of ready labour was a godsend to the builders. Many of them were monoglot Welshmen who had not yet considered attending an evening class to improve their command of English. These immigrants were fully dependent on their employer, who arranged their work and who paid their weekly wage. The negative aspect of this setup was that it kept the Welsh working class apart from the rest of the workers in the city. The Welsh speakers who had received a favour from fellow chapel members would often be penalised by receiving a smaller wage package than their Liverpudlian comrades. This exploitation was happening on a large scale, and the only changes occurred was when a flourishing Welsh builder had to hire Irish or English workers as well. This is how John Jones came to be known as 'John Drinkwater'. When they reached the middle of the week the Irish bricklayer would ask for a sub to buy a pint of beer. John Jones, who was a temperance supporter, would respond by saying 'Drink water, my boy, drink water!' The dominance of the employers in their chapel community reinforces, without doubt, their grasp on those who worked for them. They could not disagree with their employer for they were members of the same chapel, sharing the same values and realising that it was a very valuable situation for workers to be in when there was a great deal of unemployment around them. The ideal was to nurture a full-blown Christian character and improve their worldly lot. After all, John Jones and John Hughes, and later J. W. Jones and many others, were ordinary people not aristocrats. They were people who had overcome their very harsh and difficult circumstances by virtue of their Christian convictions as well as their personal ambitions. They had heard the

The home of John Jones (John Drinkwater)

Another view of Mayfield which John Jones built in 1906.

Calvinistic theology from the pulpit, the need to improve the conditions of their fellow men. Not only did God rule the world by the universal laws of nature, 'he sustains, nourishes, and cares for everything he has made, even to the last sparrow'. God's hands are in everything.

To a Calvinist, the Christian faith derives from God, who speaks to us, invites us and draws us into the society of Christ; turns us away from sin and towards holiness, and rules our world, guiding and supporting us through earthly instruments of care and determination. The Christian in his day-to-day existence can trust God and should rely on God in business as well as in church activities. His confidence should not be in himself or in the world of his earthly condition. He should be thankful for all good gifts, especially the gift of God's kindness, but should not rely on other goods easily taken away. Calvinism was the crux of their theology, and this exposition of the faith believed that the disciple could overcome his circumstances.

The Reverend William Owen, like his elders and members allowed himself to believe that one should not fall into poverty but work hard and be consistent in one's calling. It was the Protestant ethic of work that sustained them. The minister had been encouraged by the religious revival that began in south Wales in October 1904. He wrote in support of the Revival by emphasising the experience of a knowledge of Jesus and the responsibility of young people in the revival. He said in the spring of 1905:

> We are looking forward to receiving great things from our young people this year. The emotional feelings will be translated into work for Christ. Let us make sure that anyone who is neglectful gets peace, but prod everyone to approach the God of Hope.

Locally, William Owen played a key role in the Revival, and gave a great deal of support to the Reverend Dr John Williams, minister of Princes Road Chapel, the organiser of the Revivalist Evan Roberts's visit to Liverpool. The minister could signify victory in the fruits of the 1905 Revival. He mentioned seven:

1.   The souls who had sought a home in Webster Road from the 'sins of the city'. There were 33 of them.

2.   Those who had sought membership in Webster Road. He could cite 24 members.

3.   The Sunday School, which had increased with 76 new members.

4.   A generation of praying people, men and women, who had appeared as a consequence of the Revival.

5.   The renewal of every aspect of the Church in Webster Road, renewed, but it was the prayer meeting above all that was a 'means of grace'. He could say that it was 'a joy to attend these prayer meetings' and he 'could not understand those who neglected them'.

6.   The revival of the missionary witness and the chapel could take pride in the fact that the Young People's Society for Religious Endeavour was collecting weekly to maintain a missionary in North-East India. A tremendous change for the best had taken place in the attitude of the young people. They were attentive to those who neglected their religious observance and they were extremely hardworking in their efforts for the 'poor and the needy'. The Chatham Street Welsh Chapel, in co-operation with the Chapels of Crosshall Street and Webster Road, had appointed Miss Mary Williams, Earle Street, as a local missionary, so that the women of the three chapels, could bear witness effectively in a missionary setting. The first effective measure was to form a Women's Meeting amongst the female members of Webster Road.

7.   A substantial increase in generosity, as a result of the 1904-5 Revival. The Minister could say at the end of 1905: 'Nearly every one of the collections had increased substantially and some of them were quite astounding'. The leaders of the chapel were very generous, the three builders, John Jones, John Hughes and J. W. Jones, all giving £10, though the last two included their wives in the contribution, whereas John Jones was a widower. But the majority, even though the Minister had

Reverend John Williams (1854-1921), minister of Princes Road Chapel from 1895 to 1906

boosted their morale, were still contributing just £1 a year or even less. Dr Isaac E. Owens and Mrs Owens, 126 Lawrence Road, gave a guinea between them while the son of the Minister, a young academic, Dr Gwilym Owen, BA, MSc gave a guinea, and in 1911 he was made an elder, together with J.W. Jones, Garth Davies and Henry Williams, Grovedale Road.

The Edwardian Era proved to be a period of blessing for the Reverend William Owen and his flock. He was not expected to be often in his own pulpit. It is incredible to look at the list of Sunday Preachers for Webster Road in 1906 and to realise that the minister was in his own pulpit only ten times in a full year. How expectations have changed! There were plenty of Welsh-speaking preachers on Merseyside to fill the pulpit. Some of them came more than once. The congregation appreciated the company of O. J. Owen, Rock Ferry; John Roberts, David Street; E. J. Evans, Walton Park; Lodwig Lewis, Seacombe; David Jones, Edge Lane; R. Aethwy Jones, Newsham Park and Owen Owen, Anfield on two occasions. To the Annual Preaching Service they invited the Reverend Thomas Charles Williams, Menai Bridge, and the blind preacher, J. Puleston Jones of Dinorwig, near Llanberis.

Reverend Josiah Thomas (1830-1905), a member in Webster Road.

At the end of the first ten years of the Reverend William Owen's ministry the cause was very different. Indeed it was not the same Church. In 1906, only 78 members of those recorded in 1896 still remained. But in these same ten years nearly 500 members had arrived from Wales and from other Welsh chapels on Merseyside. The chapel had been extended, and the Ramilies Road Schoolroom had been built, and the sum of £2,750 of their debt had been paid. This table tells the story fully –

	1890	1906
Number of communicants	219	562
Total members of the Sunday School	243	514
Collections towards the ministry	£137-14-1½	£321-6-6½
Collections for missionary work	£9-6-6½	£46-12-7
Rent for pews	£64-2-0	£134-8-0
Total collections	£345-14-8	£757-14-10

The Welsh Religious Revival had given an evangelical as well as a missionary zeal to the community based on Webster Road. The local missionary work was quite successful under the direction of Miss Williams, and they began to organise prayer meetings in ordinary homes. These initiatives were in the hands of the young people, and it is interesting to realise who they were: individuals who later became dependable leaders, people of great faith, such as E. J. Jenkins, Cedar Grove, J. R. Jones, Mayfield and Miss C. E. Pugh, Arundel Avenue. The strongest Sunday School was based at Webster Road. There were 113 children compared with 51 at Ramilies. It is gratifying to notice that there were 56 Sunday School teachers of both sexes ready to prepare for the weekly classes in 1906. But the Minister was still concerned that there were large numbers of Welsh people not attending the chapels in

Reverend J. D. Evans of Garston

Webster Road and Ramilies Road. These Welsh people were often economically poor and according to the minister 'they cried out for help'.

These successes were forcing the leaders now to consider a new chapel on a different site. Webster Road Chapel had become too small by 1906 and the shifts of settlement amongst the Welsh population towards Allerton was making the location of the chapel less attractive. As early as 1898 they discussed the possibility of building a large new chapel on the corner of Lawrence Road and Bagot Street in Wavertree, and the Presbytery was ready to support such a move. They found that it was not easy to sell Webster Road. So they decided to enlarge the building, but, by 1906 their lack of space was a constant problem to the minister and the ruling elders. The Reverend William Owen wrote in 1906 of the possibilities as well as the dangers involved:

The question of moving ahead to buy land for the new chapel in the vicinity of Ramilies Road was discussed by the elders during the year, but after making a thorough search, we did not have the maturity to do so at that time. This matter is of the utmost importance to us as a Church and to religion in the area.

He added: 'It is a matter that calls for a great deal of wisdom to discuss it properly'. This was an ongoing matter that was discussed dozens of times, as we shall see in the next chapter of this saga.

Reverend David Jones of Edge Lane, whose two daughters became members of Heathfield Road Chapel.

Chapter 4

THE AFTERMATH OF
THE REVIVAL (1906-1915)

After the flames of the religious revival had been extinguished, it was not at all easy for the minister and his elders to cope with the period 1906-15. The Reverend William Owen expressed his views in his address at the beginning of the Annual Report for 1907:

> We are living in difficult times. Our enemies are many and aggressive. The enthusiasm of the Revival, to a large measure, has become a past memory.

Circumstances within the community were creating tension; unemployment in particular was disturbing the chapel hierarchy. Against such a background the minister concentrated on three issues.

First, the children and the young people. It was not easy for the parents to bring up their children to understand and to speak the Welsh language. Obviously, this was a most important reason for their existence as a people, the ability to speak the language of the chapel community. One of the most talented of the Liverpool Welsh, John Howell Hughes, the surgeon, who was born in Anfield in 1908, wrote of his Welsh upbringing and the disadvantages experienced after he had started in the primary school.

> Within the Welsh community the language of the home was their native tongue and English was rarely spoken and this was true in my family. It was therefore not surprising that on the first day I entered Anfield Road Primary School I understood but could hardly speak much English and when asked a question my answers were given in Welsh producing laughter from the rest of the class.

This was not an experience felt only by J. Howell Hughes but a common experience. For the leaders of the Welsh communities in the city took great interest in the children and the young people. There were 225 children in the community. Many of them became part and parcel of the church community, such as R. T. Glyn Lewis, 7 Silverdale Road, a large giant of a man but with a tender heart and a unique face, Doris Mary Thomas, 2 Wyndcote Road (later 43 Allerton Road) who also became a heavily involved person, and Winifred Annie Jones, 50 Claremont Road, who became a neighbour of mine, when she and her sisters lived nearby

John Howell Hughes

in 14 Calderstones Road. Some of the children have names that connect them with their period, such as Adelina Patti Parry Hughes, 40 Cranborne Road, who lost her small brother, Herbert Parry Hughes, one of the six children who died in that year. Of the 225 children named in the Annual Report, only one was a member in 1999 at the end of the century, namely Annie Ceridwen Griffiths, 60 Avondale Road, and later Herondale Road. In that year she moved to a nursing home in Rhosneigr, Anglesey, but retained her membership till her death in 2003.

The Church had a large number of young people between 15 and 21 years of age, people who had plenty of energy and Christian commitment. The Minister expressed the hope that this initiative and energy would be 'sanctified and consecrated to Christ and his cause'.

The second concern was focused on the poor people. This became an abiding theme also and the agenda for the Socialist movement, which was beginning to attract some of the Welsh. It is a great interest that one of the preachers invited to the annual preaching services at Webster Road in 1908 was the Reverend J. H. Howard, Cwmavon, near Port Talbot. He had been a stalwart for his friend Evan Roberts in the religious revival and later became a rising star of the Independent Labour Party, who stood as parliamentary candidate for the Labour Party in the Merioneth constituency in 1931. His autobiography, *Winding Lanes* (published in 1938), is very interesting, especially when he describes his ministry at Willmer Road Chapel in Birkenhead from 1910 to 1915, and then at Catharine Street Chapel in Liverpool between 1928 and 1941. The fact that Webster Road Chapel had invited him as a preacher to the Preaching Festival fitted in well with the social gospel that we find in the published sermons of J. H. Howard under the provocative title *Jesus the Agitator*, published by Hughes and Son of Wrexham in 1934. The minister's friend, George Lansbury, wrote an introduction to the book. His pacifism and socialist idealism comes through as well as his concern for Sunday observance. J. H. Howard combined the priorities for Sunday with a new approach. He said – 'Sunday is a precious privilege to guard. A week without Sunday would be like a year without summer, a world that had no flowers, and a child that could not smile'. Sunday was a great help to reformers: 'One secret behind the tremendous energy and accomplishments of Wilberforce and Gladstone was their strict observance of Sunday rest and worship'.

Reverend J. H. Howard

Webster Road had an active Society geared to assisting the poor inside and outside the chapel community under the chairmanship of J. W. Jones of Hiraethog, Allerton Road, who became a very well-known builder. The society was greatly helped by the local Missionary Society and individuals with enlightened consciences. Yet, as William Owen said: 'I am afraid that we could and should do much more as a church in a general manner'. In this way the Reverend William Owen was an extremely unusual Calvinistic Methodist preacher compared with many of his contemporaries, as revealed in their annual addresses presented in the chapel reports.

The third concern was focused on the building of a new chapel. The Ramilies Road schoolroom was much too small and the Presbytery gave the go ahead for them to buy a piece of land on the corner of Green Lane and Menlove Avenue. The Minister was afraid that the leaders of the Ramilies Road schoolroom would build a chapel for the members who had settled around Allerton Road and Penny Lane and leave the others around Sefton Park and the lower end of Wavertree in Webster Road. By 1909 the total number of members and children amounted to around 800 in total. Even then, the increase was small, only six, while in 1908 a decrease of three had taken place. In 1908 the number of members was 557, and the children 225, but the number of those who had left, or had been excommunicated, or who moved came to 61. But I must add that, of the 61 only 2 were dismissed as members. Discipline, an integral part of Calvinism, was regarded as essential in these Welsh communities of the Victorian and Edwardian era, but they were excommunicated usually without any written record.

In the years after the Revival the chapel timetable of Webster Road was extremely full. On the Sunday there would be four meetings: at 10 00 a.m. a Young People's Prayer Meeting, with the morning service at 10.30, then in the afternoon the Sunday School and in the evening at 6.00 another service of worship. On a Monday afternoon at 2.30, the Mothers' Union meeting took place and in the evening at 7.30 a Prayer meeting followed at 8.30 by a Reading Class. In 1907 a musical society was established; it met at 8 00 p.m. on Tuesdays. This catered for those who were keen on singing. William Davies was the Precentor while

Harry Evans

since 1901 John P. Taylor, was the organist. He succeeded John Hughes who lived at 77 Granville Road. John P. Taylor served as organist for three decades.

This period was the golden age of singing amongst the Liverpool Welsh with Harry Evans as the prince of the musical renaissance. He was the product of the rich musical culture found in Merthyr Tydfil and north Glamorgan at the beginning of the twentieth century. Born in Dowlais on New Year's Day 1873, he was appointed at the age of nine to follow Dan Price, a well respected soloist, as organist of the Welsh Independent Chapel of Gwernllwyn near Dowlais. As the conductor of Dowlais Male Voice Choir, Harry Evans won the principal prize for choral singing at the National Eisteddfod of Wales held

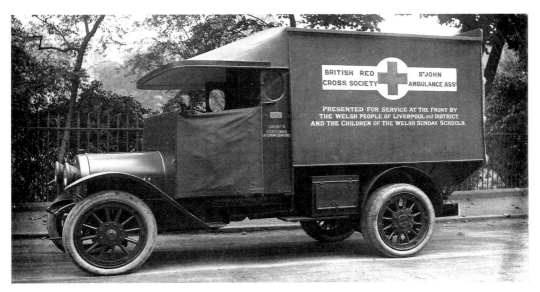

Generosity of the Liverpool Welsh in the First World War

at Liverpool in 1901. Consequently in 1904 he was invited to move to Liverpool and be the conductor of the Liverpool Welsh Choral Union. Music in Liverpool was greatly enhanced by the presence of Harry Evans and his sensitive interpretation of the music of Bach, Elgar, Vaughan Thomas and Granville Bantock. He attracted members of Webster Road to join the Choral Union. At that time 23 from the chapel were members of the choir. Today, in 2007, there are at least fourteen from Bethel Chapel who are faithful members of the choir. His premature death in the summer of 1914 in Liverpool, when he was just 41 years of age, was a momentous blow to the Liverpool Welsh musical scene; and every year I encourage pilgrims from Wales to visit his grave at Smithdown Road Cemetery. This cemetery is nearly opposite Webster Road, and I always read the Welsh *englyn* by Pedrog (the Reverend J. O. Williams) which is on the unusual gravestone, donated in fond memory of their conductor by members of the Liverpool Welsh Choral Union.

Life was not easy in Liverpool at the end of the Edwardian era. There was a decline in the number of members at Webster Road, as well as in the Sunday collections. Merseyside witnessed its greatest industrial confrontation with the transport strikes of summer 1911. A spell of unemployment, following a decade of declining real wages, brought a feeling of despondency. There were numerous confrontations between labour and capitalists, trade unionists and politicians, union leaders and their rank and file, as well as disagreements between unionized and non-unionized labour. The transport strikes of 1911 alarmed the organisers of Webster Road, and they were annoyed also at the instigators of the Liverpool strikes of 1911, namely J. Havelock Wilson, President of the National Sailors' and Fireman's Union and Tom Mann, an inspiring agitator. None of the Welsh leaders had any sympathy with Wilson and Mann and their followers, for they were men who had overcome their obstacles and had ventured confidently in their chosen trade as builders. They rejoiced at the attack of the satirical local journal, *Porcupine* in describing the conflict as a 'stupid strike'. The chapel members rejoiced at King George's Coronation. Over 165,000 people, one fifth of the population of Liverpool, enjoyed civic hospitality, and the Welsh of Toxteth as well as Wavertree joined in the celebrations. The Welsh leaders redoubled their efforts on behalf of temperance, and the Reverend William Owen was very proud to defend the witness:

> We wish the temperance movement every success and we hope that the whole church will be leavened with the principles of sobriety and that it will be strong in its opposition to the practice of drinking.

The young members fulfilled their missionary witness by door to door visitations, and inviting those who understood Welsh to re-establish their allegiance. The Mothers' Union was also involved. It was obvious by 1910 that the Webster Road buildings were in an area of Liverpool that was not as attractive as it had been twenty years earlier. The Menlove Avenue Chapel Committee had been established, with the Minister as Chairman, John Hughes, (Moneivion), Green Lane, as Treasurer, and J. R. Jones, Mayfield, as Secretary. The possibility of building a new chapel on the corner of Menlove Avenue/Green Lane was still a distinct possibility in the minds of leaders. But the members were not so enthusiastic. They promised the sum of £1,030 but by the end of 1910, only £250 had been given to the Treasurer, W. Morris Owen of 14 Sydenham Avenue. In 1910 the Sunday School had declined by 36 members. This became a matter of discussion in a weekly meeting, and they came to the conclusion that this decline was due as much to 'religious apathy' as it was to the movement of members owing to the economic climate.

Another interesting change decided by the congregation involved the monthly Communion Services. The old tradition in Webster Road was for everyone to drink from one cup, but they decided on a vote to 'have individual cups' and to follow the Nonconformist tradition. Those who led the campaign for change did so on health grounds. The decision was adjourned for a while because of the costs involved. But one of the generous members of Webster Road, Mrs Jane Davies, 39 Mulliner Street, came to the rescue and paid the sum of £30, equivalent of £300 in 2008. It was a generous act and one which was greatly appreciated.

In a community of 563 adults it is incredible to note that only two of the members died in 1910, one being the widow of Josiah Thomas, a member of a remarkable Liverpool family that included the two notable pulpit giants, Dr Owen Thomas and Dr John Thomas. The other member was less well-known, Miss Mary Hughes of Walton, described by her minister as 'one who was completely lonely, homeless and an orphan'. This is a picture of a poor Welshwoman who was part of this community but her background was known to the caring pastor. As historians we tend to give pride of place to the professional men and women, medical practitioners such as Dr T. R. Williams, 43 Halkyn Avenue. Though he was busy in his practice, he also served as an official in more that one Webster Road society and relished his responsibilities as Chairman of the Library Committee and Superintendent of the Sunday School. Another person whose life was so different from Mary Hughes's was Dr Gwilym Owen, a son of the Manse and a University lecturer, who took charge of the Welsh language class and many other commitments. One can understand how the congregation elected him as an elder in 1911, as well as two Welsh builders, J. W. Jones and Henry Williams, 13 Grovedale Road. It was decided in 1911 to give support to the pastoral commitments of the Minister by re-arranging the catchment area of the chapels into districts for the purpose of elders visiting the members. This remains the structure today and it has served the purpose for a period of 100 years. In the same years they decided to abandon the idea of building a new chapel at the Menlove Avenue/Green Lane juncture. The congregation voted by a large majority not to venture, and yet, more and more activities were held at Ramilies Road. Originally it was only intended to hold a Sunday School in the building but, by 1911, more week night meetings were held there. A Prayer Meeting was held on a Monday night with a Reading Group that duplicated the provision to be found in Webster Road. Then on Tuesday they started a Literary Society, while on Friday they had a Band of Hope, followed by a Musical Class. This took place at Webster Road as well.

In 1911 the Minister lost his beloved wife. This was one of eight deaths amongst the members during the year, and four of them were young people in the prime of their lives. I came across the grave of Mrs A. Owen, the minister's wife, and her bachelor son, Dr Gwilym Owen, in Smithdown Cemetery in quite a poor condition. I arranged with one of the staff to clear the saplings that were sprouting from the grave. I am glad that this has been done. We as a chapel paid for the clearance. I noticed then that the Reverend William Owen had not been buried with his wife in Liverpool, but in Conwy.

The decision to abandon the chapel in Menlove Avenue was quite a disappointment to the minister, but he responded by telling them that they had to face the issue, and that in time they would receive the strength to fulfil the vision of the new chapel.

The Minister suffered ill-health for most of 1913 and early 1914. It was at this time that his son, Dr Gwilym Owen, moved as Professor to the University of Auckland in New Zealand. The elders had to prepare on his behalf the address for the Annual Report of 1913. In this sense the community was strong. They baptised 13, and the number of communicants at the end of 1913 was 541, even after losing 64 members. But I noticed that 88 members had not contributed a penny to the ministry, and of the 58 who left, only 20 contributed, which totals 126 members who had made no effort whatsoever to sustain the fabric of the church or contribute towards the sustaining of the ministry. They were people who had entirely forgotten their chapel responsibilities.

The minister, the Reverend William Owen was concerned at the situation in 1914, when it was quite obvious that there was a tendency for the Liverpool Welsh to settle in the northern suburbs of Liverpool. He maintained that for the last 18 years the church had grown mainly because the Welsh tended to migrate to the Wavertree/Sefton/Allerton area, but now there was an obvious trend to move to north Liverpool.

The First World War was casting its shadows over everything that the chapel community in Webster Road had stood for, and 31 young people joined the armed forces. The first casualty was John David Jones, Bective Street, who had joined a battalion of the Royal Welsh Fusiliers. He was killed at the Battle of the Mons in September 1914. The minister moved to 101 Arundel Avenue, his new abode, from 11 Greenbank Road. He stated in 1914: 'The church is called to care for the suffering humanity and to comfort the bereaved, let us be ready and kind hearted to fulfil our important responsibilities'.

The Minister decided to set up Ambulance Classes in the Ramilies Road Schoolroom so that they could train the young with necessary skills to treat suffering civilians. In 1915 the minister decided to leave the chapel for the churches of Tabernacl and Y Gyffin, near Conwy, and he looked back with satisfaction at a ministry which had lasted for nearly twenty years. It was hard for him to leave Liverpool after all those years of labour. After all, in this period, he had baptised 269 children at Webster Road, had prepared 170 young people as communicants, and had ministered in the funerals of 112 of his members. He had been a good friend to the young people. In his last but one address William Owen underlines the bond of friendship established by him with the younger generation: 'I cannot but look upon them as if they were my own children. It is sad for me to think that so many of them, in obedience to the call of their country, are today on the field of blood – in the navy or preparing for the great campaign'.

The caring shepherd felt for his young flock, and gave specific guidance to the elders on the precious lives that were now in mortal danger in the theatre of war. He stated to his members: 'Remember that letters should be sent constantly to them. To send a letter to brighten the life of a young man as a soldier in the trenches of France or wherever he is, is as much a service to Christ as anything an Archbishop can do'.

William Owen and his second wife left with the best wishes of the community, which literally extended from Lodge Lane to Penny Lane. He received from the chapel members a watch with a golden chain and in addition his wife received a silver brooch. The membership numbered 219 in 1896, when he came as minister, but by 1915 there were 552 members, an increase of 333, and the total membership (including the children and those preparing for membership was 750. In 1896 it was 329 while in 1915 it had risen to 750, an increase of 421. The total collection in 1896 totalled £348 while in 1915 it had risen to £706, an increase of £358. The statistics reflect the success story and a very interesting chapter was now closing before the next ministry was to begin. The Reverend William Owen died at Conwy in 1922 and the Presbyterian Church of Wales lost one of its most loyal ministers, one who believed with Jesus, 'What shall it profit a man if he gain the whole world and lose his own soul', or life? Between the years 1914 and 1918, Britain and its allies lost 908,371 men, reported dead or missing, an episode which disturbed the Reverend William Owen. He believed that each one of the ten million Europeans (including his own young people from the Liverpool Welsh community), who fell in battle, was a precious child of God. He gave two decades of loyal service to the Liverpool Welsh communities of Arundel and Wavertree.

Gwylfa Chapel in Blaenau Ffestiniog where the Reverend Robert Davies preached often at the services before moving to Liverpool.

An Anglesey Chapel which had nurtured leaders of the Webster Road Chapel

River Teifi in all its glory.

The village immortalised by the Liverpool Welsh poet, William T. Edwards
(Gwilym Deudraeth, 1863-1940) and the birthplace of R. J. Jones, Eirianfa, an elder.

A symbol to remind us of the translators of the Bible into Welsh located at St Asaph.

The Cathedral of St Asaph associated with the translation of the Bible into Welsh which meant so much to the members of the Welsh chapels in Liverpool.

Chapter 5

THE MINISTRY OF THE REVEREND DANIEL DAVIES (1916-1923)

At the end of 1916 the church at Webster Road extended a call to the Reverend Daniel Davies, minister of Nasareth Welsh Presbyterian Chapel in Pentre, near Treorchy, in the Rhondda Valley, to minister in Liverpool. He responded to the invitation and in April 1917 he moved with his wife to 20 Langdale Road.

In the period between the departure of William Owen and the arrival of Daniel Davies, the elders and members of the chapels made a strenuous effort to clear the remaining debt of £500 on the buildings at Webster Road. As a community they had paid the money they had borrowed on interest. It was a difficult time. Five of the young people died on the battlefield in 1916, and they also lost a godly soul in John Bryan, 36 Cranborne Road, who in his final illness suffered like Job of the Old Testament. The testimony to him was as follows: 'He possessed mature spiritual experience and a strong faith in Almighty God'.

When Daniel Davies came to his new pastorate he had responsibility for 554 members, and 73 of them were in the Army or the Navy. Members of the Young People's Society cared for them and were in constant contact with those who were serving their country in uniform.

It was not easy to move to a large church in a bustling port in the middle of the First World War. Daniel Davies realised fully the problems they faced and mentioned them very soon after he moved to Wavertree. These were his concerns:

a.   The difficulty in leaving the home to attend meetings in mid winter. Today senior members tend to mention this concern, but this was in 1917 when the chapel had scores of youngish people active within its walls.

b.   Families who are worried for their loved ones in active service, 73 who had volunteered for service, and who now were in danger of life and limb. The minister understood the reluctance of their parents and others to frequent the services. While understanding his concern, it could be argued that it was in the chapel and its fellowship the greatest comforts could be found.

c.   The long trek for those who had settled in Allerton to come to the services at Webster Road and the inadequate facilities for them at Ramilies Road Schoolroom.

Reverend Daniel Davies

The Reverend Daniel Davies could be scathing at times. He felt at the end of the war that many of the members had grown too apathetic with regard to religion. Chapel goers, he considered, were often worried about their own mortal lives rather than their inner spiritual lives. These are his words in translation: 'Form and ritual and order took our attention, our souls were not crying for God, for the living God'. Church leaders welcomed the end of the hostilities and the Minster responded: 'Peace has never been so precious, many hearts were lifted and sunshine came instead of the night'.

The church had been very generous towards the needs of soldiers and the ministry acknowledged the successful efforts, in particular those of the young members. In 1918 the chapel had lost three young children, Idwal Jones Griffiths, (Fallowfield Road), Mair Eluned Williams, (Gainsborough Road), and Mabel Jones, (Plattsville Road) and tragedy was not unusual in those days. At this present time medical expertise is far more advanced

R. J. Evans of Wellington Avenue

The Reverend Daniel Davies welcomed the new era, and saw a large increase in the Sunday services, when those who had been on service in the War returned to civilian life. At least two services were held to welcome back youngsters of the chapels, and others who had been on the battlefield. Gifts were presented to them in appreciation of their efforts. The minister himself lost some time through illness, and was grateful for the kindness shown to him.

In 1919 the chapel elected three new elders in the persons of R. J. Evans, 36 Wellington Avenue, David Griffiths, 32 Micklefield Road and George Jenkins, 46 Karslake Road. Owing to ill-health, W. Morris Owen, who gave valuable service, resigned from being an elder.

It is interesting to note that in 1920 two different collections were made, one which totalled £8-0-7 to assist the poor and the other which totalled £15-16-4 to help the children of Vienna in Austria. The minister saw 1921 as a year to be proud of in Liverpool and especially amongst the Welsh of the Webster Road community. They had increased their generosity and spirituality and had paid the ultimate price of sacrifice in the First World War. A plaque was unveiled on 20 February 1921 for thirteen young men from Webster Road Chapel who had lost their lives in the conflict of 1914-1919, and their names are all recorded. One agrees with the Reverend Daniel Davies as to the importance of the plaque: This is a witness to the love the 'church has for its young people and the admiration for their service and sacrifice for their country'

William Davies the precentor

The minister and his elders decided to hold an Evangelical Mission. They invited an evangelist from the Rhondda Valley, namely the Reverend John Owen (ap Glaslyn: 1857-1934), musician, and author who had been converted during the Revival of 1904-05. He was the son of Richard Jones Owen (1831-1903) a cultured local historian, who was known in the Beddgelert – Penrhyndeudraeth area by his bardic name of Glaslyn. His son ap Glaslyn was ordained a minister by the Welsh Presbyterians in 1919 and spent the rest of his life ministering within the East Glamorgan Presbytery.

In October 1921 the Evangelical Campaign under the leadership of ap Glaslyn began in Webster Road. In few words the minister mentioned that the reasons for his visit were to create an awareness amongst the Liverpool Welsh of the 'value of God's Grace in saving the sinners', remembering the strength and experience of the evangelist 'who himself had been saved'.

Compared with the religious revival of 1904-05 they did not reap a large harvest in 1921. A few came afresh to the faith and more of them heard the Gospel in its evangelical mode. The year had its tragedies amongst members in the Webster Road community. Little Dan Lloyd Jones, Menlove Avenue, died at the age of four and the young man, William Owen Roberts, 4 Edington Street, also died; in addition the church felt the loss of a young father in the person of D. Griffith Roberts, 103 Kenmore Road, at sea. His wife and parents, David and Annie Roberts and his small children, Eleanor Mary and David Glyn Roberts, mourned his tragic passing.

Early in 1923 the church made a significant decision to buy land to build a new chapel in Heathfield Road. The Reverend Daniel Davies urged them to fulfil this vision, though one gathered that he would not remain to oversee the transfer from Webster Road to Heathfield Road. They had bought a large piece of land on the corner of Heathfield Road and Smithdown Place, where a house called Dudlow Cottage stood. They paid for this land and then they bought an additional piece of land, all for £2,778.

In the last full year of Daniel Davies's ministry, the precentor, William Davies, 49 Ramilies Road, retired after 30 years of faithful service. A testimonial was presented to him and the eldership invited R. J. Jones, 14 Calderstones Road, Henry Owen, 16 Harthill Avenue and W. Penry Williams, Calderstones Road to succeed him. As it happened these three lived near Calderstones Park, a considerable distance from Webster Road. But near enough to walk when the church moved to Heathfield Park.

George Jenkins of Karslake Road

Of the eight funerals in which Daniel Davies officiated, one was that of Iorwerth Davies, 16 Mayville Road, an ex-soldier. He died from war wounds, leaving a widow and a son John Ifor Davies, who later became a teacher at the Calder High School, and after his early retirement, a clergyman who gave tremendous service to the Anglican Church of All Hallows in Allerton and the Anglican Churches of Lixwm in Flintshire, from where his wife Nesta (née Davies) hailed. One of the last christenings in the ministry of Daniel Davies was on New Year's Day 1922 when Alwena Davies, 44 Dovedale Road was brought into the fold. One cannot but recognise the vast contribution which she and her family made to the chapel at Heathfield Road until her retirement when she moved to Rhos-on-sea. Her death, at the end of 2006, brought to an end a chapter of dedication for which one can be grateful.

At the end of 1922 the Reverend Daniel Davies decided to accept the call to Tegid Chapel in Bala, one of the most important causes in the history of the denomination. At the end of 1922 Webster Road had on its books 606 members, the largest number during his tenure of office.

When I first came to Liverpool, he had many admirers amongst leading members of the chapel, such as Mrs J. Pugh Davies, and she often referred to the children, Aeron and Emrys, who became ministers of the gospel like their father, and the daughter, Mair, who married a minister. The Reverend Aeron Davies served the Welsh for years in the Wallasey -

David Griffiths, an elder

Birkenhead area and the other son, the Reverend Emrys Davies, Llandrindod, served as a Chaplain in the RAF, while his sister, Mair, married the Reverend J. Harries Hughes, Pontypridd, twin brother of Dr R. Arthur Hughes and both became Moderators of the Presbyterian Church of Wales. Their father, the Reverend Daniel Davies, served the Welsh of Ramilies Road and Webster Road for six years, a period when his dynamic preaching was well received. His efforts brought results in most aspects of the witness. Wherever one turns, according to the Reverend Daniel Davies, God's powers is manifested and his presence is made apparent in his son, Jesus Christ, and in the circle of his disciples. Our great God does care for his children. He secures forever those who are His. It was a positive Gospel which, according to Mrs J. Pugh Davies, gave the congregation comfort and commitment from his ministry.

A glimpse of a street in the village of Croesor in Merionethshire - the shop and a house for sale.

The village of Cilgeran in north Pembrokeshire, the birthplace of George Jenkins, an elder and a Liverpool Welsh builder

The Babell Chapel, the spiritual home of George Jenkins at Cilgeran as a boy.

An old Welsh farmstead with a symbol of modernity.

Chapter 6

PREPARING FOR THE NEW CHAPEL AND ITS COMPLETION (1923-1929)

It was an exhilarating experience to the Webster Road community to have a successor to the Reverend Daniel Davies. A call was extended to the Reverend Robert Davies, BA, minister of Carregddu Welsh Presbyterian Chapel in Blaenau Ffestiniog. He and his wife, his son Mr R. Maldwyn Davies and daughter, Miss Gwyneth Davies, came to live in the new Manse at 16 Russell Road, a pleasant road off Ullet Road. The house had been bought by the chapel for £723. The actual cost of moving their furniture and contents from Blaenau Ffestiniog came to £22-5-0.

The new minister soon settled down, and it became clear that he was the right person to give leadership on the important task of moving to a new building. He warned the flock that they had a 'mountain to climb' but that 'nothing was impossible for faith and love' to overcome. They collected the sum of £4,174-12-8 in his first year as minister towards building the new chapel, but he warned them of the huge task ahead. They lost 31 members and concern was expressed, that because of the severe economic conditions in the country,

One of our neighbours in Smithdown Place.

Welsh people were migrating from rural north Wales to Wavertree, Sefton Park and Allerton areas of Liverpool seeking work.

It was also sad to lose very talented people in their prime of life. The medical practitioner, Dr Richard James Jones, Clynnog, Allerton Road, son of the Reverend James Jones and Mrs Jones, Croesywaen, Caernarfonshire died in his early twenties. He was the brother of Dr Emyr Wyn Jones, the Liverpool Welsh cardiologist who contributed so much for the eisteddfod movement and Welsh history. Dr R. James Jones had recently married one of the young women of the church, Miss Gwladys Jones, daughter of Mr J. W. Jones and Mrs Ellen Jones, Hiraethog, Garth Drive. They had everything going for them on their wedding day on 3 January 1922. Both settled in a delightful house some hundred yards from the home of Mrs Jones's parents and joy came to the hearth in December

Reverend Robert Davies

when a daughter Elinor Wyn (later Betws-yn-Rhos) was born, to be baptised on 30 December 1922. Dr R. James Jones was a promising Welsh poet and a volume of his poetry was published. He was an asset to the Welsh Christian movement.

It was individuals like him who were the backbone of the local branch of the League of Nations. The chairman was J. R. Jones of Cintra and J. Llewelyn Jenkins, 86 Grant Avenue was Secretary. Both later were elected as elders. In the year 1924, 75 members of the chapel had paid subscriptions to become members of the League of Nations branch.

From the beginning the Reverend Robert Davies was determined to be a conscientious pastor to his flock. His hope 'was to know every member and every attender, not only by his appearance but by his name, as well as his characteristics and his relationship within the fabric of life'. The young people were very supportive of his ministry. The young people of Webster Road in 1924 were full of initiatives, supporting the Literary Society, Welsh League of Youth, League of Nations, the Sunday Schools, the drama group and summer-time activities. This is the tribute of the minister: 'If it were not for them our week-night meetings would often be thinly attended. It is wonderful to see them in the *Seiat* [Society] and the Prayer Meeting: and who in the near future will be the leaders? It will be them'.

It was right to make these observations. Webster Road Chapel was a relatively young church as far as members were concerned. The Reverend Robert Davies acknowledged that it was the middle aged who carried the largest responsibility and the largest share of the financial burdens. He adds this sentence: 'We have no one who is old, but some are on the threshold of seventy, but may they keep in mind that it is not by the number of years that one should count the quality of life'.

A large number of young people were working for the Sunday School in Ramilies Road under the guidance of Sam Rogers, whose two brothers became ministers in the denomination, the Reverend A. H. Rogers, Cilgeran and the Reverend G. W. Rogers, who came to live in Allerton to be with his son's family in the 1960s. There were 42 adults involved in the Ramilies Road Sunday School while there were 43 in the Webster Road Sunday School, a total of 85 individuals, all convinced of the need for religious education. In the Sunday School there was the notable Platt family of 126 Alderson Road, namely Evan Platt and his wife and sons, Thomas Richard, Ivor, who was accepted by the Presbytery as a preacher on trial in 1924, and Glyn Platt. Thomas Richard and Ivor Platt, and eight others, were in charge of the Band of Hope which catered for the children. An annual picnic was held usually in June. In 1924 they went to Sefton Meadows and the expenses amounted to £27-10-8. The cost of hiring the bus was £15-0-0 and the tea cost £12-10-8.

In 1924 R. D. Roberts, 19 Russell Road, son of a well-known Presbyterian Minister in Merioneth, the Reverend David Roberts, Blaenau Ffestiniog, died. The brother of R. D. Roberts was the well-known pacifist, the Reverend Dr Richard Roberts, one of the founding members of the Fellowship of Reconciliation during the First World War before he emigrated to New York and later to Toronto in Canada.

It was decided to establish a committee with wide-ranging agenda for the new chapel in Heathfield Road. According to the rules of the Presbyterian Church, the minister is expected to convene such a committee, and the mega builders were appointed officers - J. W. Jones as Treasurer, John Jones, Mayfield, a Vice Chairman and his son, J. R. Jones as Secretary. They amalgamated the Building and the Finance Committees and one of the precentors, R.

Dudley Institute was situated in this area.

J. Jones, 14 Calderstones, became Secretary of the Buildings Committee. The committee had eight other members, all of them builders, Henry Davies, Dovedale Road, John Hughes, Moveivion, E. J. Jenkins, Rowland Jones (eldest son of J. W. Jones), Thomas Jones, Queen's Drive; T. W. Thomas, Allerton Road (father of Doris and Eunice Thomas) and Thomas Roberts, Stalybridge Avenue.

The Finance Committee was a large committee under the chairmanship of Owen Hughes, Secretary of the chapel with J. R. Davies, Dovedale Road, as Secretary. It consisted of twelve men and thirteen women, including the minister's wife and Mrs Backhouse, housekeeper to the family of John Jones at Mayfield, Dudlow Lane. This made a total of 25. I noticed that not every one of the elders was a member of the New Chapel Committee. One does not see the names of William Davies, Henry Williams, R. J. Evans, David Griffiths and George Jenkins. Ill-health was the reason for the absence of R. J. Evans and William Davies but the wives of David Griffiths and George Jenkins were members of the Committee also. This was a large committee, as far

Penny Lane.

as numbers were concerned, but it had been chosen carefully in order to get representation from likeable members of every section of the chapel community.

The details of those who contributed to the building of the new chapel include very generous donations that came through the efforts of J. W. Jones in 1923 and 1924, a total of £1,250 in 1923 and £250 in 1924, making a total of £1,500. John Davies, 32 Crawford Avenue, contributed the sum of £250 in 1923; Owen Hughes £50 in 1923 and the same figure for 1924, and George Jenkins, the builder gave £250 in 1923 and John Jones, Mayfield, the generous sum of £1,000 in 1924. But no one could be compared to J. W. Jones and his family. Three of his sons gave £50 each, Rowland, W. Glyn and John Trevor Jones – and, the youngest Howell Vaughan Jones gave the sum of £5. The precentor, R. J. Jones, Eirianfa, £100 in 1923 and another builder, T. W. Jones, a cheque for £100 in the same year. The cigarette company, W. D. and H. O. Willis Ltd, Bristol, gave a guinea in 1924 in view of the fact that they were originally staunch Congregationalists!

1925 proved to be an important landmark, the end of a chapter, and the beginning of a new and interesting story. The last service was held in Webster Road on the first Sunday in August under the ministry of the Reverend Seth Pritchard, Cwmtirmynach, in Merioneth. The following Sunday they held their services in Dudley Institute, Blenheim Road, under the ministry of the Reverend E. Arfon Jones, Denbigh. Then on 17 October 150 bricks were laid at the Heathfield Road site by the children of the chapel, and one of the few who remembers that event as a participant is Miss Dilys Griffith, Patterdale Road. The children were addressed by Miss C. E. Pugh, Llefenni. A fortnight later, on 31 October, the foundation stones were laid by three of the officers of the chapel, Owen Hughes, Salisbury Road, Secretary, John Jones, Mayfield, Treasurer, and J. W. Jones, the main instigator behind the whole project. The new chapel was designed by the Liverpool company of Richard Owen and Son, and the building was to be built by John Williams, Collingwood Street. They received the sum of £2,200-5-5 for the sale of the old chapel and its buildings in Webster Road.

The historian of the cause, His Honour Judge J. E. Jones, mentions the old quarry bought from the estate of the Marquis of Salisbury, which was filled with stones and waste material by a builder who was a member of the chapel. To meet the requirements of the planning authority the frontage of the chapel had to be refocused creating a problem that still exists. The original design was to build the chapel facing Church Road, but it had to be built facing Penny Lane by the insistence of the planning authority, which means that it has to brave the onslaught of constant wind and rain. For this reason the wall behind the gallery always needs attention. We have spent some fifty thousand pounds since 1968 on trying to cope with this problem, which has still not been rectified.

The large schoolroom was built before the chapel sanctuary. In the beginning, after moving to worship in Dudley Institute, the children who attended the Sunday School at Webster Road joined the children of the Ramilies Road Sunday School, while the adults met at Dudley Institute. As both buildings were near to each other, no difficulties were experienced by the superintendent or by the teachers. Because of the lack of accommodation, a number of meetings of the Literary Society and the Reading Group were cancelled. Even worse than the lack of space was the lack of time, since a large number of committees dealing with

The kitchen at the Heathfield Road Chapel.

matters concerning the new building had to be held. A Bazaar to raise money was held in St George's Hall in the centre of Liverpool on 24-27 November 1926.

One of the able organisers for the Bazaar died before it was held. She was Mrs Catherine Davies, 49 Ramilies Road, wife of William Davies, an elder since 1900, who died on 8 April 1926. She was greatly respected for her strong personality and her long- standing service to Webster Road and to the Ramilies Road chapel. She was one of the main organisers of the earlier Bazaar held in 1899 and did a great deal of work organising for the 1926 Bazaar. Among the ten members lost there was a baby of 14 months, Gwilym, son of Mr and Mrs W. R. Jones, 394 Queen's Drive, and Vivian a native of Caerwys, who worked as a maid for the J. W. Jones family at Hiraethog in Garth Drive; Nellie Parry, a teacher in the Sunday School, and Miss Ella Williams, 12 Newborough Avenue, who died of TB in the Chest Sanatorium at Frodsham. The minister said of her that she had 'given valuable service to the Sunday School, loving the children like a mother, praying regularly for the young and in return they all prayed for her during her long illness. She was well-loved by a large section of the congregation and when we heard of her passing we were filled with sadness'.

On 2 July 1925, Robert Jones Evans, 36 Wellington Avenue, died, a person who had given distinguished service as an elder since 1919. A gentle and kind character, R. J. Evans was highly regarded for his public prayers. A godly man who looked forward to the new chapel, he personified Presbyterianism at its best. In view of the huge cost of building the new chapel, many different methods were devised to raise money. Members paid a shilling each for their names to be inserted on a linen cloth. Their names are still precious reminders for most of those that have now been recalled to higher service. On 24-27 November the Bazaar held in St George's Hall proved to be a huge success. There were six stalls named after the areas where the members lived. A profit of £407-18-3½ was made by the Allerton stall and £135-9-4½ by the efforts of Wavertree. The Mossley Hill stall was the most successful with £514-0-4; Sefton succeeded in making a profit of £334-6-4½, with Woolton slightly ahead with a total of £357-3-11. The stall selling food and ice cream made a profit of £140-1-6. The strength of the bazaar was the way in which co-operation was motivated between the Welsh Presbyterian churches on Merseyside, which sold a large number of tickets, contributing gifts and buying from the stalls.

Contribution made by the Presbyterian Chapels on Merseyside	£	s	c
Anfield Road	143	2	6½
Belvidere Road	87	1	0
Chatham Street	117	10	8
Bethlehem, Douglas Road	83	10	9½
Edge Lane	105	2	9½
Fitzclarence Street	114	18	9
Garston	31	16	6

Laird Street, Birkenhead	91	9	6½
Rake Lane, New Brighton	100	2	6
Newsham Park	106	13	0
Parkfield, Birkenhead	33	9	11
Peel Road, Seacombe	10	15	6
Princes Road (on top of the list)	212	13	7
Rock Ferry	5	11	0
Seacombe	16	19	0
Peniel, Southport	25	10	4
in addition, goods to the value of	8	5	0
Stanley Road, Bootle	141	13	9
Walton Park	40	8	0
Crosby Road South, Waterloo	64	18	6
West Kirby	164	1	6
Woodchurch Road	23	10	11
Total	**£1769**	**0**	**1**

I notice that those Welsh chapels on the outskirts of Liverpool, namely Widnes, Runcorn, Huyton Quarry, Prescot, St Helens, St Helens Junction, Ellesmere Port did not cooperate in this scheme. If West Kirby chapel could contribute £164-1-6 then it is feasible to expect the two Welsh Presbyterian chapels of St Helens and St Helens Junction could have assisted, even if the donation were as small as those from Peel Road and Rock Ferry.

The expenses of the Bazaar were very high. The chapel had to pay £86-12-6 for the hire of the hall, they paid £176-5-7 for the entertainment, namely the Silver Band of the Welsh Guards. The preparation and hire of the stalls came to £103-0-0, the advertising and the printing to £96-10-3, while the insurance came to £2-15-0. The general costs are recorded as £11-12-0, hiring the cash registers for the six stalls £4-16-0, making a total of £520-18-10. The financial statement was audited by J. Llew Jenkins who later became an elder, and T. Lloyd Williams, whose fellowship the author was fortunate to enjoy together with that of his wife, Mrs Sidney Williams in their home near All Hallows Church in Greenhill Road. Both paid tribute to the work of the two Treasurers, J. R. Jones and Rowland Jones, sons of two of the main instigators of the whole project, the building magnates John Jones (John Drinkwater) and J. W. Jones.

Other important meetings were a means of raising money. An important institution in Welsh Nonconformity until the end of the twentieth century in most large chapels was the preaching service. This was the climax of the year's preaching. In a city such as Liverpool, the standard of proclaiming the Word of God was high, as a number of outstanding preachers resided within its boundaries. In the period 1923-1927 there were at least four outstanding communicators of the Word. The most notable was the Reverend Dr J. G. Moelwyn Hughes,

MA. Following him as an itinerant star preacher one would name Daniel Davies, minister of Webster Road until 1923; Currie Hughes, the young minister of Peel Road, Seaforth and a native of Anglesey, and R. Aethwy Jones, Newsham Park, who spent his whole ministry in his first pastorate in an area where there was a strong Welsh presence.

Liverpool churches endeavoured to attract some of the denomination's most celebrated communicators. Did they succeed? In 1923 they invited the Reverend Llewellyn Lloyd, who later became minister of Chatham Street Welsh Chapel in Liverpool, and E. P. Jones of Cardiff, then in 1924 two very exceptional preachers, the Reverend M. P. Morgan of Blaenannerch in west Wales and the Reverend W. R. Jones of Holyhead came to Liverpool. In 1926 they invited a former minister, the Reverend Daniel Davies to preach on Saturday, 2 October, and at two services on Sunday, 3 October (an obvious honour to him). He was exceptionally powerful in his ministry during that weekend. In 1927 they invited the Reverend Dr T. Charles Williams of Menai Bridge but he died a few days before the event on 29 September, only five days before the *Cyrddau Mawr* (Important Meetings). The church officers succeeded in getting an unusual prophet in the person of the Christian Socialist, the Reverend John Morgan Jones, MA of the English Chapel of Hope in Merthyr Tydfil. He served the church in Merthyr Tydfil for 37 years, a town renowned for its left-wing politics since the days of Henry Richard and Keir Hardie. J. Morgan Jones's nephew, the Reverend Morgan R. Mainwaring (who was considered a possible minister for the Heathfield Road Chapel in 1948) wrote an impressive article on him in a volume on Welsh pacifists, edited by the present writer under the title, *Herio'r Byd* [Challenging the World] (Modern Welsh Publications Ltd, 1980). The collections

The heating system.

at these preaching services were transferred to the fund for building the new chapel. In the period 1923 to 1925 the sum of £27-16-5 was transferred, then in 1926 £11-15-4, and then in 1927 £12-18-1. In addition carol singers were organised in that period to travel around the area and they transferred substantial sums, £28-1-2 for 1923 to 1925 and £14-10-6 for 1926. A further £4-7-3 was raised by a lecture delivered by a fine preacher from Llansanffraid-ym-Mechain, the Reverend W. M. Jones, and late of Liverpool. Through all these efforts, and the sale of Webster Road Chapel for £2820-5-5 and a further £699 for the sale of Ramilies Road Schoolroom, all the efforts came to £19,004.

The church had elected two new leaders in 1925, J. R. Davies, Dovedale, and R. J. Jones, Eirianfa, Menlove Avenue, two who gave valuable service to the community.

The chairs for the elders.

Though the church had a large number of members, they were quite reluctant to elect too many elders. The average number for the period 1900 to 1925 was three, that is how it was in 1911 and 1919, and two in 1925, and even subsequently there was very little change.

The new chapel was officially opened on Saturday, 26 March 1927. However, a fortnight before it was opened, they realised that there was not enough room in the *Sêt Fawr* (Elders' Pew), which meant that that they had to move the pulpit further back, so it was partially under the organ loft. Moreover two days before the official opening they realised that the pulpit did not have a ledge. They had to place one made of metal till one of the chapel members, a fine craftsman, prepared a beautiful ledge in oak. This has been part of the pulpit ever since.

The facilities in the new chapel were remarkable. It had a room for the Minister, a room for the elders, two rooms for the Sunday School, a small compact schoolroom, a large schoolroom, a kitchen, toilets for men and women and a library. The library in Webster Road had been well-served by librarians such as Emrys Roberts, 32 Cantsfield Street, and, daughter of the elder, R. J. Evans, namely Miss Dilys Evans, 36 Wellington Avenue. The author remembers well the library stamp and the rules pertaining to the library, but to his disappointment the books had long disappeared, before he arrived in Liverpool.

The Society meetings were beginning to lose popularity with the majority of the members, because religious experience was not a subject that chapel members were keen to discuss. One useful and encouraging note was the contribution and the support of the young people. Only two members were lost in its first year in its new home out of 611 members. But the two who died reflected on the high quality of the membership. The first person to die was Mrs Ann Jones, 6 Belhaven Road, on 12 February, before the chapel was opened. She was nearly 80 years of age and her zeal for Calvinistic Methodism was evident to all her contemporaries. Mrs Ann Jones knew more than most of her contemporaries about the life and work of its ministers. She remembered the great preachers such as the Reverend Dr Thomas Charles Williams, Menai Bridge, and she had provided hospitality on a Sunday to many of these men of prayer and holiness. The other person who died at the beginning of July was Leslie J. Rees, 26a Smithdown Road; very little could be said of him besides that he never sought the limelight and attended the services infrequently. He was an apathetic member, representing those who have been on membership lists of every chapel and church since the days of the Apostles. The first baptism in the new chapel was on 30 April when Dyfi Gwenda Thomas, 59 Granville Road, was accepted into the care of the chapel, and another three were christened during the year, a total of six for 1927. The first wedding took place on 1 June when Arthur Davies, 9 Ramilies Road, married Florence May Owen, 18 Mapledale Road. Another wedding took place on the threshold of Christmas, on December 21 between Thomas Jones Parry and Mary Jane Jones, both living at 35 Charles Berrington Road, off Heathfield Road.

1928 was a year of pleasant surprises. The response to the collections was excellent and it was decided to collect towards the suffering of the miners. This effort came to £20-10s-0p. Clearly Heathfield Road was a generous church and so it proved throughout the years. The chapel's debt continued, to the constant worry of the minister. This was his call on 28 February 1929: 'If everyone responded according to his ability we could clear a large amount of the debt in 1929'. But he was not heeded, although he was quite authoritative in his manner and strong in leadership. The church was like a fruitful garden, with growth and harvest on every side, but a reluctance to clear the debt. The Sunday School flourished, a large number attended on Monday night as well as at the activities for the rest of the week. They flocked to the societies, the Literary Society, Young People's Society, the League of Nations Society and to the local branch of the North Wales Women's Temperance Union, the Drama group and the Tonic Sol-fa and the Welsh Language Classes. This was a flourishing community with some individuals more active than others. Miss Doris Thomas, 43 Allerton Road, was in the forefront of the Temperance Witness, while Miss Megan Price and Richard Williams were in charge of the young people. The chapel had extraordinary caretakers in Mr and Mrs William Owen. The Band of Hope did sterling work with the children and they decided to send an annual sum of money to assist the missionary endeavour in North-East India. The Poverty Campaign flourished under the chairmanship of Robert Thomas, 8 Beckenham Avenue, with Miss Gertrude Hughes as Secretary. She lived at the Manse and made a substantial effort to bring the needs of the starving masses to her fellow members. The Flowers Committee, which was as effective then as now, had Miss Laura Jones, Bristol Road, as their Secretary.

The chapel suffered great losses; fourteen died, and the Minister said of one of them, Mrs Laura Jane Jenkins, wife of the elder George Jenkins, 46 Karslake Road: 'Wherever she went she brought comfort and the remembrance of her is everlasting'.

On 3 September Mrs T. W. Thomas, mother of Doris and Eunice

Copies of the 'Brython' newspaper.

Thomas, died. She had been a faithful member and had contributed regularly to the activities of the chapel and to the services. The new chapel flourished with excellent congregations on Sunday, mornings and evenings and a large gathering to the Sunday Schools in the afternoon. Let me remind you of the words of the Minister for 1929: 'There is great support for the Monday night Prayer meeting. Of all the weekly meetings, besides the Sunday services, this is the most well attended and popular gathering'.

Three important aspects of the ministry of the Reverend Robert Davies were:

(a)   the Temperance witness

(b)   the Peace witness

(c)   the evangelisation witness for Christ.

This sentence summarises his philosophy: 'We are saints, and as saints we should co-operate with God to bring his wonderful deed to fruition, which is to win the world to Christ and our Lord.'

A new Hymn Book for the Presbyterians and Methodists in Wales, appeared in 1929, a valuable volume which brought an extra dimension to the Sunday services. The chapel received 54 members in 1929 and lost 53. Amongst the new members there were two who had laboured as missionaries in Lushai in North-East India. The Reverend D. E. Jones and Mrs Jones had moved to 5 Tanat Drive, Allerton, a house built by the elder J. W. Jones and his company. He called the road Tanat Drive as his wife came from Brithdir, outside Llanrhaeadr-ym-Mochnant in the Tanat Valley in north Montgomeryshire. The number of communicants at Heathfield Road Chapel stood at 629 on 1 January 1930, an increase of one on the preceding year. But the number of children attending the chapel was decreasing from 119 to 108. It was sad that twelve of them were deleted from the list of members as they had not supported the chapel in any way.

The debt on the chapel stood in 1929 at £7466-15-7, which was equivalent £11-17-5 for every member. Amongst the six who died in 1929 there was a young boy named Thomas Emlyn Parry, 35 Charles Berrington Road, a favourite with his contemporaries, and a Welsh poet, Isaac Roberts (ap Carog) of 32 Towers Road, and one of those who acted as producer of the local Drama Group. When one views the list of teachers in the Sunday School, one is impressed, since there were 23 individuals ready to prepare weekly classes for the adult Sunday School and 14 in the children's section. I noticed that every one of the elders in 1929, except for John Jones, Mayfield, acted as a Sunday School teacher, as well as taking responsibility for the financial, cultural and spiritual life of the community.

Great excitement was experienced on 12 September at the wedding of two who had been brought up in the chapel, Rowland Owen Jones, Hiraethog, Garth Drive, and Blodwen Jones, Eirianfa, Menlove Avenue, son and daughter of two of the elders. By 1929 there were three young people preparing for the Christian Ministry from Heathfield Road. These were D. Jones Hughes, York Avenue, Great Crosby; Ivor Platt and John Trevor Jones, 41 Plattsville Road. The minister could inspire his congregation to service with this encouragement: 'Our God deserves from us our best for his sake and his kingdom, and I am certain that our efforts will not be in vain in the Lord'.

Reverend Albert Evans-Jones known as Cynan, who wrote and arranged the Good News Pageant at St George's Hall, Liverpool from 6-9 May 1931. Involved in the pageant were 350 actors from the Welsh chapels - an indication of the incredible activity in the cultural life of the Welsh chapels of Merseyside.

Trevor Jones as a ministerial student in the 1930s

*Dr R. Arthur Hughes and Mrs Nancy Hughes on their wedding day
(7 January 1939) at Palm Grove Wesleyan Chapel, Birkenhead. They set
sail from Birkenhead to Calcutta and Shillong on January 28. He began
his duties as a surgeon at Shillong Welsh Mission Hospital on St David's Day.*

Another photograph from the archives of the 1930s.

Harvest Festival at Heathfield Road Chapel in the 1930s.

Chapter 7

THE ACTIVITIES IN THE THIRTIES

Throughout the thirties the chapel at Heathfield Road was full of enthusiasm to win more members. Lack of attendance at chapel by the Welsh was discussed constantly. It was decided, in the summer of 1930, that two dozen young people act in the tradition of the Mormon Church and visit potential new members amongst the Welsh people. These would go, two by two, and invite the Welsh people in Liverpool to start afresh to read the Bible and support chapel activities. The young people had a prayer meeting every Sunday morning at 9.45 a.m. and usually these gatherings were organised by J. R. Davies. These gatherings were a means of inspiring a number of young people to take part in prayer meetings and for some, perhaps, to consider a call to the Christian ministry. The chapel had a number of lay people who preached regularly. One who was remembered for his ministry when he died on

The first Presbytery open meeting to be held at the Chapel.

Originally a schoolroom belonging to the Welsh Independents at Grove Street.

12 June 1930, was Robert Dodd, Elm Hall Drive, a native of Rhosllannerchrugog but who had lived in south Wales before he moved to Liverpool.

At this time it was with sadness that the death of a nine year old lad, John Ronald Thomas, 22 Elmsdale Road, was recorded on 6th December. When his Missionary Box was opened at the end of the year, they found the sum of £2 3s 8d, made up of pennies, three pences, six pences and shillings. This had been a generous response by a child and his memory is preserved in this volume.

The chapel received 21 to communion from amongst the young people of Heathfield Road Sunday School, a large number. In addition, there were 18 from the Liverpool Welsh churches and 36 largely from Wales itself, making a total of 75. No one came from outside Christian communities and the adherents, who were not members, had, by this date, largely disappeared from the congregation. Adherents, who were not actually members, had been a phenomenon in Nonconformity but this was no longer a feature. In 1930 fourteen left for other churches in Liverpool, 26 to other churches, 2 to foreign countries, one was excommunicated and three members died, making a total loss of forty nine. One can see from the statistics that the communicants had increased from 629 to 655, that is 26 new members. This was the largest number in the history of the cause, which started in the Windsor area. But one fact was of serious concern, the falling numbers of children. In 1921, the number of children came to 162, but by 1930, they had decreased to 93.

The chapel community collected £1,345 6s 10d for the buildings at Heathfield Road, £143 10s 5d towards the cost of the organ and £96 13s 8d was received, towards the costs of seating, from the young People's Society and £201.11s.9d from the local drama group. In Webster Road seats were provided for 'sinners', that is the Welsh people who were not respectable with regard to their dress or their morals, including individuals who regularly frequented public houses. But in Heathfield Road Chapel the 'sinners' pews' had disappeared by this date. Yet, there was one slight change: half

Allerton Police Station built by John Lewis, a member of the Chapel.

The work of John Lewis.

a crown a quarter was charged for the seats in the two wings, and one shilling and nine pence a quarter for those who sat in the centre of the sanctuary.

In 1930 a special meeting was held to consider the possibility of reducing or deleting the chapel debt. The sum of £3,000 was promised. These promises were to be paid to the Treasurer, John Jones, Mayfield, over a period of three years. It is of interest to analyse this list of promises, with John Jones himself making a promise of £1,000; and J. W. Jones and his wife the same sum. The next highest amount came from wealthy builder, Mr. Thomas Roberts and Mrs. Roberts, Monfa, Harthill Road, with a promise of £250; Mr. and Mrs. R. J. Jones, Eirianfa, pledged the sum of £200. The debt amounted to £5,536 18s 5d in 1930, that is £8 9s 0d a member.

Members who attended Heathfield Road Chapel enjoyed a regular ministry and in 1931 a Missionary Pageant was held 6-9th May. The children, young people and the women took part in the preparations and the Pageant was produced by the preacher-poet, the Reverend Albert Evans-Jones, who by 1931 had assumed the bardic pseudonym, 'Cynan', by which he was subsequently known. During the last years of the twenties, thousands had sat entranced at Caernarfon and Conwy Castles as the historical pageants that Cynan had written and directed were performed. So, in the Spring of 1931, there were great expectations when Cynan came to Liverpool to present his pageant, *Good Tidings*. The children were used to performing on the stage for they were expected to learn and recite a verse in the weekly *Seiat*. They had been nurtured in the Band of Hope before becoming fully fledged members of the chapel. They were also taught tonic sol-fa notation and encouraged to compete in the Liverpool Welsh Eisteddfodau and concerts. One of the important events was the staging of the National Eisteddfod of Wales in Liverpool in 1929, when the activities were held in Sefton Park. A Liverpool Welsh Children's Choir was established and a number of children from the chapel became members. They remembered this experience for the rest of their lives.

The style of John Lewis as a builder

In 1931 an opportunity was given to the congregation to vote on the possibility of choosing more elders. After a secret ballot J. R. Jones, son of John Jones,

Allerton Fire Brigade Station erected by the Welsh builder, John Lewis.

Mayfield, and J. Llewelyn Jenkins were chosen, both prominent figures in the Liverpool Welsh community. These two men had been greatly involved with the construction of Heathfield Road Chapel. Both were Sunday School teachers and also carried the *Sêt Fawr* tradition, as I have mentioned earlier, of teaching elders.

The total chapel membership at the beginning of January 1932 amounted to 663, an increase of eight over the preceding year. It is interesting to note that a number of collections had been arranged in support of missionary work, towards the work of Miss Andrews. These raised the sum of £19 15s to keep a native teacher in North-East India under the auspices of the Linen League. There were very few churches more supportive of the Foreign Mission work than this church and it has proved to be so until our own days. The need to support poor people financially gained the adherence of a sizeable number of members and, in 1932, they collected £3 17s 1d to assist the Christian Churches of Syria. The collection towards the Good Tidings Pageant came to £400 5s ½d with £243 18s 0d coming from those who were known as supporters. All these are listed under the heading of Connexion and Public Collections, under the care of the secretary, W. Phillip Davies, 34 Heydale Road. I have very happy memories of the time when I visited his widow and daughter in their home. His widow lived to a grand old age and I used to receive a wonderful welcome each time I visited her. In this period, some members sat in the gallery, twelve of them in 1931, mainly young men and women who had come to work in the city. Amongst these I notice the name of Tom Bennion, a native of Montgomeryshire, who spent a whole lifetime in the employment of J. W. Jones and who became overseer for the building company.

The minister, the Reverend Robert Davies, had his own views and he was quite well versed in what was happening on the world stage as well as in the Welsh community of the city. In his verdict on 1932 he could state: 'Look at 1932 as the year of promise and disappointment. A large number of promises were made in the course of the year but very few of them were implemented'. He quotes a paragraph from one of the commentators of the

Fallowfield Road

The small schoolroom of Heathfield Road.

Anglican Church, Canon F. R. Barry: 'We sit and starve in the midst of plenty, content with the economies of Bedlam – not because any sane man believes in them, but for sheer lack of facts in anything else – while the world slips down from chaos to catastrophe'.

This was a somewhat devastating comment, but what the minister implies is that anyone who has authority in the church or the world receives criticism. 'They attack', he said, 'religion and religionists for they have no salvation.' Yet to him and his members there was an answer, even an escape from sin, and an alternative to the failure of politicians to safeguard the working class from unemployment. The answer to the inevitable weaknesses of the individual is to be found in a healthy relationship with God in Jesus.

Moreover, the Minister raises another important point. Though acknowledging the salvation and the spirituality that belonged to religious services, he asks the question which often comes to leaders of chapels and churches, 'Are we, as members, appreciative of the spiritual and cultural provision as we should?' By 1932 the spiritual meetings were less popular than they had been a decade earlier. These are the words of the Reverend Robert Davies:

> Let me say, and say it in all truth, that the number in comparison who attend the spiritual meetings in the week nights – the Prayer Meeting and the *Seiat*, the power house of the spiritual life of the church, are relatively small. Oh! it would be wonderful to see, as in the days of old, the room full and everyone eager to approach the throne of grace and ready to express what God had done for them in his extravagant love.

The most important Church event, the General Assembly was held on 10-12 May, 1932. The General Assembly had, over the years, come to Liverpool regularly but this was the first time it had come to the Allerton and Childwall area. The usual centres had been Princes Road, Chatham Street and the Anfield Road Chapels but now a new centre had been added to

Ministers (Reverend J.Hughes Morris and Reverend David Jones) and elders of Edge Lane Chapel..

the list. The General Assembly, as we see in the photograph, was a large gathering of ministers and elders of the Connexion.

The Church at Heathfield Road placed a great deal of emphasis on the Peace Witness. A number of meetings were held and they invited some outstanding speakers on behalf of Peace and Disarmament. Resolutions were prepared and passed and sent to those who governed in church and politics. No church could do more than this; the community expressed the Gospel of Peace in its voice and in its welcome to the Welsh people. The Reverend Robert Davies expressed himself in no uncertain terms on the matter:

> Every member of the Church of Christ should oppose war and be supportive of peace. It is in the time of peace that one should condemn war and not when the conflict is bleeding and paralysing us. Remember them too, so support every movement geared to peace. Then, if the sad day comes, and it will be a sad day, we will have at least a peaceful conscience that we have done our best to try to avoid war in days of grace and in the appropriate time.

This was useful advice and a concern that is still relevant. This advice could not be surpassed as an important item for society, especially when Adolf Hitler and his followers were demonstrating their intentions and threatening the world from their Alpine fortress in Germany.

The chapel at Heathfield Road was gaining new members every year. Forty eight joined, 37 from other chapels, eight from the fold of the church and three from the Welsh community in 1932. Thirty nine left and five died; and amongst them was Mrs. Mary Hughes, Moneivion, Green Lane, wife of the elder, John Hughes. The Church received in memory of the late Mrs. Hughes a gift of a Peter Williams Bible. This Bible had been prepared by the eighteenth-century Methodist Revivalist, the Reverend Peter Williams, which was published in 1779. I would like to know what happened to that Bible, as today, it is a very special item, in particular the biblical commentary on every chapter by Peter Williams (1723-1796) himself.

In 1933 the Reverend Robert Davies celebrated ten years as minister of the church. When he came in 1923, he came to fulfill a long thought-out vision. With the land having been bought, the architect appointed, the plans were in hand and a large sum of money already deposited in the bank, and he chaired the meetings and oversaw the whole design for the new chapel. During this decade (1923-1932) he baptised 58, he received into communion, from the Sunday School and the Welsh Society, at least 144, 70 were lost through death and there were 58 marriages. Four new elders were elected and four were preparing for the ministry, namely David C. Edwards, 28 Bagot Street; D. Jones Hughes, Great Crosby; Ivor Platt, Alderson Road, and J. Trevor Jones, 41 Plattsville Road.

The Minister underlined a theme which he has not mentioned a great deal, namely the valuable contribution of the women. It was a long overdue tribute, for it was they who were in charge of the temperance witness; they were enthusiastic on behalf of the Mission Work and from one Sunday to another prepared the flowers to beautify the sanctuary; it was the women members who arranged the Fair in 1933 to help the church to pay off its debt. This had been something that was of great concern to the Minister, almost an obsession. We cannot forget his words in the Annual Report for 1932: 'It would be a delight to see the four thousand [pounds] disappear like snow under the rays of the sun.'

The Minister now looked forward to a new spirit, like spring after a hard winter, to revive them in their commitment. The debt was of constant concern to the minister. But a large number of the 670 members in 1933 responded, especially the women. There were other concerns that needed attention, such as the contribution of £16 6s 6d to have a fitting memorial to a famous preacher from Anglesey who had ministered at Princes Road Welsh Chapel in Liverpool, Dr. John Williams, Brynsiencyn; £33 12s 0d towards the testimonial of another outstanding preacher from Anglesey, who had served in the Chatham Street Chapel in Liverpool, the Reverend W. Llewelyn Lloyd; £7 0s 0d to the Fund in memory of the late Reverend W. J. Jones, Manchester; and the large sum of £269 9s 0d to the Testimonial Fund for Owen Hughes, who had been Secretary of the Church for forty years. But the main support came from the women members such as Mrs. Jane Williams, 17 Russell Road, who gave, between 1926 and 1933, a loan of £300 towards the Debt Fund without any interest. The Garden Fête and the Welsh Fair was a success and the Treasurer, Mrs. Mary Lewis, Green Lane, aunt of Mr. R. T. Glyn Lewis (a real gentleman and a faithful member during my ministry), received the sum of £177 15s 6d. The Garden Fête was held at Mayfield, Dudlow Drive, and followed by the Welsh Fair, which brought a profit of £140, which included efforts from every section of the church. Amongst the new members who arrived in 1933 from Anglesey, was Mrs. A. M. Farr. She moved in October to 33 Wheatcroft Road where she remained until her death. For many years, I called regularly to see her and her husband, a seafaring man with a passion for collecting stamps.

1935 was a year of celebrating two hundred years since the birth of Welsh Presbyterianism and the contribution of the Methodist Revival. It was indeed a revolution when five young men were responsible for the Revival preaching, although not one of them came near Liverpool. Their names have been carved on the pages of Welsh religious history: Howell Harris, the

The General Assembly of 1932.

74

Our Methodist neighbour of Elm Hall Drive.

organiser par excellence; Daniel Rowland, the preacher; William Williams, the hymn writer; Howell Davies, evangelist and Peter Williams, the Biblical commentator. They were the best known of dozens of preachers who were called to proclaim and disperse the good news of the Gospel. It was good to remember the past but Heathfield Road could not forget the present and two meetings were held with regard to Peace. These were addressed by Fred Llewelyn Jones, Liberal MP for Flintshire, and Rhys J. Davies, Labour MP for Westhoughton.

The church was glad to hear that Ivor Platt, mentioned earlier, had completed his ministerial training and was now to be ordained and called to minister at the Presbyterian Church of St. John's, Runcorn. J. W. Jones was honoured with a number of important responsibilities in the denomination – President of the Building Committee of the North Wales Association, Treasurer of the Missionary Fund for the Disabled and Elderly. His sister-in-law, Miss M. E. Owen, Greenhill died, a good example of Montgomeryshire charm; and six others, including a leader of the chapel, William Davies, 8 Heydale Road, a precentor for 32 years and an elder since 1901, who died on 30th December, 1934. Another hardworking leader who died was D. J. Price, Clwydian, 4 Stockville Road whose daughter, Mrs. Megan Pugh, remained extremely loyal during my ministry. He died on 10 February 1934 and on 2

J. R. Jones, Cintra.

J. Llewelyn Jenkins

In memory of Reverend David Jones.

April, his daughter, Margaret or Megan, as she was better known, was married to the chemist, Francis Vincent Pugh, whose shop was near the traffic lights where Smithdown Road meets Allerton Road. Like his daughter, D. J. Price was a committed, extremely hardworking, treasurer of the Chapel League of Nations Society and a member of the Poverty Campaign and other committees. Thomas Roberts, Harthill Avenue, a pioneer of the cause, died at his home, Monfa. Generous and a well established builder, he had been a great asset to the religious cause. It was a tragedy for the chapel to lose a young lad of eighteen, John Thomas, 12 Stamfordham Grove, one that believed in the fundamentals of the faith. Another tragedy took place on Saturday, 22 September, 1934, in the Gresford Colliery, near Wrexham, when 265 miners were killed, one of most serious explosions in the British coalfield. Altogether 261 miners, three members of the rescue team and one surface worker were lost, creating a network of sufferers – 164 widows, 242 children without a father and 132 dependants. At least 1700 men became unemployed as a result of the Gresford disaster.

A Choir of the Liverpool Welsh of 1929.

Two Welsh nurses.

Heathfield Road Chapel like so many other chapels, was affected, as many of the members originated from villages around Gresford and Wrexham, such as Coedpoeth. It was a disappointment to learn that the authorities decided to leave the bodies of the miners in the colliery. The Lord Mayor of London opened an appeal and there was also a fund in Wrexham. Heathfield Road Chapel collected £49 3s 6d from 114 of its members. Every member of the family of J. R. Davies, Dovedale Road, contributed, as did the families of Arthur Thomas, 11 Fallowfield Road, and T. W. Thomas, Allerton Road. The sums ranged from £5 given by John Jones as well as by J. W. Jones and his wife down to a shilling from others. Some forty shillings contributed to the Gresford Fund collection came from children and the young people of the chapel community.

In 1935 twelve members passed to glory: dependable women such as Miss Elen Williams, 71 Grosvenor Road; Miss E. Roberts, 59 Brookdale Road; Miss Mary Ann Evans, 20 Central Road; Mrs. Ackerley Lewis, Childwall Valley Road; Mrs. Jane Jones, 50 Heathfield Road. Then on 30 March, Ellis Morris, 50 Claremont Road, died and on 3 April, Dr. Richard Arthur Jones, Awelon, Allerton Road, a Welsh medical practitioner, and on 24 June, Emrys Jones Williams, 9 Ramilies Road, the son of the Reverend and Mrs. Afonwy Williams, Barmouth. It was a great loss to the chapel community when Henry Davies, Dovedale, Calderstones Road, died, for on his hearth he had nurtured a young man who became a Minister of the Gospel in Nottingham, Pennsylvania, the Reverend William H. Davies. His theological training was in the United States of America where he received a thorough education. A Biblical enthusiast and a Sunday School stalwart, Owen Davies, 20 Olivedale Road, was greatly mourned, and so was Captain William Williams, Artro, Wheatcroft Road, Allerton, who died in hospital at Alexandra, Egypt, after falling ill on his ship.

Our Anglican neighbour of St Barnabas.

The chapel members were thrilled in 1936 to receive the news that two young men had responded to the call of the ministry in the Presbyterian Church of Wales, namely Alwyn Jones, the son of the Reverend and Mrs. D. E. Jones, and Trefor Davies Jones, son of Mr. and Mrs. Thomas Jones, 23 Beckenham Avenue.

Another young man had already dedicated himself to the same calling, a few months earlier, namely H. Godfrey Jones, son of Mr. and Mrs. Richard Jones, Bird Street. His father, Richard Jones, had been for years the caretaker of Webster Road Chapel. Every one of these three who had decided on a unique calling was indebted to four factors: faithful parents; a home where the chapel had a high profile; a strong community of worshippers and a dedicated minister such as the Reverend Robert Davies.

The community at Heathfield Road lost six more members during 1936. On 20 March, Hugh Morgan, 77 Nicander Road, died and then on 20 June and 26 October two well known Welsh builders, Thomas William Thomas, 43 Allerton Road, and John Jones, Mayfield, Dudlow Lane. Both have been mentioned often in this volume. Owen Jones, 75 Cranborne Road, was remembered with affection, when the news spread of his passing on 20 October and also William Jones, Monfa, Harthill Road, on 13 December. The Minister only mentions the death of John Jones, Mayfield, but as one reads the list we come across the name of the Minister's own son, on Saturday 11 July. Maldwyn Davies had walked his sweetheart home and he was struck by a motor car in Brodie Avenue. His father did not mention his name in the usual section of the Annual Report and one can understand this omission. This was a horrific loss to them as a family. It occurred in the year that the chapel was celebrating fifty years since its inception in Webster Road. The celebration meeting was held on Tuesday, 5 October, 1937 and the chapel produced a useful booklet of 63 pages adding to the story as prepared and printed in *Hanes Methodistiaeth Lerpwl* (Volume 2) by the Reverend J. Hughes Morris. But this turned out to be a missed opportunity as one of the elders, such as the long serving

Elders and minister (left to right) second row, Henry Williams, George Jenkins, David Griffiths, J. R. Davies, R. J. Jones. Front row (left to right) William Davies, John Jones, Reverend Robert Davies, Owen Hughes and J. W. Jones.

Reverend Dr J. G. Moelwyn Hughes,
outstanding minister in Merseyside
from 1917-1937..

Owen Hughes, could have been invited to prepare an account that would have made a considerable additional contribution to the story. However, I hope that this volume will fill the gaps and help complete the story.

The minister, the Reverend Robert Davies, in his address for 1937, mentions what had made the year memorable. At last the chapel debt had been cleared. They had attempted to clear all debts by the Jubilee on 5 October but this had failed. Two days earlier the chapel had held its Annual Preaching Service and had invited an excellent preacher from south Cardiganshire, the Reverend M. P. Morgan, Blaenannerch, to be the guest preacher. Today, the Annual Preaching Service has disappeared in Liverpool but in those days such events were great crowd pullers. Nonconformists shared the belief that on these occasions, congregations came together for essentially only one purpose: to worship by hearing *y Gair*, 'the Word of God', addressed to them from their pulpit. This was the very reason for the existence of the building: it is the kernel around which the saints and sinners gather for inspiration, salvation and conviction that they are in God's house.

The following Sunday, 10 October, the two brothers, J. R. Jones and W. H. Jones, handed over a cheque for £1,250 in memory of their late father, John Jones, Mayfield. The minister expressed gratitude when he remarked: 'The last sum is the most difficult to move, but salvation came through one generous gift. May the kind brothers accept our genuine thanksgiving.'

The situation had been saved by the generosity of the Mayfield family and 1937 blossomed into a rosy year. The chapel received, through membership, the transfer of 55 new members, an increase of nine since the preceding year. It accepted a further 31 new members from the rural Welsh chapels of north Wales. At the end of 1937 the chapel had 691 members, the largest number in the whole history of the cause. The Sunday School, after the difficult years of the early thirties, was now beginning to renew itself. The number of adults increased from 193 to 220 and children under fifteen increased from 62 to 67. There were two reasons for these increases, namely the arrival of new members to the chapel and, secondly, the attraction of the Sunday School syllabus, to study the Gospel of Matthew. Seven members died in 1937, including two generous members, namely John Davies, Bryn Golau, Druidsville Road, and the builder, Thomas Jones, Newlands, Childwall Abbey Road.

The Church was still growing in 1938. It received 44 to communion but lost, through removal, 35, and 6 due to death, a total loss of 41. But there was an overall increase of 3 members. The Church numbered 689 members and 83 children at the end of 1938, an incredible figure compared with 2007.

But 1939 brought its pain and distress from which the cause never fully recovered. On 3 September, Neville Chamberlain proclaimed that the United Kingdom would go to war against Germany. The war and subsequent restrictions affected the chapel meetings, the collections, and even the atmosphere within the church. This was the experience of the minister, expressed in a fine Calvinistic sentence: 'Some lost their faith, others became fearful and forgetful, but the elect stood firm in spite of the calamity.'

Five members from the church died, amongst them, Mrs. Jane Williams, 17 Russell Road, one of the oldest members of the chapel who had shown generosity to Heathfield Road Church. More members left than joined the chapel. When one remembers those who left Liverpool between September and December the chapel had done quite well. A large number of children were sent away as evacuees to the safety of the Welsh countryside. The number of children declined from 62 to 44. This was just the beginning of evacuations. In the next two years at least 200,000 adults and children were moved from England to safer places in Wales.

Young people were now recruited in large numbers into the Armed Forces. The other big change had been the decision of the Reverend Robert Davies to retire at the end of 1938. After sixteen years of faithful service, he decided to move to live in the picturesque town of Llangollen on the River Dee. He and his wife and their children had been successful and energetic in Liverpool. A farewell service was held for them as a family on Monday, 15 January, 1939. He was presented with a cheque for £50 as a symbol of good wishes by the chapel. The Sisterhood bought a silver tea set for Mrs. Davies as an appreciation of her efforts over the years. The minister wrote in Welsh, a number of verses to wish the community well in seeking a successor. He had loved his work and his flock and he hoped and prayed that they would be able to find a successor who would serve faithfully the 'gospel of God . . . concerning his Son' (Romans I, verses 1-3). The minister had been faithful to the missionary preaching 'that Christ died for our sins in accordance with the New Testament scriptures'. In the preaching at Heathfield Road the saving events had been announced in the pulpit from Sunday to Sunday; Jesus was proclaimed as Lord and Christ; men and women of all ages were summoned to repent and receive forgiveness through the Son of God. An extraordinarily rich ministry had come to an end amongst the Welsh and they were soon surrounded by gloom, darkness and the potentially destructive forces of the Second World War.

Rev J. D. Evans and Mrs Evans and a Sunday School Ladies Class at the end of his ministry in 1942.

Young women of Heathfield Road Chapel, including Miss Eunice Thomas who is our oldest member at 99.

Reverend Aled Davies of Dovedale Road, a product of Heathfield Road Chapel.

The village of Ysbyty Ifan, the birthplace of the notable elder David Griffiths whose home was destroyed in the Blitz

Heathfield Road in all its glory.

Chapter 8

THE WAR YEARS AND THE NEW MINISTER DR. R. GLYNNE LLOYD (1939-1947)

The Second World War was a stressful time for the inhabitants of Liverpool. In every way, it meant tremendous changes and increasing fear as the bombs dropped, especially in May 1941, with the potential destruction of many of the chapels and churches. The chapel of Heathfield Road did not receive any damage and services were held throughout the war, except for Sunday, 11 May, 1941 which followed a week long period of bombing by the Germans. A large number of bombs were dropped around Wavertree Park, known as the Mystery, to the bottom of Smithdown Road, destroying shops and houses as well as the Post Office. One of the cluster bombs fell on the home of the hard working elder, David Grifiths, killing his wife on 4 May, 1941. The whole church extended its sincere sympathy with the Secretary of the Church in the sad loss of his wife and home. The Minute Book of the Elders' Meeting, together with the rest of the contents of the home, was destroyed in the Griffiths' house at 32 Micklefield Road. David Griffiths then moved to live at 32 Mapledale Road off Allerton Road.

The war affected every aspect of the work of the church. The church declined in number and financial support during 1940. It lost 48 members and every chapel collection showed a decrease during the year; nevertheless the total amount of all the collections was only £95 less than the total had been in 1939.

Nearly 70 members joined the Army, the Navy or the Air Force as well as other vital services. The chapel supported them well by correspondence and sending parcels to them. These actions were meant to comfort them and remind them of the community at home based at Heathfield Road Church which had been a spiritual home for them from the days of their childhood. Though the chapel had no minister to care for the members, the elders, all ten of them, were doing their best. In addition, there were three able ministerial students; H. Godfrey Jones, 18 Earlsfield Road; Trefor Davies Jones, 23 Beckenham Avenue and R. Aled Davies, 44 Dovedale Road. The number of communicants at the beginning of 1941 was 642 and though there had been a loss, nineteen new members were received.

Reverend Dr R. Glynne Lloyd.

There were five baptisms during 1940; three of them are well known names to me, namely Edward David Bennion (Woolton) who taught for years at the Quarry Bank Comprehensive School where John Lennon was a pupil; Elizabeth Pyke Kilgour, the youngest child of the remarkable Kilgour family, of 1 Arranmore Road, Mossley Hill. It is good to know that today she is very active in her local Anglican Church in the heart of the Cheshire countryside; and John Bryn Thomas, who lives in Speke, near his mother, Mrs. Eunice Thomas (who died in 2007), a native of Coedpoeth.

Five weddings took place in 1941, more than usual. The first was on 27 March when Enidwen Jones, 96 Queen's Drive, and Leonard H. Bowden from Neath, were married. They remained members for the rest of their lives and lived in Hunt's Cross, a suburb on the outskirts of Liverpool, but near to Woolton Golf Club where they both enjoyed many friendships and of course, the impressive green golf links. Enidwen's parents, Mr. and Mrs. D. T. Jones, were extremely supportive of the Chapel; and her brother, David Arthur Jones, keeps in touch with us to this day from Norfolk where he still receives our community newspaper, *Yr Angor*. Her other sister, Elizabeth Myfanwy Jones, moved to Llŷn. This family had deep roots in the history of Liverpool Welsh. On 15 November, the marriage took place of Norman J. Newton, West Derby, and Gwyneth Lloyd Roberts, 30 Earlsfield Road, two who relished their connection with the Welsh Presbyterians in Liverpool and afterwards at Trinity Chapel, Swansea, and later Siloh, Llandudno. I well remember staying at their home when I was engaged with the Preaching Service at Trinity Chapel, Swansea. At that time Norman Newton was in charge of the large Smith's Crisps Factory at Fforest Fach, an establishment which has now been closed.

The pulpit was well served throughout 1941 by many ministers from Merseyside. These included the Reverends Easter Ellis, Walton Park; Llewelyn Jones, Douglas Road; J. D. Evans, Garston; W. Llewelyn Evans, Edge Lane; Coningsby Lloyd Williams, Anfield, and ministers from Wales, including the Reverend R. Jones, Amlwch; the theologian Reverend James Humphreys from Capel Mawr, Rhosllannerchrugog; the Reverend Richard Lloyd, Rhyl and the pacifist, the Reverend T. H. Williams from London. Amongst the list of visiting preachers it is interesting to see the name of the Reverend Tecwyn Parry (1912-2006). He began his ministry in the Welsh Methodist circuit of London on the first Sunday in September 1939 at City Road Chapel. The congregation did not hear him at City Road that morning in 1939 as the Air Raid siren blasted out, (indicating that the War had started) at the very moment when Tecwyn Parry was reading out his text for the sermon. The congregation disappeared to the

John Owen
R GLYNNE LLOYD

The life and work of the 17 th century Puritan divine.

The plaque which commemorates those lost in the Second World War.

shelter. When the City Road Chapel had been burnt by the bombs at the end of 1940, there was no longer any need for two ministers in the London Welsh Methodist Circuit and Tecwyn Parry moved to Lincolnshire to serve the Methodist Church there. From Lincoln he came to preach on Sunday 18 May, 1941 at Heathfield Road. Another minister who travelled a long way to Liverpool on Sunday July 13 to proclaim the Gospel at Heathfield Road in Liverpool, was the Reverend Trevor O. Davies, M.A., lecturer in the Presbyterian College at Trefecca in the heart of the Breconshire countryside.

1941 was a most difficult year. Due to the War, the chapel lost ground when, in particular, many Welsh people moved back to Wales for the support of their own families. The gifted writer, Kate Roberts of Denbigh, in a letter to J. Saunders Lewis, dated 17 April, 1941, mentions how members of her own family from Bootle, her brother, John Evan Roberts, and his wife, Margaret, and the family left Merseyside when the horrific bombing by the German Air Force began. This is what she said: 'By this time my brother and his family were living with her, [that is their mother, Catrin Roberts, 1854-1944] – he had lost his work because of the bombing of the cotton warehouse and they feared that worse could happen to them as individuals.'

Eventually, this family returned to Liverpool, but that was not true of a large number of others who had moved to the safety of Wales for the same reasons. As many as fifteen left Heathfield Road without even bothering to ask for their membership letter. Many of these were young women who had been in domestic service, and though the elders made strong efforts to get in touch with them, they were unable to gather any information about the majority of them.

There were the inevitable losses through death, including that of the medical doctor, Dr. T. R. Williams, of 79 Ullet Road, and J. R. Lloyd, Calderstones Road, two who had given a great deal of service, in particular in the days of Webster Road Chapel. Further losses included Owen Griffith, 60 Avondale Road, and Richard Jones, 23 Eddington Street, who had been members for years and were extremely faithful; also E. Henry Evans, 37 Kingsdale Road; Mr. William Pritchard, 3 Purley Grove; Mrs. Owen Thomas, Green Lane; Miss M. L. Owen, 4 Truro Road, and Mrs. M. Jones, the wife of J. W. Jones. On 10 January, we lost John Derek, the little child of Mr. and Mrs. A. W. Roberts, Arfon, Towers Road. This was a tragedy. When I came as minister to Liverpool, Mrs. Roberts was housebound and her husband, Mr. A. W. Roberts, a printer by profession, was her carer. He did this work very much on his own. Often, I have thought that if Derek had lived he could have been a great comfort and assistance to his ailing parents. But it was not to be. When the final call came to both, I travelled with the funeral

The large schoolroom

company to lay them to rest in Caernarfon. During 1941 four of the young people were made members but only one child was baptised during the year.

During these war years it was nearly impossible to hold spiritual meetings despite attempts to schedule them on Saturday afternoons. But the response was disappointing and dismal. These are the words, (in translation) of the Elders: 'But only a small number faithfully attend these meetings. Special efforts were made with the Sunday School, with William Owen, Chapel House, as Superintendent, O. Cledwyn Williams, Foelas, Greenhill Avenue, as Secretary; and twenty teachers in charge of the adult classes. Mr. G. T. Griffith, 21 Fallowfield Road, was the Superintendent of the Children and Young People's Sunday School; with five teachers and Arthur O. Roberts, Heydale Road, in charge of the singing. Even with such a provision the average attendance was often as low as 32 on a Sunday afternoon'.

But there was an encouraging note of hope during 1941 in that the chapel was able to persuade the Reverend Dr. R. Glynne Lloyd to move from the East Glamorgan Presbytery to be the minister of Heathfield Road Chapel. He began his ministry in Liverpool on the first Sunday in April 1942. A native of Corris, a quarrying village in Merionethshire, from where his parents, Mr. and Mrs. D. R. Lloyd, moved to London in 1922, he stayed behind to complete his studies at Tywyn School, and then went on to the University of Wales at Aberystwyth, where he graduated with Honours in Philosophy. From there he moved to the United Theological College, also in Aberystwyth, where he received a Bachelor of Divinity degree from the University of Wales. From Aberystwyth he moved to New College, Edinburgh, to conduct research on the Puritan divine, Dr. John Owen, who had been chaplain to Oliver Cromwell and the only non-Anglican Chancellor of Oxford University. It was a pleasure for

Elders and minister. Back row (left to right), J. Edward Jones, David Williams, J. Llewelyn Jenkins, John Lloyd, Evan Edwards. Front row (left to right) J. R. Davies, David Griffiths,, Reverend Dr R. Glynne Lloyd, R. J. Jones and J. R. Jones.

me to prepare the Reverend Dr. Lloyd's research findings for publication in 1972, in the volume published by Modern Welsh Publications Ltd. of Pontypridd and Liverpool under the title, *John Owen – Commonwealth Puritan*. After Edinburgh, R. Glynne Lloyd studied at the Universities of Marburg and Tübingen in Germany. It was from Siloh Chapel, Aberystwyth, with the support of the minister, the Reverend Dan Evans, the elders and the members, that he first entered the ministry. Ordained by the Association in the South held at Bwlchgwynt Chapel, Tregaron, he was first called to be minister of Penuel Chapel, Ferndale, in the Rhondda Valley. His brother, John Meirion Lloyd, was called to the Christian ministry by the London Welsh Presbytery. Their father, D. R. Lloyd, had been an elder in the Welsh chapels of Mile End and Walthamstow. In the Presbytery held in London on 27 May, 1942, the Reverend R. Glynne Lloyd was congratulated on gaining his PhD from the University of Edinburgh. By that time he had started his ministry at Liverpool. In a short address he expressed his appreciation of the call to Heathfield Road Chapel in March 1942:

> I admire you as a church for your dedication to all the responsibilities in difficult days. Because the difficulties of this period have not made you cease your witness, it is a privilege for me to be a co-worker with you. I hope that our church will be a home to the Welsh in exile who need comfort and strong defence against the temptations of the world and a safe guide to the truth in Christ.

No-one could have expressed it better and this numerically strong church was very fortunate to have this scholar from a remarkable London Welsh family as its next minister.

The special Committee of women, which had been in operation during the war years had not been disbanded. This had been the means of keeping the church in contact with those away on active service. Its Chair was Mrs. R. O. Jones, Burnham Road, with Mrs. J. Parry Williams, Menlove Gardens South, as her deputy. Miss Doris Thomas acted as Treasurer and Mrs. Helen Jones, Fron Eilian, Sinclair Drive, as Secretary. Seven women acted as the Executive: Mrs. Gwenno Bouch, Cassville Road, a native of Blaenau Ffestiniog, who had first come as a young person to work in T. J. Hughes, London Road; Mrs. J. R. Davies, Dovedale Road; Mrs. J. Pugh Davies, Druidsville Road; Mrs. D. P. Hughes, 38 Mayville Road (she lived in nearby Rutherford Road when I came to the city); Mrs. J. R. Jones, Allerton Drive, a wife of a well known estate agent; Mrs. Charles Parry, sister of Mrs. Cathy Jones, and Miss Laura Jones, Mill View, Bristol Road, Wavertree. This active Committee purchased, in 1941, goods to the value of £23 9s 2d, in order to create items that could be sent to the soldiers, sailors and airmen. They held a concert and made a profit of £8 3s 0d. The church's young people helped when they contributed the sum of £4 5s 0d. In spite of the continuing difficult circumstances, they succeeded in arranging meetings in the schoolrooms throughout the winter months of 1941-1942. They arranged concerts, *nosweithiau llawen*, hymn-singing sessions and a large number of debates and discussions on the relationships between the church and society. For teenagers in the 14-21 age group, they created another society with the title, *Cylch yr Aelodau Ieuainc* (The Young Members Circle).

In the Annual Report of 1942, we find that there was a small increase in membership. After war had broken out, the church had suffered membership losses. One has to remember that previous increases had been due, to a large extent, to the influx of past members from Fitzclarence Street Welsh Presbyterian Chapel in Everton. This had been destroyed by the bombing and the Presbytery decided not to build a new chapel. Dr. R. Glynne Lloyd reflected a widely held view at this time: ' We sympathise fully with them as a result of the damage that led to the closure of this important church that they belonged to and we hope that they will be happy and contented in our midst.'

Among those who came from Fitzclarence Street Chapel was Miss Gwen Griffiths, Erskine, 15 Childwall Mount Road (later Deepfield Road, Wavertree) and her sister, Nancy Griffiths (who left in 1944 to serve at a hospital in Cairo and subsequently in California). Also their brother, Trefor Griffiths, who later became an elder in the Welsh Chapel at Crosby Road South, Waterloo, Liverpool, and died at Menai Bridge in 2007. Another brother was Ifor Griffiths, who became the

Foundation stone laid by J. W. Jones.

The influential elder, J.W. Jones.

Secretary of the Chapel, as we shall see. Heathfield Road also welcomed Mrs. Lloyd Jones, Arwel, Mosspits Lane, and her talented daughter, Miss Nansi Lloyd Jones. The daughter was extremely fond of the books of the historian, A. L. Rowse, especially his classic, dealing with his childhood in Cornwall. Mr. J. E. Salisbury, and his wife, Mrs. A. Salisbury, also moved to Woolton. Their roots were in the English Presbyterian Church at Orrell, near Bootle in the Lancashire and Cheshire Presbytery. Mrs. Salisbury's brother was an elder at Orrell Presbyterian Church of Wales for years. Before the end of the year the family of Glyn Eirion Peters and Mrs. Morfudd Peters moved to 42 Avondale Road and both of them, as well as their son, Gwynfor, were an integral part of our community for the rest of their lives.

In 1942 a number of the children returned to Merseyside from the Welsh countryside. The minister now began the practice of giving an address to the children in one of the services, usually in the morning service but sometimes in the evening service at six o'clock or in the afternoon service held in the winter months.

The chapel lost twelve members through death, some who had been brought up in Liverpool such as J. Bleddyn Edwards, Claremont Road. After a fatal road accident he left a widow and five children. Another Welsh patriot was J. E. Haslam, Lister Crescent, who exercised a long and influential witness with the Liverpool City Corporation. William Roberts of Beauclair Drive, was brought up in Liverpool and for years had been the Treasurer of Fitzclarence Street Chapel. Others who returned from the Welsh countryside included R. T. Williams (Llwyn Ithel, Corwen), who was steeped in the scriptures and was always ready to participate in the prayer meetings.

During 1942 the sad news arrived of the disappearance of two of the young people on active service. Arthur Idwal Jones, Streatham Avenue, had served with the Royal Air Force as a pilot, but his plane was lost. He was a man of charm and one of whom the church was really proud. This was true, also, of John Owen, Chapel House, Heathfield Road Church. He served in the Merchant Navy but his ship was destroyed at sea. This happened also to Edward Trevor Davies, Hallville Road, in August 1946. Three hardworking, good living persons, faithful to the chapel were sacrificed as a result of war. The Minister addressed the members in their sorrow, asking them to continue to support the chapel: 'With the church there is healing for the world in its wounds, and through us the community of Christ fulfils its mission. This is our honour and responsibility.'

Four young people were accepted into the community of the church in 1942. These were Eryl Wyn Bouch, 1 Cassville Road; Gwynedd Owen Davies, Mayville Road; Beryl Davies, Page Bank Road, and Geoffrey H. Evans, 133 Allerton Road. The daughter of Mr. and Mrs. J. R. Jones, Cintra, Mair Hughes Jones, married Arthur Wheeler Parry, 43 Druids Cross Gardens, on 17 October, the first wedding for Dr. R. G. Lloyd at the chapel. In addition, he baptised, on 5 July, David Vaughan Jones, Dunbabin Road; on 6 September, Gaenor Roberts, Maelor, Heydale Road; on 10 September, John Manzine, 23 Karslake Road; and on 4 October, Enid Wyn Williams, 47 Barndale Road. Enid Wyn Williams has had a high profile career within the BBC in London as producer of plays and other programmes, mainly on Radio 4. Gaenor Gregory (neé Roberts) has retained her membership of our church, although she now lives in Bebington and comes regularly to our Sunday service. She is one of the few of her generation who has continued to give us loyal support throughout the years.

In 1943, the Chapel Committee known as *Pwyllgor Cysuron Rhyfel*, mentioned earlier, was again fulfilling valuable witness. During the year the chapel heard that Sergeant Gwilym H. Griffiths (brother of Miss Dilys Griffiths, Wavertree) had been taken prisoner by the Italians in Sicily and Captain Charles Parry, OBE, 6 Dulas Road, was also a prisoner. The families and the church were extremely distressed.

In addition to the practical work by the ladies, the chapel held a Prayer Meeting every Tuesday afternoon on behalf of those who were serving their country in the Armed Forces. In addition, a Prayer Meeting and a *Seiat* were held regularly on Monday and Thursday evenings during the summer and in the winter a Prayer Meeting was held on a Monday alternating occasionally with a *Seiat*. Meetings of the Young People's Society were held on Wednesday evenings throughout the winter. On Thursday nights the Young Members Circle met and they dealt with a specific syllabus: the theme for the first course focused on the 'Coming of Jesus' as recorded in the Old Testament. Four courses were held. Also, in 1943 Dr. R. Glynne Lloyd started a branch of *Corlan y Plant* (Children's Fold) in the church for the summer months. Because of the war situation the *Corlan y Plant* meetings were not held in the winter months. Occasionally, on a Sunday morning, a special service for the children was held. This made use of the extensive material produced in the monthly Presbyterian Children's magazine, *Trysorfa y Plant*.

A number of the leaders and members of the church became influential within the northern Association of the Presbyterian Church of Wales. The builder, J. W. Jones, was elected Chairman of the Elders' Meeting and Chairman of the Building

Evan R. Edwards

David Williams

Committee; David Griffiths, another elder, was made a member of the Missionary Committee; and Mrs. J. Pugh Davies, Calderstones, became a member of the Temperance Committee. Within the Liverpool Presbytery, J. R. Jones was invited as Treasurer of the Forward Movement and his fellow elder, J. Llewelyn Jenkins, Treasurer of the Loan Committee.

During 1943, two of the young ministerial students were ordained. The Reverend R. Aled Davies, M.A. began as Minister of the Presbyterian Church of Scotland at Kirkwall in the Orkney Island, and the Reverend H. Godfrey Jones, BA, BD, as minister of the Connexion at Dinas Cross in the north Pembrokeshire Presbytery, a chapel which no longer exists. Aled's sister, Nansi Mai Thomas, was waiting to go out to join her husband in Shillong. She had been nurtured in the chapel community where she had given splendid witness to every aspect of the Christian Gospel. Membership losses through deaths were as the previous year: twelve supportive members whose roots were in the life of the Welsh language community of Liverpool.

The Church continued to receive substantial support on Sundays, though there were obvious gaps in the list of preachers. Today, we are able to complete the list of preachers before the middle of summer in the previous year. When the Annual Report was published in 1942, with the Sunday engagements, there were twelve Sundays for which the Pulpit Secretary had been unable to find a preacher. In 1943 war time conditions, including petrol rationing, meant fewer preachers coming from Wales. The minister, himself, preached in his pulpit only fourteen times. Today, the minister serves the pulpit on twenty five different Sundays. Amongst the visiting preachers in 1943 were the Reverend R. Bryn Williams, Llanberis (his sister Mrs Glenys Jones, 7 Meldrum Road was a member), as well as the Reverend Heber Alun Evans, Llangeitho, one who was extremely helpful to me when I prepared for the examination for Ministerial Students. The Reverend Heber Evans had to travel a long way to reach Liverpool, as I know from my own experience. Amongst the other preachers, there were the Reverends D. Ffoulkes Roberts, Llandudno, and T. Byron Hughes, Beaumaris.

During the year 1944 a Union of Parents, Teachers and Supporters of the Children was formed in Liverpool with the intention of meeting at least once a year. It was decided, to prepare a monthly newsletter for the Welsh chapels on Merseyside. The Welsh language newspaper, known as *Y Brython* and published in Bootle, had ceased in 1939. In these circumstances the Welsh League of Youth branches decided to produce a newsletter to be called *Y Glannau*. This was highly appreciated between 1944 and 1959, when *Y Bont*, a new monthly magazine, appeared, then from 1979 onwards *Yr Angor*. The Young People's Society at Heathfield Road decided to become a branch of the Welsh League of Youth to be known as *Aelwyd y De,* a significant step but quite appropriate when one remembers that one of the inspiring leaders of Urdd Gobaith Cymru, R. E. Griffith, had been brought up in the chapel before the family moved away to Abercynon in south Wales. The church celebrated the long service of Owen Hughes, 88 Salisbury Road, as church secretary as well as congratulating him on reaching fifty years as an elder of the church. He had been a member from the very beginning in Webster Road, Secretary of the Church since 1890 and remained in that position for fifty seven years. It also extended its best wishes to the Reverend Trefor Davies Jones, B.A., B.D., on his induction as minister of Bethel and Sardis Chapels at Bodorgan, Anglesey. One of the young people, Miss Olwen Thomas, Fallowfield Road was married to the Reverend J. D. Williams, a native of Penuwch in Cardiganshire and the successor of the Reverend W. N. Williams, affectionately known as Nantlais, the hymn writer and evangelist, at Bethany Chapel in the industrial town of Ammanford, on the virtual edge of the anthracite coalfield. Olwen was highly thought of as a minister's wife in Ammanford.

The chapel lost nine members during the year. One of them, Dr. E. R. Evans, 40 Menlove Avenue, was a well-loved medical practitioner. Captain David Wynne Jones, 2 Allerton Drive, also died. He had been badly injured when the British troops arrived in northern France and he never recovered from his wounds. The next member we need to mention among those who passed away is John Lewis, 37 Courtland Road. He had been an excellent builder and his work can be seen today in Mather Avenue, that is Allerton Fire Brigade's Station as well as the Police Station. It was also a tragedy to lose a young nursing sister, Evelyn Evans, from the Smithdown Road Hospital. In addition we need to pay tribute to J. P. Taylor, 109 Salisbury Road, who died on 3 December. He had been an organist from 1901 until 1939, thus serving a period of thirty eight years. When he decided to retire, his place was taken by three people, Miss Nansi M. Davies, Miss Mary Davies, 18 Fallowfield Road, and Miss Margaret E. Owen, 19 Russell Road. In 1944 the team of organists was strengthened by the contribution of Miss Alwena Davies and Miss Gwen Griffiths, 42 Fallowfield Road, Wavertree.

Another family suffered immensely as a result of the war, namely Mr. and Mrs. D. P. Hughes, 38 Mayville Road, when their son, Ivor, died as a result of his wounds. In 1944, the chapel established a Welcome Home Committee with the minister as Chairman and Norman Newton, 14 Beverley Road, as Secretary. The elders, as well as the Ladies War Effort Committee, were co-opted along with ten

John Edward Jones

men of the chapel. Miss Doris Thomas, Allerton, was asked to be the Treasurer of the new committee. As an orderly, staunch Presbyterian community, Heathfield Road Chapel was ready for the end of the war. Dr. R. Glynne Lloyd summed it up when he said: 'Even the issues we fought for declined during the war years. The life of so many homes declined but Christ can restore them. The freedom of people was curtailed and, indeed, freedom is useless unless a person knows how to use it fully.'

In 1945 the chapel published two issues of its newsletter and Idris Foster, Head of the Celtic Department in the University of Liverpool, accepted the invitation to edit the publication. The chapel lost two elders, both dying during the month of August. On 12 August, it mourned the passing of Henry Williams, 13 Grovedale Road, Allerton, and then on 25 August, the remarkable J. W. Jones, Greenhill, Allerton Road. Both had been elected elders in Webster Road Chapel in 1911, as noted earlier; and both had served as Moderators of the Liverpool Presbytery. Seven other members were lost. Amongst these were two young men, E. R. Parry, 44 Mosspits Lane, and Luke Backhouse, 4 Welbeck Avenue, both dying from war wounds. Luke Backhouse had spent two years in the Military Hospital of Johannesburg but he died just as he was on the verge of being transferred back home from South Africa to Liverpool.

There were five christenings witnessed during 1945. On 4 March, Daniel Jones, 4 Winchfield Road, was baptised. He grew up to be a delightful person and he became an integral part of the community. It was sad to lose him so early in his life and I paid tribute to him at his large funeral held in Gwernafield, near Mold. Amongst the six weddings witnessed in the chapel there was a unique occurrence in the union of John Edward Jones, 23 Beckenham Avenue, and Katherine Elizabeth Edwards, 15 Dulas Road, on 8 November. Both had been born and brought up within the chapel community and after their wedding they settled in the local area and gave sterling service. Nearly two years later their first child, Glenys Wyn Jones, was born. In that same year, John Edward Jones and David Williams, 29 Mayville Road, were elected elders.

1946 was a year of tremendous activity particularly the welcoming back home of all those who had served in the Second World War. As an acknowledgement of the community's gratitude, each received a Bible (with their name printed on it) as well as a cheque for five pounds. A number of them became involved enthusiastically in the life of the chapel, while others stood on the sidelines. Very successful meetings were held every Tuesday by the Young People's Society as well as the opening of the large schoolroom for games, especially the playing of squash, on Thursday nights. There was no need for any young Welsh person to feel lonely in Liverpool on a Tuesday or Thursday. In addition, by 1946, a branch of *Yr Urdd* had been established and an opportunity to take part in all the activities of the Welsh League of youth – the drama festival, the campaign to sell Welsh language books, the Urdd Eisteddfod and other cultural events. One of the most notable preachers of his age, the Reverend Dr. Martyn Lloyd-Jones of London came to preach. It was a notable service attended by a large congregation, with the preacher proclaiming with fervour the Word of God. He was regarded as one of the most gifted Free Church preachers of his age. For thirty years he was minister at Westminster Chapel, one of London's most celebrated Nonconformist churches. The preaching of Martyn Lloyd-Jones made a remarkable impact on his fellow Welshmen. An estimated 7,000 heard him at the 1935 *Sasiwn* (Presbyterian quarterly meeting) at Llangeitho. Our Heathfield Road Chapel, which held 750, was full to capacity when he visited us. Dr. Martyn Lloyd-Jones had left Harley Street and a promising career as a consultant physician in private medicine for a Mission Chapel in the depressed area of Port Talbot in south Wales.

In 1946, the church had an opportunity to choose more elders on Sunday evening, 14 April, when Evan Edwards, a lecturer at the University of Liverpool, was the only person elected. He had been, as mentioned earlier, an enthusiast for the social witness and his particular concerns were important contributions for the monthly gathering of the elders. But the church leaders were disappointed that only one person had been elected by secret ballot at a time when the community had lost one if its elders in the death of George Jenkins, who had been an elder since 1919. He was a native of Cilgerran in Pembrokeshire, had been a builder by trade, and a wise leader of his community. Eight other members also died in those twelve months.

During 1947, thirty one individuals joined the community, but the chapel lost the services of the editor of the newsletter, Professor Idris Foster, on his appointment to the Chair of Celtic at Jesus College, Oxford. The congregation also voted on the proposition that the visiting preachers who ministered from the pulpit on Sundays should wear the robes that were worn generally in the Presbyterian Churches of England, Scotland and Ireland, namely a cassock, gown and Geneva tab. The matter had arisen two years earlier when the two sisters, Miss C. E. Pugh and Mrs. J. Pugh Davies, had decided to donate vestments for the resident minister as well as vestments for the visiting minister. The elders had been reluctant to give a lead on the issue and the issue dragged on for twenty four months. In the end, the congregation decided to adopt what can only be called a 'High Presbyterian' standpoint. I do not know of another Welsh-speaking Presbyterian congregation where the wearing of vestments is the norm, though for the last twenty years it is not expected of visiting preachers. I have a deep respect for the Presbyterian order of service and also for the memory of the two sisters, in particular, Mrs. J. Pugh Davies, whom I had the opportunity of knowing well in her declining years. But the decision of the congregation was an important one. The Reverend Dr. R. Glynne Lloyd, the Reverend E. Watkin Jones and I all continued to wear vestments in the pulpit. Will our successors?

1947 saw the passing away of one of our pioneers, Owen Hughes, 88 Salisbury Road. He is remembered as a wise leader, an excellent secretary since 1890, a frequent visitor to the sick, a dependable Sunday School teacher, a friend to the young and an elder since 1894. In other words he lived for the chapel, he and his sister being present at every meeting. As he had similar qualities and dedication, J. R. Davies, who had moved from Dovedale Road to Gwynfa, opposite Calderstones Park, was invited to become the successor of Owen Hughes as Secretary of the Chapel.

The other loss was the decision of the Reverend Dr. R. Glynne Lloyd to accept a call from the United States of America. He left at the end of 1947 to serve as Pastor of Moriah

Presbyterian Church, Utica, New York State, a chapel where one of the ministers of the Liverpool Presbytery, the Reverend Llywelyn Jones, Douglas Road, Anfield, had ministered for a period during the 1920's. It was obvious that travel was in the family blood. Dr. R. Glynne Lloyd went to New York State, whilst his brother, John Meirion Lloyd, left Catharine Street Chapel, Liverpool, to be a missionary in North-East India. Dr. R. Glynne Lloyd and his wife, Mrs. M. Lloyd, were extremely popular, as were their children – Gareth, Aeron and Margaret. It was at Liverpool that Margaret Lloyd was baptised on 15 July, 1946, a week before the baptism of John Wynne Jones, 7 Meldrum Road, one who has given long service to the administration of the University of Wales, Bangor. At the time of writing, he is Secretary of the Welsh Presbyterian Chapel at Beaumaris, in Anglesey. The popularity of the minister and his family was remembered by J. R. Davies when he commented on 'the large congregation that gathered in this farewell service, when every aspect of the church life was represented.'

The chapel officers decided immediately to seek a successor. The congregation elected members to serve on the Pastoral Committee and even though the number of ministers within the Connexion was declining, they soon achieved success. In a probing article the Treasurer of the Chapel, J. Llewelyn Jenkins, made this observation, 'At this time there is a scarcity of ministers for our Connexion and it is envisaged under the new structure of the Sustentation Fund, a more effective method will be introduced for the ministers that we already have.'

The new call was extended to the Reverend E. Watkin Jones, B.A., from the pastorate of Deiniolen in the heart of Snowdonia. He began his ministry on Sunday 24 April, 1949.

The organ that was inserted during the ministry of Reverend E. Watkin Jones

The organ which has been a great asset to the Presbyterians of Heathfield Road Chapel.

The centre of the large sanctuary, the pulpit and the organ.

The Chapel House built by the men who worked in the building industry.

John Edward Jones with D. Ben Rees and W. Elwyn Hughes in 1987, the minister congratulating both for 40 years service as elders in the Liverpool Presbytery of the Presbyterian Church of Wales.

Chapter 9

THE MINISTRY OF THE REVEREND E. WATKIN JONES (1949 – 1967)

The Reverend E. Watkin Jones, B.A., was the epitome of wisdom. He was a native of Blaenau Ffestiniog and a small number of the congregation in Liverpool had known him from his youth. He had spent thirteen years as minister in Anglesey and Caernarfonshire. By 1948 he had matured as a minister with a great deal of experience that was highly relevant for a large chapel in a city that was in the process of recovering from the destruction of the Second World War.

His wife, Mrs. Jane Jones, was a native of Llanddaniel-fab, Anglesey, and she was extremely supportive of her husband's duties. They had no children and therefore she was able to direct all her energies to the work of the church, in particular visiting the sick, and the activities of the Sisterhood. The number of communicants on 1 January, 1949 amounted to 595 and each one was expected to pay the sum of 2s 6d a year as a levy to the Sustentation Fund which had come into existence at the beginning of July 1948. This was a new system adopted by the denomination as a whole. The purpose of the scheme was to provide a salary of £350 a year for every minister in the large towns and £300 for those who worked in rural areas.

Reverend E. Watkin Jones.

It is of interest to look at the contributions made by members in Heathfield Road Chapel for 1949. All those who contributed did so conscientiously, though the majority of members had not understood the guidance given by the Treasurer, who had suggested that, in addition to the Ministry Fund, they should contribute an additional 2s 6d to the Sustentation Fund. Out of 595 members only 69 had contributed also towards the Sustentation Fund which came to a total of £80 3s 0d. Contributions towards the Ministry and the Whitsun Preaching Festival fluctuated considerably. The leaders of the chapel suggested to the members the amount needed but even this turned out to be misleading for married couples. For example, the sum of £25 was received from one of the elders but the contribution was in the name of his wife and himself which meant that only £12 10s 0d each had been given. Nevertheless, this was the highest

Henry A. Williams.

individual contribution in 1949. The only two who contributed generously, and independently, were Captain Thomas Meirion Edwards, 44 Arundel Avenue, and Miss Ann Evans, Brynawel, Llanrwst. Capt. T. M. Edwards gave £10 to the Ministry, and £1 to the Sustentation Fund while Miss Evans contributed £10 to the Ministry and a further ten shillings to the Sustentation Fund. The majority of the members had given only between £1 and £5 each.

Two events took place in the ministry of the Reverend E. Watkin Jones, which received a great deal of publicity. The first was an opportunity to communicate the Gospel to the Welsh nation when BBC Wales recorded the morning service on 18 June, 1950. Secondly, the chapel still had no pipe organ. As we have noted, there was a small chamber organ, which had been used regularly between 1930 and 1949. It was felt in 1949 that, with a new minister at the helm, a chapel with a

Members of the North Wales Association which met at the chapel in November 1950

J. R. Davies.

large congregation like Heathfield Road could afford a better organ. So, after contacting the Directors of the famous company of Rushworth and Dreaper, a new, large pipe organ was purchased for just over £6,000, a huge sum in 1950 (equating to £50,000 in 2007). To build a similar organ today would cost the church around £100,000.

In 1950 the chamber organ was given to an English Chapel in Buckley, Flintshire. After the task of building the new organ, the building itself was renovated and to celebrate the arrival of the new organ a concert was held on 26 June. The guest organist on this important occasion was the famous Dr. Caleb Jarvis, FRCO who was vociferous in his praise for the new instrument. At the concert, the soloist was Miss Ceinwen Rowlands from Anglesey, who brought delight to the audience. The new organ was now available for the several meetings held by the Association in the North in November 1950. The Moderator was the Reverend R. Dewi Williams (1870-1955), Principal of the Preparatory College for Ministerial Students at Clynnog and Y Rhyl for twenty two years. He had written *Clawdd Terfyn* in 1912, which became a best seller in Welsh. Among those ordained at this Association was the Reverend Idwal Jones, minister at Salem, Laird Street Welsh Chapel in Birkenhead, when he died suddenly on 22 November 1983. I contributed a chapter on his life and work in the bilingual volume, *Alpha and Omega: The Witness of the Welsh Presbyterians in Laird Street, Birkenhead 1906-2006,* published by Modern Welsh Publications in 2006.

In the fifties, the church suffered losses through death and through members moving back to Wales. By 1955, the membership had fallen to 520, a loss of 75 since 1949. The numbers of children fell to 65 compared with the 84 recorded five years earlier. The Sunday School had declined from 213 in 1950 to 170 in 1953, a loss of 43 of its students. Whereas the chapel community had been growing from 1890 to 1945, it was now facing a completely different period, a time of anxiety and disillusionment. But, in the 1950s, there was still a large number of young people who came to Liverpool, the majority to fill positions in Liverpool schools after completing their teacher training in Wales. These young teachers were keen to preserve the Welsh language and culture. Thus, leaders of Welsh life were quite optimistic about the future of the Welsh language within the Welsh communities of Merseyside. Some, like the Reverend Llewelyn Jones, minister of Bethlehem Chapel, Douglas Road, felt that the situation was better in the Liverpool of the 1950s than it had been when he returned home from Utica, New York State, in the early 1930s. 'Indeed,' he said, when presenting the Presbyterian witness on Merseyside to the Association in north Wales in 1950, 'the situation

Owen Hughes.

is much better than it was two generations ago'. Another leader, the Reverend D. Hughson Jones, minister of the Welsh Independent Chapel at Park Road, Dingle, stated that in his view the Welsh language and culture was now stronger in Liverpool than it was in Treharris in east Glamorganshire and even in Cardiff. He had moved from Treharris to Liverpool as a minister in 1934 and this was his honest observation, 'What struck me in Liverpool was its Welshness. I heard more Welsh in Church Street than I had heard on the streets of Cardiff.'

The situation has changed dramatically in Cardiff since then, as there are now at least 32,000 Welsh speakers in the capital city of Wales. The situation had also changed before the Reverend E. Watkin Jones had arrived in Heathfield Road. After the end of the Second World War a large number of talented young Welsh-speaking teachers had started their careers in Liverpool and through their enthusiasm it was decided to establish a number of Welsh language centres, eight in all, across the city where children could be taught Welsh on Saturday mornings. Unfortunately, this scheme survived for only a number of years. Improved transport links and the availability of the motor car meant that these young teachers returned home at weekends. So, one after another these centres were closed, to the disappointment of many, as it denied the children their chances of learning and improving their knowledge and use of the Welsh language.

In reviewing the 1950s, the Reverend E. Watkin Jones emphasised three important points. Firstly, the annual loss of members which occurred as people retired and decided to move from Liverpool back home to Wales. A case in point was the decision of the elder David Williams, Mayville Road, to return in 1953 to Port Dinorwic. He had been a prominent leader of the chapel. For years he had held Welsh language classes every Wednesday at the school room; and also he assisted on Fridays with the children's *Corlan* as well as teaching a class of young people in the Sunday School. In July 1954 David Griffiths, another elder, decided to return to Wales. He was a very charismatic leader, a hard working activist, steeped in the scriptures. David Griffiths spoke with authority in an Association meeting or in the Presbytery or in a Sunday service where he presided and made the announcements. He was the official announcer for our chapel. Elected an elder in 1919 he served as Moderator of the Presbytery in 1941 in a difficult year for him personally as a result of the bombing, which had occurred earlier. He moved from Liverpool to Penmorfa, near Tremadog. David Griffiths gave his testimony at the *Seiat* on the last Sunday he lived in Liverpool, emphasising his faith in his Saviour, reminding the congregation 'that he had given himself to Jesus Christ the night he was accepted as a fully fledged member in the chapel of Ysbyty Ifan', and that he had

Arthur O. Roberts (Alaw Penllyn)

made a valiant effort to be faithful to that vow for the rest of his life.

Then, in 1955, on 22 January, John Richard Jones, Cintra, Menlove Avenue, died. His name has appeared often in this book and so has that of his father, John Jones, Mayfield and his brother W. H. Jones, Gwydrin, Dudlow Drive, who died on 21 February 1949. J. R. Jones was an extremely active person in the life of the Liverpool Welsh, the county of Anglesey, as well as in Wales generally. I am glad that I prepared an entry on him in my book, *Cymry Adnabyddus,* published in 1978, as well as in English in the *Oxford Dictionary of National Biography,* published in 2004.

The chapel had opportunities to elect more elders in 1953 and 1955. In 1953, Griffith R. Jones, Allangate Road, Aigburth, and R. Glyn Williams, Garthdale Road, Allerton, were elected. G. R. Jones had married his second wife on 11 April, 1949, one of the supportive members of the chapel, namely Miss Jennie Thomas, 21 Stand Park Road, Childwall. R. Glyn Williams was the son of a minister and his wife, Hannah Williams had been a member since the 1930s when she moved to Liverpool from Anglesey. Then, in 1955 the chapel elected four new elders, namely Goronwy Davies, Ifor Griffiths, R. D. Jones and Arthur O. Roberts, each of them highly talented. Three of them had moved from Wales to Liverpool. Ifor Griffiths was the only one who had been born in Liverpool but who could write Welsh in a correct manner. He was a perfectionist.

A year later the chapel mourned, in a period of twelve months, the passing of three elders of great distinction, R. J. Jones, Eirianfa; Evan Edwards, Mayville Road, Allerton and J. R. Davies, Gwynfa, Calderstones Road. R. J. Jones had been extremely active and an elder since he was first elected in 1925. Generation after generation of Welsh children are indebted to him. He gave of his utmost to the Sunday School and had been enthusiastic as a precentor and in ensuring a new pipe organ for the chapel. J. R. Davies had been elected as an elder the same year as R. J. Jones. He was fully committed and one of the most constant of visitors to the sick and the bereaved. It was he who encouraged young people to attend the Prayer Meeting at 9.45 a.m. on Sunday mornings. Out of this gathering, a large number dedicated themselves to the Free Church as well as the Anglican ministry. Moreover, his son became a Presbyterian minister, his eldest daughter a missionary and his youngest daughter, Alwena Davies, became an elder at Hermon Welsh Chapel, Rhos-on-Sea, which she served until her death early in 2007. The third leader was Evan Edwards, M.A., B.Sc., Mayville Road, a man who gave of his best to the Sunday School work and to movements such as the United Nations. Then, in 1959, R. D. Jones, a well known Welsh playwright, left us to move to Tremadog on his appointment as headmaster of the primary school there.

Idris Lloyd Williams.

In 1960 fifteen members of the chapel died and amongst these, one deserves particular mention - Arthur O. Roberts, known in the Gorsedd of the National Eisteddfod of Wales as *Alaw Penllyn*. He died in the prime of his life. He had served as an extremely useful person dealing with matters concerning the fabric of the chapel and all its buildings. He was faithful to all the demands on his time. He had worked diligently with our children in *Y Gorlan* and the Sunday School and he was always looking forward to the Christmas activities. His loss was still evident when I came to Liverpool eight years later; something which is not often mentioned even with regard to our leaders. In 1960, two more elders were elected by the congregation, namely Howell Vaughan Jones, the son of J. W. Jones, and the banker, Idris Lloyd Williams, Ballantrae Road, Allerton.

The other issue that the minister highlighted is that Welsh families were no longer moving to Liverpool, as they had done after the First World War and, to a lesser extent, after the Second World War. Nevertheless, some were still arriving in smaller numbers to strengthen our community. An example of this was the coming of the Reverend Dafydd Hughes Parry and his wife, Nan, and their daughter, Nia, in 1961 to live as near as they could to the chapel at 101 Penny Lane. In his welcome, E. Watkin Jones, said, 'They have already settled and are faithful and active in our midst'. This situation has persisted for forty six years in the case of Nan Hughes Parry; and now her grandchildren are bringing her a great deal of pride and comfort through their involvement in our Sunday School.

Thirdly, the Reverend E. Watkin Jones raised an important issue when discussing the young, 'The practice for many of them is to spend the weekend in Wales from Friday night until Sunday afternoon when they return to study and to teach.' This trend had increased

Reverend R. Leslie Jones and Mrs Beryl Jones who were members at the chapel between 1957 and 1961.

The Foreign Mission offices.

by the end of the sixties but, as we shall see, there was to be a tremendous success amongst the young people as far as chapel involvement was concerned by the early 1970s.

The chapel experienced another great loss in 1961 when J. Llewelyn Jenkins, one of the most faithful elders, died. On 17 November, the Reverend and Mrs. R. Leslie Jones left Liverpool on accepting a call to the Presbyterian Church of the Crescent in Newtown, Montgomeryshire. It was a loss to Welsh Presbyterianism in Liverpool, as both had been involved in the activities of the chapel. The Reverend R. Leslie Jones had served in the Foreign Mission Office in Falkner Street and later he became an influential figure in the Connexion, honoured by being elected Moderator of the General Assembly. At the beginning of 1962, the Reverend Herbert Jones Griffith, B.A., of Rhosllanerchrugog, was elected to be his successor and he and his wife, his daughter and his son, became members of the chapel.

Another elder, Idris Lloyd Williams, Ballantrae Road, was remembered long after his death on 3 June, 1962. He, and his wife, Mrs. Gwladys Lloyd Williams, and their two daughters, Gwenfron and Bethan Lloyd Williams, as well as their sons, Hywel and Roger Lloyd Williams, had come from Bala to live in Allerton in 1953. Mr. Lloyd Williams had been a bank manager at Bala, and an elder in Capel Tegid.

1962 proved to be a year of great activity. The 75th anniversary of the building of Webster Road Chapel was celebrated and a valuable booklet, giving an outline of the efforts made by the Welsh community in establishing that chapel, was written by Owen Evans and printed by the Liverpool Welsh publisher, Hugh Evans of Bootle. A meeting was held in November to highlight these celebrations. Earlier that year in the month of June, the General Assembly of the Presbyterian Church of Wales was welcomed again to Liverpool, when visitors from all over Wales stayed in the homes of members. A welcome tea was prepared by the ladies of the chapel and on this occasion the Lord Mayor of Liverpool, Alderman D. J. Lewis (who worshipped regularly at the chapel), as well as the Anglican Bishop, Dr. Clifford Martin, and the Moderator of the Free Church Federal Council, the Reverend T. C. Chesnutt, attended as guests. Large congregations attended every public meeting, especially as the Davies lecture was given by one of the most erudite ministers in the city, the Reverend Ifor Oswy Davies. He dealt with the theology of Karl Barth, a theologian whom he had learned about as a ministerial student at the University of Bonn in Germany.

The chapel was invited, for the second time by BBC Radio Wales, to record its morning service on Sunday, 23 September, under the guidance of the minister. Four young people of

A Liverpool Welsh Dinner.

the chapel were accepted as members, namely Glenys Wyn Jones, Sinclair Drive; Siân Helen Thomas, Barndale Road; David Jones, Chapel House, and Huw Merfyn Jones, 21 Wyndcote Road. Two were baptised on 1 April: Keith Jones, Breeze Hill, Bootle and on 16 September, Sioned Wyn Jones, the eldest daughter of Louie and Humphrey Wyn Jones, Wheatcroft Road. Sioned was the daughter of another family that had moved from Caernarfonshire to teach in Liverpool at the end of the 1950s.

1962 was an entirely different world from that of 2007. The attractive booklet on the history of the cause was printed at a cost of £134 but sales only brought in £127; thus a small loss was recorded. The cost of printing this volume today is huge and will entail a great effort to make it break even. The amount spent on insuring the church had amounted to £70 in 1962, but the premiums amounted to £2035.16 in 2006. The Treasurer, Mr. Howell Vaughan Jones, paid £35 for the maintenance and tuning of the organ. In 2006 these costs amounted to £349.00. The local expenses for staging the General Assembly came to £27 but the cost of holding the annual church court and paying for the accommodation today amounts to thousands of pounds. In 1962, the Heathfield Road Chapel, with its 435 members, paid £854 to the Central Office of the Presbyterian Church of Wales, but in 2006 this same payment, for 149 members, increased to £29,296. Members contributed towards the upkeep of the ministry the sum of £1319 in 1962 but this increased to £18011.35 in 2006. The BBC paid the chapel £10 for broadcasting the morning service in 1962. Indeed, 1962 was an entirely different world from that of today!

On 23 January, 1963, the Lord Mayor of Liverpool and the civic leaders came to the chapel, a tradition which has grown over the years. As mentioned earlier, Alderman D. J. Lewis was a Welsh-speaking Welshman, who attended regularly on Sunday mornings, proud of his allegiance to the Presbyterian Church of Wales since his schooldays at Tabernacle Welsh Presbyterian Chapel in Aberystwyth.

Another successful evening was held in the large schoolroom when the local drama group performed a Welsh play. This drama company known by the Welsh name for Heathfield, '*Maesgrug*', has been a valuable asset to the local community. Men of talent have been amongst the company's producers, such as William Owen, Chapel House; T. C. Davies, Dovedale Road; D. Elwyn Williams, Caernarfon, and H. Wyn Jones. Its talented actors included Morus O. Roberts and Jane and Emrys Hughes, Aigburth.

The Reverend E. Watkin Jones was delighted with the large number of other ministers who were members of the Heathfield Road chapel. By 1964 these numbered four; the Reverends Dafydd Hughes Parry and Robin Wyn Griffiths, both schoolteachers; the Reverends G. W. Rogers, who had retired, and H. Jones Griffith, who served in the Presbyterian Missionary Office in Falkner Street, where, in earlier periods, both the Reverends D. R. Jones and R. Leslie Jones had been part of the team.

On 27 July, 1964, Gwenfron Ceris Williams was married to Joshua Hine, a Liverpool schoolteacher. Mrs. Gwenfron Hine, has over the years, been a godsend to thousands of patients at the Liverpool Cardiothoracic Hospital in her role as a regular visitor. At this particular hospital is Robert Owen House, named after the orthopaedic surgeon, Professor Robert Owen, Old Colwyn. This accommodates families from Wales, from the Isle of Man and from the north of England who have come to be near their loved ones whilst they await or recover from a heart operation. This important facility is greatly appreciated and deserves mention as our chapel has been involved in raising funds.

Elders and minister. Back row (left to right), Glyn Davies, Griffith R. Jones, Howell V. Jones, Ifor Griffith. Front row (left to right), Goronwy Davies, Owen Evans, Reverend E. Watkin Jones, John Edward Jones and R. Glyn Williams.

Only one new member from amongst the young people was accepted in 1964, on January 5, namely Melfyn Jones, 22 Centreville Road. The chapel still had 403 members in 1964 despite having lost 22 members, eight to other churches, eight who moved without asking for their membership transfer, and six who died. Generosity still prevailed and members of the Sunday School collected the sum of £14.5s.9d to keep a native teacher active in the mission field in Jamkon, India. Another Presbyterian minister joined as a member in 1965, the Reverend Alun Williams from the Welsh Chapel in Rhosddu, a district in the town of Wrexham. He moved to Liverpool on his appointment as Home Secretary to the Mission Office at Falkner Street.

The minister baptised five babies during the year: Eirian Hughes Parry, Manor Road, Woolton; Gwenan Wyn Jones, Wheatcroft Road; Tomos Alwyn Jones, Edenfield Road; Alun Edwin Jones, Chapel House, and Ceri Anwen Rogers, Greenhill Road. Only one of these five still remains in our community, namely Eirian See, who remains very much involved in chapel life with her husband Phillip and their children, Thomas and Olivia, an integral part of her witness. The deaths of five members were mourned, including Miss Gwladys E. Pugh, who had been so generous to the community at Heathfield Road, in her presentation of funds for preaching gowns.

The pleasant task of extending hospitality to visiting preachers fell, as today, on the shoulders of a few members, including the Minister himself and the elders. In 1965, for example, the pleasure of looking after the visiting minister for lunch and tea depended upon seven families. Today, in 2007, we need to provide much more hospitality than in 1965. In 1965, only six ministers needed hospitality, the Reverends W. Brothen Jones, Caernarfon;

Reverend I. Oswy Davies and the Elders of Belvidere Road chapel.

Hywel Jones, Gellifor; Alun Lewis, Colwyn Bay; E.C. Jones, Y Bala; Isaac Parry, Colwyn Bay (late of Birkenhead), and Alan Wyn Roberts, Holywell. Others, such as the Reverend S. O. Tudor, Colwyn Bay, had their own personal arrangements. His daughter was married to Dr. Maldwyn Jones Griffith and lived in 2 Livingston Drive. My friend, the Reverend E. Emrys Evans, Mountain Ash, stayed with Mr. and Mrs. Ifor Griffiths in 29 Charles Berrington Road. It was at their home that he stayed during the General Assembly in 1962 and they became great friends, with the result that he would travel every two years from the Aberdare Valley to preach in Liverpool. The Reverend Trefor Davies Jones, Llannerch-y-Medd, stayed with his mother, Mrs. T. R. Jones, in 17 Duddingston Avenue.

Alderman D. J. Lewis.

Every aspect of the life of the church is important and Heathfield Road Chapel was well organised. Nothing took place before a great deal of prior consideration. There were secretaries for the pews; the Visiting Committee had its convenor in the person of Mrs. Gwladys Lloyd Williams and, after she left for Anglesey, we appointed Mrs. Elan Jones, who still fulfills the responsibility. The elders appointed a team of men to be in charge of the Sunday morning and evening collections. In 1965, eight members were invited, namely W. T. Jones, Ivydale Road, a joiner and a remarkable craftsman; Roger Lloyd Williams, son of an elder, who today farms at Llanfihangel Glyn Myfyr; Glyn Davies, Ruthin, a biochemist and who was the Superintendent of the Adult Sunday School; Robert Jones, Merrion Close, Woolton, a pharmacist and a native of Anglesey; Vincent Roberts, Superintendent of the children's Sunday School; Glyn E. Jones, Granard Road, son of the well known elder, Dafydd ap Jones, of Douglas Road Welsh Chapel; Alan W. Jones, Edenfield Road, and his brother, Daniel Jones, Winchfield Road, a precentor in the Adult Sunday School. Of the eight mentioned, four have since died and another four have moved from Liverpool (three to Wales and one to Stoke-on-Trent). Such movements are typical of the urban Welsh Society in Liverpool, particularly since the Second World War.

In 1965, Elan and R. Emrys Jones moved from the Dingle to the Chapel House to take up their position as caretakers following the retirement of Mr. and Mrs. W. J. Jones. R. Emrys Jones began his work on 1 February and he served some eighteen years as the chapel caretaker. Joy was expressed when the saintly Reverend G. W. Rogers celebrated forty years in the Christian ministry. A mention was made of this achievement in the Presbytery and at the Heathfield Road Chapel where his family was fully involved.

In September, the resignation of Mr. W. Llewelyn Lewis, ARCO, who formerly had been organist and choirmaster at Sefton Parish Church, was received. An extremely able organist, his stay at Heathfield Road was rather short, because on his retirement from Cranes, the piano company, he and his family moved to the outskirts of Liverpool to settle at Lydiate.

The elders decided to advertise for his successor. In the meantime, the precentor, W. G. Jones of Eardisley Road, was asked to consult a few competent musicians who were members of the chapel community including Miss Gwen Griffiths, Fallowfield Road (who had taught generations of children the rudiments of music, especially the playing of the piano); Miss Alwena Davies; Mrs. Gwladys Lloyd Williams; and Mrs. Megan Davies, Roby; as well as one of the young people, Miss Glenys Wyn Jones. The chapel had given prominence to music as a form of praise. Rushworth and Dreaper always tuned the pipe organ and pianos regularly. In 1965 they were paid the sum of £17 for this work.

One candidate only, namely Mr. Denis Humphries, FRSA, of Beddgelert responded to our advertisement for an organist, and he was invited to travel to Liverpool on 6 November. The ministers and elders met him and they had a fruitful discussion, when it was realised that he would need to secure a post in the city of Liverpool before he could accept the post. He was given an opportunity to play the organ and given two months to find full-time employment elsewhere to which he gave his assent. By 29 November, the Elders' Meeting, on the basis of information supplied by the minister, decided not to sign an agreement and to leave the matter in abeyance.

It is interesting to note that in the minutes of the Elders' Meetings, it was recorded that in their December meeting it was a tradition to chose two elders and three members from the congregation to constitute *y Pwyllgor Enwi*, whose function was to select individuals to act on the chapel committees. It is obvious that this practice ceased at the completion of the ministry of the Reverend E. Watkin Jones.

On the first Sunday of January, 1966, five young people were accepted as members, namely Hywel Rhys Davies, Woolton (later a barrister in Canada); Ann Griffiths, Willowdale Road (who now lives on Anglesey); Glenys Ann Williams, Centreville Road, a schoolteacher who married another schoolteacher, Phil Daniel, (who later became Headmaster of Springwood Primary School); Glenys Ann Williams, Karslake Road, who now lives in Sudbury, Suffolk; and John Richard Williams, Wellington Avenue, a teacher at Derby, who had been the Chairman of the Derby Welsh Society, and during his year of office, he invited the author to be his guest speaker for the St. David's Dinner, which was remembered with gratitude for the hospitality and welcome that was received.

On Saturday, 26 March, 1966, John Lloyd, Cynfal, Hilltop Road, Childwall, the oldest serving elder, died at the age of 86. He had been associated with the chapel community for seventy years and was one of our pioneers. John Lloyd had given sterling service to the Sunday School. During his lifetime he was prominent amongst the Welsh builders of the suburbs of Childwall and Allerton. His minister prepared a well-deserved tribute for the Elders' Meeting in April.

The young were still coming in large numbers to Heathfield Road Chapel and *Urdd y Bobl Ieuainc* [League of Young People], received support from the Presbytery through the enthusiasm of the Reverend William Jones, minister of the Welsh Presbyterian Church of Stanley Road, Bootle. In June, the elders considered a letter from the Reverend D. Hughes Parry, Secretary of the Union of Welsh Sunday Schools on Merseyside, to start a kindergarten for children under five years old on Wednesday mornings from ten to twelve o'clock supervised by Mrs. Nan Hughes Parry and Mrs. Joyce Griffiths. The request was granted. As both of the organisers were ministers' wives, the chapel did not expect any payment.

The need for more leaders was expressed on 25 September when the congregation again voted on the proposition to elect more elders. Two were elected, namely Owen Evans, Montclair Drive, who was already an elder in the denomination, and Glyn Davies, Roby, whom we have mentioned above in his capacity as an officer of the Sunday School. At one of their meetings during this period the elders decided to refuse an invitation from the Welsh Chapel in Garston to hold united Sundays in August, which had arrived via the District Meeting. Instead, it was decided to welcome members from Garston Chapel, if they wished, to attend the normal service at Heathfield Road Chapel.

In 1966, it was obvious that the care for the buildings took up a great deal of the elders' time. In addition to damage caused by the weather, vandals were beginning to cause destruction to the building. In November 1966, the roof above the small schoolroom was destroyed but fortunately this was restored through the connections of Howell Vaughan Jones with the company of J. W. Jones. This saved a great deal of effort for the Maintenance Committee. Permission was given before the end of the year for the Treasurer to transfer money in the Drama Group account to the General Fund on the understanding that if, on a future date, the Group decided to revive the drama activities, the church would provide finance.

At the Elders' Meeting on Monday, 3 January, 1967, a letter from the Reverend E. Watkin Jones dated 2 January, was read stating his intention of retiring from the Ministry at the end of the year. However, he intended to continue living within the Presbytery. He acknowledged and was grateful for the excellent co-operation he had enjoyed with the elders for over eighteen years. The letter was received with sadness. A special meeting was held on Sunday, 8 January, under the chairmanship of John Edward Jones, when the following options were announced:

1.   the officers should invite the minister to reconsider his intention to retire at the end of 1967;

2.   if he did not accept this invitation to reconsider, then the elders would inform the congregation the following Sunday, as it was impossible to keep such a decision a secret from the members;

3.   that three months should be allocated to prepare for his successor.

It was decided to ask John Edward Jones and Ifor Griffiths to discuss the resignation letter with the Reverend E. Watkin Jones. The minister promised to reconsider his decision during the week and that if he did abide with his original intention, he would inform the church the following Sunday. On Sunday, 5 January, the minister informed the congregation that he and his wife, had considered the elders' requests carefully and prayerfully but that finally they had decided to retire at the end of 1967. The Church Secretary, Ifor Griffiths, informed the Secretary of the Presbytery, the Reverend Cledwyn Griffith, of the situation and asked for permission to select a Pastoral Committee. On Sunday, 14 May, under the careful eye of the Reverend W. D. Jones of Edge Lane Welsh Chapel, they chose eight men and women to assist the eight elders as a Pastoral Committee. Those chosen by the congregation were Miss Alwena Davies, Gwynfa; Miss Doris Thomas, Allerton Road; William Jones, Meldrum Road; Dr. D. A. Price-Evans; H. Wyn Jones; the Reverend D. Hughes Parry; O.E. Roberts, Childwall; and G. Vincent Roberts, Ramilies Road. Of the original sixteen members of this Pastoral Committee, only three are alive today. These include Glyn Davies, who now lives at Ruthin in the Vale of Clwyd; Emeritus Professor David Alan Price-Evans, a remarkable scholar and medical practitioner, who retired from Saudi Arabia in 2007; and Humphrey Wyn Jones, who serves at present as Church Secretary and an elder.

The question of having a permanent organist still remained on the chapel agenda and another effort was made in July 1967 to advertise the vacancy in the *Daily Post, Goleuad* and *Y Cymro,* but there was only one candidate who expressed an interest. Miss Margaret (Peggy) Owen wanted to retire from the rota of organists and she was given a testimonial for her long service. A meeting was held on 11 September, under the chairmanship of the minister when the failure to find an organist to accept the whole responsibility for morning and evening services for fifty two Sundays a year was discussed. They were able to persuade the same team of organists to undertake the work with the addition of Mrs. H. Jones Griffith.

On Sunday night, 31 December, 1967, a large congregation gathered for the last service of the Reverend E. Watkin Jones as minister of the church, after eighteen and a half years service. The Presiding Elder invited Mrs. Watkin Jones to sit with her husband in the *Sêt Fawr*. The Secretary of the Elders' Meeting, Mr. Griffith R. Jones spoke, as did J. Edward Jones, the only elder still carrying on the responsibilities since E. Watkin Jones had arrived as a minister back in 1949. At the end of his address, John Edward Jones presented a beautiful leather case with notes and a cheque for £480 to the Reverend and Mrs. Watkin Jones. The Minister responded. Owen Evans expressed his appreciation of the work done by R. Glyn Williams who was the treasurer of the Testimonial Fund and reminded the congregation that £480 was a very generous expression of their appreciation: nearly as much as the salary of a minister for the whole year in 1967.

When we appraise the ministry of E. Watkin Jones we can highlight several achievements. First, there was his faithfulness to his pastoral responsibilities for the church. This was his strength. In a period of nearly nineteen years, he had baptised 82 children, officiated at the marriage of 41 couples and he had prepared 67 young people for full membership. He had also ministered at some 180 funerals. He and his wife were conscientious visitors of the sick. The majority of the chapel members then lived within walking distance of Heathfield Road – in Penny Lane, Allerton Road, Dovedale Road, as well as Herondale Road, Briardale Road, Mayville Road, Reedale Road, Winchfield Road, Patterdale Road, Deepfield Road, Charles Berrington Road, Elm Hall Drive, Olivedale Road, Berbice Road, Centreville Road, Bristol Road, Allerton Drive, Meldrum Road, Wembley Road, Henley Road, Green Lane, Menlove Avenue, Eardisley Road, Coventry Road and in Sinclair Drive. This situation has changed. The Reverend E. Watkin Jones, was a minister who depended on public transport and through patience and foresight would always arrive for his duties on time. He received a great deal of support from a number of elders who owned a car. The only elder who could not drive was R. Glyn Williams; all the others could and they looked after their minister. But he could easily walk from his Manse to most of the named streets where members lived. He had been fortunate in having a church whose members lived mainly in the Allerton/Smithdown area. Secondly, he was an accomplished preacher, with a clear voice, who prepared conscientiously for the pulpit. He was not in great demand elsewhere as a guest preacher, but he enjoyed high esteem within the chapels of the Liverpool Presbytery. Thirdly, both the Minister and his wife took a great deal of interest in every visitor, in particular, the Welsh students who attended the services. Yet, there is no mention that he prepared for their fellowship, which seems to have happened after he had left. Indeed, Glyn Davies raised the matter in the Elders' Meeting on 11 September 1967, for he had noticed a sizeable number of young people present in the Sunday evening service: 'It would be a good idea for us as a church to organise a meeting in one of the schoolrooms after the service so that they and us could get to know each other and we could do so over some light refreshments.'

This suggestion was well received but it was not implemented for nearly another year. It was one of the priorities that I have implemented as will be mentioned shortly. Fourthly, the Reverend E. Watkin Jones maintained the highest standards of his vocation over many years. He was not very happy with too much publicity for his endeavours, but it seems that he never had a fraternal meeting with the priests and other clergy of the Allerton-Mossley Hill area. Both the Minister and his wife wished for a simple gathering to mark the end of their ministry. The correspondent to *Y Bont* (The Bridge), the monthly magazine of the Liverpool Welsh in that period, wrote: 'They do not at any time seek publicity or attention with regard to the work achieved by them.'

The ministry of the Reverend E. Watkin Jones had been a valuable one. In the final Farewell Service, it was stated, 'your (the Minister's) place will be empty in every aspect of the life of the church.' In his last address for the year 1967, the departing Minister rose to the occasion and wished his successor strength and health to fulfill the responsibilities of the ministry. The number of communicants on 31 December, 1967, stood at 381, with 50 children. Thirty six members had left (this included eight members who had died) and 10 children had left the church. Though it was still a relatively large church in Welsh Presbyterian circles, from now on it did not seem at all possible to stem the decline that was to be experienced during the rest of the twentieth century.

The church was saddened to hear the announcement on Sunday, 4 February, 1968, of the death of the Reverend Dr. R. Glynne Lloyd. After leaving Liverpool he had served as pastor of Moriah Presbyterian Church, Utica, New York State for 18 years; and in 1966 he joined the academic staff of Utica College of Syracuse University as Assistant Professor of Philosophy. A tribute to him was delivered by J. Edward Jones and our sympathies were extended to members of his family on both sides of the Atlantic.

From now on there was a great deal to be done to attract a new minister but from a scrutiny of the minutes of the church, it is clear that all suggestions for new things were left 'until a new minister arrived.'

Chapter 10

THE CALL TO LIVERPOOL FROM THE CYNON VALLEY

Liverpool had been known to me since the Second World War when the evacuees came from Liverpool and East Grinstead to our midst in Llanddewibrefi and to live in our homes. Between 1 and 4 September, 1939, at least 1647 children and mothers arrived in Aberystwyth from Liverpool. Those that suffered from infectious diseases, such as whooping cough, were kept back at Tan-y-Bwlch mansion with the nurses that had accompanied them. The rest were made welcome in homes in Aberystwyth and in remote rural villages such as Llanddewibrefi. It was an eye-opener. As we came to know the Scousers, we discovered new things. There was no-one from the Liverpool Welsh community amongst them. The majority of them, however, were nearly all from Anfield and Everton and had surnames, such as 'Verdun', or were related to another branch of the Celtic family, the Liverpool Irish. These were the descendants of the thousands who had left the Emerald Isle during the Potato Famine between 1845 and 1849. Many of these Liverpudlians became Welsh speakers and a few of them stayed in the village or came back when they had grown up to be adults. Though I came to know the Liverpool children, I had never been near the city as a child – though in

Dafydd, Meinwen and D. Ben Rees

my grammar school days I once went to London for the celebrations for the Festival of Britain in 1951. Moreover, as a theological student between 1959 and 1962, I never received an invitation to preach in one of the Welsh chapels on Merseyside. Even after qualifying and accepting a call to minister at Abercynon and Penrhiwceibr in the Cynon Valley, Liverpool still remained a distant city, a city associated, above all, with the Beatles.

The activities that I became involved with in the Cynon Valley and in Cardiff filled my life. These were crusading days. In 1963, I succeeded with others, in preventing the blond Welsh girl from Llanelli, Mandy Rice-Davies, from coming to perform in a working man's club at Ynys-boeth. In that summer I began a Welsh publishing house, Modern Welsh Publications Ltd. That was an exciting venture, especially when I decided to publish illustrated books for children printed in the Netherlands, Prague, Budapest or Sofia and imported in their

114

thousands through the port of London to Teifi House in Abercynon! Travelling to Cardiff, especially to the television studios of TWW and BBC, occurred frequently. In addition, there were opportunities to organize large rallies and pilgrimages within the denomination through the Young People's League and my ecumenical work in the valleys, as well as involvement with the Labour Party.

It is true that nothing changed my life as much as the tragedy that occurred on 21 October, 1966, in Aberfan, where I had, some months previously accepted responsibility for the chapel at Disgwylfa in Merthyr Vale. It was a day that gave ministers of religion in Aberfan and Merthyr Vale a challenge that words are inadequate to describe. Yet, at the same time, it was an opportunity to minister the comfort of the Gospel of Christ to families in two villages that had been devastated by the tragedy. My great friend, the Reverend E. Peris Owen and I gave our best to the task of caring for families who had lost 116 children. A total amounting to 144 adults and children were lost when the buildings of Pant Glas Primary School were overwhelmed by tons of coal-tip slurry. The headmistress of the school, Miss Jennings, was suffocated in her room. Her sister was the secretary of the nearby Quakers' Yard Comprehensive School where my wife, Meinwen, was a full time teacher and where I served regularly as a chaplain and, for a time, I taught scripture to forms five and six. That sad morning I rushed to Aberfan from Abercynon with hundreds of other men, mostly miners

Mrs Jean Edwards holding Dafydd together with her fellow members from the Welsh Presbyterian Chapel of Abercynon in south Wales.

from the nearby colliery of Merthyr Vale, to try and rescue those who had been buried by the landslide.

Earlier that year I had been canvassing for my friend, Gwilym Prys Davies, who was standing as the Labour Party candidate in the famous by-election in Carmarthenshire. His wife, Llinos, was from Abercynon and her parents were always involved in the chapel activities there at Tabernacl. The election result turned out to be a historic victory for Gwynfor Evans and *Plaid Cymru*, though no one was more pro-Welsh than the Labour candidate. But the crisis of the pound, the decision of the Labour MP, Megan Lloyd George, to stand in the General Election a few months earlier when she was dying of cancer, the closure of collieries in the Aman and Gwendraeth Valleys and the enthusiastic campaign of *Plaid Cymru* members was enough to disillusion a large segment who usually voted for the Labour Party.

Overall, 1966 proved to be a difficult year but, before the end, the good news arrived of the

LLYFR GWASANAETH
(IEUENCTID)

Trefnwyd gan

Y Parch. HARRI G. PARRI, B.A., B.D., Porthmadog
a'r
Parch. D. BEN REES, B.A., B.D., Abercynon

Golygydd: Y Parch. WILLIAM MORRIS, O.B.E., M.A.

Llyfrfa'r M.C. Caernarfon
1967

A volume of services for young people prepared by Reverend Harri Parri and D. Ben Rees in 1967.

birth of our eldest son, Dafydd Llewelyn. He had a great welcome in Abercynon. When I came home the night of his birth from Aberdare hospital, there was a group standing outside the Post Office in Carnetown with my mother-in-law, the post mistress Mrs. James and others waiting for the news. I remember pressing on the horn of our first car, a Ford Anglia, for half a mile as I rejoiced in the good news that a son had been born to the Manse on the threshold of Christmas.

The following summer, when the National Eisteddfod was held in Bala, we stayed in our denomination's Holiday Centre at Tresaith on the Ceredigion coast. I had been heavily involved in the decision to set up this Centre, as well as in establishing the Layman's Centre at Trefeca, the original home of the eighteenth century Welsh Revivalist, Howell Harris, often known as the 'greatest Welshman of all times.' Our son, Dafydd, was taken from Tresaith to Bala for the National Eisteddfod and we all rejoiced, in the achievement of Eluned Philllips from Cenarth in winning the Crown at the Eisteddfod for her poetic work on the subject of *Corlanau* [Folds].

Sometime that summer I received a phone call from a minister that I had known in Ceredigion, the Reverend William Jones of Bootle, asking me a direct question, 'Where are you preaching a week next Sunday night?' I answered Tabernacl, 'Abercynon'. 'Good', he said, and he put the phone down. I did not think more of this phone call until five minutes to six that particular Sunday night. I was waiting by the door of Tabernacl Chapel when I saw a large Rover car being driven slowly up Margaret Street and parked nearly opposite the chapel. By the time I had arrived in the pulpit there were three strangers sitting at the back of the chapel. This was not unusual. Often, I would see someone or other from Cardiganshire, on their way back from Cardiff or elsewhere, turning up in our services. In nine out of ten cases they would be known to me. But, this time it was different. I had never seen these three men who were worshipping with us. We welcomed them in the *Seiat*; and at the end of the service I went out to shake hands with the congregation. Two of the three wore spectacles but the third did not. The first two, (Howell Vaughan Jones and the Reverend Dafydd Hughes Parry, as I discovered later) did not want to engage in conversation just in case I realised from where they had come, but the third (Vincent Roberts) was one that seemed prepared to chat. '*O ble rydych chi'n dod?*' (Where are you from?), I asked. As he was on the verge of answering, Dafydd Hughes Parry said, on behalf of the three, '*Diolch yn fawr iawn. Nos da.*' (Thank you very much. Good night).

I pondered about this visit for several days. Then everything became clear when I received an invitation to preach at Heathfield Road Chapel, Liverpool. On Saturday, 18 November, 1967 I began my long journey north. I caught a train from Abercynon to Merthyr

Some of the young people from Hermon Presbyterian Church of Wales, Penrhiwceiber in 1967.

Tudfil and then a bus all the way to Liverpool. As we approached Wrexham, I could see that the weather was deteriorating and it became worse in Chester. By the time we approached Merseyside, there was thick fog. I remember arriving at the Crosville Bus Depot in Edge Lane. There was no other passenger on the bus except myself but I could see two elderly persons in a car waiting for me. When I came out of the bus station, the two introduced themselves. The car driver was Goronwy Davies, and the other person R. Glyn Williams with whom I was going to stay for the weekend. In the fog it was not easy to find the car and the subsequent journey from Edge Lane to Garthdale Road was something of a nightmare. Goronwy Davies was not the best driver on the roads of Liverpool but he was miraculous that night! We arrived safely at our destination in Allerton to a warm welcome from Mrs. Hannah Williams.

This was to be the beginning of a close relationship with both Hannah and Glyn Williams. Their house was home from home. Mrs. Williams had a meal waiting for me. She was a native of Llanbedrgoch, Anglesey, but her husband was a native of Liverpool. He had been brought up in the home of the General Secretary of the Foreign Mission, the Reverend R. J. Williams. We shared so much in common: the Connexion and its ministers, the missionary work, the witness for the Gospel, Liverpool Football Club and the Liverpool Welsh who had settled to live in the streets of Liverpool between Smithdown Lane and Smithdown Place. The conversation was in both Welsh and in English as in most of the homes I visited in my pastorate in south Wales. Mrs. Williams spoke in Welsh but her husband mixed both languages. It was a great introduction to Liverpool and when I went to bed at 11p.m. I felt completely relaxed.

Breakfast was at 9 a.m. the following morning. We were within walking distance of the chapel, about half a mile, according to the host; but he wanted us to arrive in the Minister's Room at least a quarter of an hour before the service began. Mrs. Williams was not coming: she was going to prepare lunch, the mid-day meal, for us.

We left the house at Garthdale Road at ten minutes to ten and walked across Elm Hall Drive, up Garthdale Road, to Allerton Road, which was a fine road with shops on both sides. R. Glyn Williams pointed out to me, the Post Office across the road and, next door to it, the funeral undertakers, Pearson and Collinson. He referred to the two brothers, Henry and Pat Pearson, who were in charge of the funeral company and told me that they were fluent speakers of Welsh. They had learnt Welsh as evacuees in Llŷn. We walked on, and at the corner of Mapledale Road and Allerton Road we met one of the faithful band, Samuel A. Rogers, a devout, God-fearing member of the chapel. I was introduced to him. Within another hundred yards we met two sisters, the Misses Doris and Eunice Thomas, and I was informed that one of them was a member of the Pastoral Committee. Then, after crossing Queen's Drive, I saw a number of other people walking in the same direction. Clearly, they were all on the way to morning service.

Within a further two hundred yards I had my first sight ever of the building that was going to play an important part in my life. Two of my fellow ministers in Glamorganshire, the Reverends E. Emrys Evans, Mountain Ash, and J. R. Ebenezer, Cilfynydd, who had attended the General Assembly in 1962, had told me of this unique building. But, when I first saw it I was overwhelmed. I saw the huge doors standing open and, though there was at least quarter of an hour before the start of the service, there was a large number of people walking up the steps into the beautiful chapel. Both of us continued up from Smithdown Place to the start of Heathfield Road and turned into Auckland Road and used the other entrance to enter the chapel. We arrived at the Minister's Room where there were seven men waiting for me, all immaculately dressed. Each introduced himself. Within a short period of my ministry in Liverpool I soon came to value their support and assistance.

Everyone was glad that the fog had lifted and emphasised to me that this did not happen very often. Immediately, I recognised Howell Vaughan Jones and I referred to his recent visit to Abercynon. He paid a special tribute to Dafydd Hughes Parry, stating that he knew the location of every Calvinistic Methodist Chapel throughout Wales; and, also, the football grounds of teams that had played against Everton. I realised there and then that key people in the Welsh chapel supported Liverpool City Football Team while others were committed to Everton. This would have to be kept in mind if the opportunity were given me to move to Liverpool.

Prayer was offered before we went into the main chapel. Then, when we entered, I was impressed by the size of the assembled congregation. From the pulpit it looked an impressive gathering but I felt completely at ease. That morning my sermon was based on the experiences of the prophet Elisha at Gilgal. He had been able to take the poison out of the cauldron. It was obvious that the congregation appreciated the freshness of approach in my sermon, which emphasised the need for us, as disciples, to redeem society of its failings by our commitment to Christ. For them the illustrations that I used were new and different. On the way out one of the members said to me that he had never heard anyone before mentioning from the pulpit the Liverpool Jewish Socialist, Sidney Silverman, constant mentor of Jack and Bessie Braddock. John Morgan Davies, Stoneycroft, made the comment and in time came to be one my most dependable friends.

I spent at least twenty minutes chatting to various members of the congregation at the end of the service. Then we walked back to Garthdale Road. In the afternoon I was expected to return for the Adult Sunday School, where I would meet more dedicated members of the chapel. The large Schoolroom was a hive of activity with six adult classes with one woman and five men teachers. I noticed that three of the elders were in charge of the classes: Goronwy Davies, Ifor Griffiths, who had corresponded with me, and Griffith R. Jones. The woman teacher was Mrs. H. Jones Griffith, wife of a minister, while the other class was under the guidance of W. R. Williams, Queen's Drive, who, though looking frail, was widely regarded as a Biblical exponent of the first order. I was placed in the class of William Jones, Meldrum, a retired sergeant in the Liverpool Police Force. To be in his company was an educational experience. He recalled, vividly, the sermons of various preachers from south Wales as well as north Wales and there was no end to his recollections. I took to him immediately and we became great friends for the next decade.

The Superintendent of the Sunday School was R. Emrys Jones, Chapel House. His Deputy was Glyn Rowlands, today living in Benllech, Anglesey; and we all became close friends. Peter Green was in charge of the singing. He had migrated to Liverpool from the Corwen area; and it was a rare treat to hear him singing the hymn. It was also very pleasant to be presented to the teachers of the Children's Sunday School. This is where I recognised the third member of the visiting team who had been in Abercynon, Vincent Roberts. His daughter, Helen Hughes Roberts, was the Secretary of the Sunday School. Today she lives in Ruthin, near her mother, who lives in Bala. I cannot claim that I remembered the names of all the teachers of the Children's Sunday School but within a year I had come to know Alwena Davies, Louie Jones, Mrs. Cathy Jones, wife of John Edward Jones, Nan Hughes Parry (and her husband, Dafydd Hughes Parry, was present that afternoon), Ceri Roberts and Mary Williams, Hornby Lane, who has been a versatile member of our chapel since she came from the Lleyn peninsula as a young person in 1948.

As I walked back from Auckland Road to Garthdale Road at a quarter past three, I was glad to have met the Sunday School. Like the hymn writer, Nantlais, I felt that we should acknowledge the contribution of the teachers and the adherents who studied God's word. It is sad to realise today that the Adult Welsh Sunday Schools in Liverpool, as everywhere else, have declined. Indeed, at Heathfield Road Chapel they have ceased to exist. Back in 1967 the Sunday School was an attraction to a significant sector of the chapel community but today they are only part of our history.

By the start of the evening service I felt completely relaxed. I preached on the Gospel of the Parable of the Mustard Seed and I still remember my conversation at the end of the service with a family from my home territory in Ceredigion, Jenkin James, Woolton (a native of Tregaron), and his wife, Mrs. Margaret James, who was from Llanddewibrefi. Another person with whom I had a conversation at this time was Ieuan Griffith, a native of Penmaenmawr, who worked in the large Ford Motor Company factory at Halewood. Indeed, he and his wife, their daughter, Gwyneth, and his son, Gareth, had settled in the extensive settlement, known as Halewood, on the outskirts of Liverpool. My hosts, R. Glyn Williams and his wife, had been well pleased, and judging from the ways in which I had conducted the services, they even thought that I, as one of three on trial, had a good chance of being called to Heathfield Road as minister.

At the beginning of the New Year in 1968, I received the official invitation from the Pastoral Committee and they stated that they would like to meet Meinwen and myself. I had no option but to drive from Abercynon to Allerton, which meant staying a night away from home in Abercynon. We travelled through the Midlands, knowing that Howell Vaughan Jones would meet us at the restaurant in the motorway service station at Sandbach in Cheshire. He would then lead us to his home near the All Hallows Anglican Church in Allerton. After arriving we had the privilege of meeting his wife, Gwen Vaughan Jones, or, as she was called by many of her early friends, 'Gwen Tegla Davies'.

Tegla, preacher and literary genius, was one of my heroes. The first time I met him in the flesh was in the National Eisteddfod of Wales in Llangefni in 1957. He was then

Florence and O. E. Roberts.

well over seventy years of age. It was an experience to listen to the Reverend Edward Tegla Davies speaking without notes, delivering his adjudication on the novel competition. With his saintly countenance, his mop of white hair and his blue eyes keeping us all under his spell, he was one of Wales's most outstanding literary figures. Tegla Davies had died the year before our visit and so our shared *hiraeth* for him brought us close to Gwen and Howell and their young daughter, Nia. In effect, we became part of the family of Howell and Gwen Vaughan Jones and our visit to Liverpool on this occasion was a great assistance to us as we contemplated moving there from Glamorganshire.

I well remember that evening. Both of us travelled in the company of Howell Vaughan Jones to a Chinese restaurant in Liverpool's Hanover Street to meet members of the Pastoral Committee. Everyone who could make it was there and I well remember Owen Evans keeping the conversation alive around the table. One member who made a particular impact on me was Owen Elias Roberts, an outstanding writer on scientific matters in Welsh. I knew that we were on the same wavelength as I had read many of his articles and knew of his contributions to Welsh life on Merseyside.

After the meal, it had been arranged that I was to meet the full Pastoral Committee in the Elders' Meeting Room at Heathfield Road Chapel. I got out of the car in Penny Lane and walked to the meeting whilst Howell Vaughan Jones took my wife to their welcoming home.

That Pastoral Committee was a happy one and I had the feeling that the meeting was keen that I should accept any call that they might make on me. No one had any intention of laying down boundaries to my ministry, which was so encouraging. I remember O. E. Roberts saying, ' Manchester is very near and you can carry on with your Welsh language television activities'. I could hardly believe what I had heard because most leaders within chapels had quite different views. But it seems that in Liverpool they had a more urbane open-minded approach.

The next morning it had been decided that we would meet a few key members of the Pastoral Committee at the Manse, namely Howell Vaughan Jones in his professional capacity as director of the building firm of J. W. Jones; Alwena Davies and Doris Thomas as extremely practical people who held the interests of the chapel uppermost. The morning passed rapidly before we had to leave for the long journey back to Abercynon. Both of us had been pleasantly surprised but the formal call had not yet arrived. We had to wait, as Ifor Griffiths told us in another letter. He had a great gift for preparing letters in both languages. The actual vote to call me as their new minister took place on Sunday, 24 March, 1968, under the joint guidance of the Reverend W. D. Jones, who proved to be an excellent mentor, and Arthur Thomas (elder in Anfield Road), both representing the Liverpool Presbytery. The church now formally extended its call to a young minister and his family as it had done in 1917 and in 1942. Previously, the Reverend Daniel Davies had moved from Pentre in the Rhondda, the Reverend Dr. R. Glynne Lloyd from Ferndale, whilst I was now called to Liverpool from Abercynon. Heathfield Road Chapel was unique in another sense: it had given a call to three from north Wales and three from south Wales.

We decided to hold the Induction Service on Thursday, 18 July, 1968, at 7.30 p.m, but the ministry was to start on the first Sunday in July. I was expected to be present for the Welsh Day in Jericho Lane, Otterspool, on the first Saturday in July and to preside at the Children and Young People's Service in Liverpool on Sunday morning. I had travelled up from Glamorganshire at the beginning of June and arranged the Induction Service in the company of the elders. This meeting was held on Tuesday, 4 June, and all aspects of this important occasion were well thought out. The Induction Service itself, held under the chairmanship of W. D. Owen, Wallasey, was a memorable one. The chapel was full of people, even a sizeable number in the gallery. A bus conveying well wishers came from Glamorganshire, as well as a coach from my home village of Llanddewibrefi. Everyone who took part excelled, and, in particular, Arthur Jones, who was an elder at Tabernacl Welsh Presbyterian Chapel, my old chapel in Abercynon, a godly, cultured ex-coal miner.

The church arranged an official Welcome Meeting for us as a family in the large Schoolroom on 13 September. The barrister, John Edward Jones, spoke on behalf of the elders, R. Emrys Jones and Vincent Roberts represented the Sunday Schools, Mrs. Moraned Williams, Chalfont Road, represented the Sisterhood, and H. Wyn Jones spoke on behalf of the Literary Society. As we shall see in the next chapter, we had travelled a long way to minister the Gospel in Liverpool.

Mimosa Celebration in Liverpool 1965 - in the photograph three members of the chapel, Lena Jones, Olwen Roberts and Gwladys Lloyd Williams

The pews that were comfortably full at this period.

The chapel before the vandals had their field day in the period 2003-2007

Chapter 11

THE MINISTER OF HEATHFIELD ROAD (1968-1975)

I became involved immediately in the task of getting to know the members in their own homes, and it was arranged that one of the elders would accompany me. By Christmas this introductory task had been completed and I received a warm welcome from everyone.

Between September and December I had to preside at three funerals. On 1 September Mr J. E. Salisbury, Heyscrofts Road, Woolton died quite suddenly. I had visited him and together with his wife he had been present in the evening services that I had conducted in July. On 25 November Mrs W. G. Jones, Eardisley Road died and then on 23 December, W. R Williams, Queens Drive. It was at their home that I first met the Reverend Cyril John, the minister of the Welsh Baptist Chapels of Earlsfield Road, Wavertree and Edge Lane, Liverpool. He was a great conversationalist and he knew my mother-in-law, Mrs Sarah A. Llewellyn, widow of the Reverend Arthur George Llewellyn (1903-1960). He had followed him as the Welsh Baptist minister at Cwmgors, near Pontardawe. I expected that my mother–in-law would have insisted on attending the Welsh Baptist chapel in Earlsfield Road, Wavertree. But she decided not to do so. She remained faithful to Heathfield Road Chapel, where over the years she attended the morning services with her two grandsons; and then on Sunday nights she looked after them so that her daughter could attend the evening service.

One of the most important decisions I made at the outset of my ministry in Heathfield Road was to re-arrange the work of the young on a permanent basis. The number of young people that were then attending the evening service was around fifty. But there were some within the Welsh community and in the Young People's League who wanted to centralise all the activities on the premises of the Catholic Church, based on Seel Street, in the heart of the city. In my first Elders' Meeting on 9 September, it was suggested that I should give a lead and thus ignore the special meeting arranged for the young people on Sunday 15 September in Seel Street. Indeed, it was decided that I would announce to them that we were going to have a regular Sunday evening Young People's meeting in the small schoolroom. This was an important

Reverend J. Meirion Lloyd.

Maesgrug Singers at Southport with Gwyn Parri Huws, Mrs R. M. Williams, Siân Parri Hughes and Reverend R. M. Williams.

decision, with the result that my wife, Meinwen, arranged with the young wives to prepare light refreshments for the students, young teachers and other young Welsh people who had come to the service. This meeting became one of the most important gatherings within the chapel for the next seven years.

So many in the congregation contributed to the success of our chapel work. The responsibility was not just on the shoulders of the minister and the elders. It was encouraging to have the contribution of a number of experienced craftsmen to carry out maintenance work within the Manse and the Chapel. I had the co-operation of four of these immediately, W. J. Jones, ex chapel caretaker, Hugh John Jones, who had worked in the same firm as Ringo Starr, and Emrys Williams, a true gentleman. The last three lived near each other in Centreville Road, just three hundred yards from chapel. Another member, Danny Jones, Winchfield Road, was willing to join the team with R. Glyn Williams, who had a great skill in dealing with people as convenor. One of the most active and kind persons during this early stage of my ministry was Miss Alwena Davies. In 1956 her family had donated to the chapel a reading stand in memory of her father, J. R. Davies, and in 1968 she decided to give a new sink unit in the kitchen in memory of her late mother.

I became very involved in ecumenical church work within Liverpool, the Merseyside Free Church Council, and I attended, on behalf of our church, a Conference in the ancient town of Conwy on 6 and 7 December 1968. This ecumenical involvement brought me into the activities of the Council of Christians and Jews, and to start a network of chapels and churches which became known as the Mosley Hill and District Council of Churches. Today, I am the only one of the original pioneers who still remains as a minister in this locality.

My wife and I had so many plans for a range of different activities, as we sincerely believed that this would strengthen the Welsh community. In the first week of the New Year I arranged prayer meetings for the first four nights. Even today we usually hold two prayer meetings, but in 1969 we had four, with a large enough number of men and women to take part, that we did not need to ask the same person twice. Those involved were invited to prepare, by choosing a portion of Scripture, two hymns, and a prayer. The minister presided and the collections were given to the foreign mission.

A great deal was expected from the Minister. I had been warned of this by the Reverend E. Emrys Evans, Aberdare, the great friend of Ifor Griffiths; this turned out to be very true. No appeal was placed before the congregation without inviting the Minister to convey it. I used to make appeals on behalf of all kinds of campaigns, different meetings, and the literature of the denomination, such as the weekly newspaper, *Y Goleuad*, the magazines, *Y Drysorfa* and *Y Traethodydd*. We also received the weekly *Faner* and the monthly *Barn* and they were all supported.

Dissatisfaction was expressed at the end of 1968 that the Presbytery/Pulpit Secretary had not placed me in my own pulpit on the first Sunday of February and October. Our elder, Goronwy Davies, who responded to my preaching with constant words of encouragement, was annoyed, and he prevailed upon his fellow elders to agree with him. The minutes of the Elders' Meeting sums up the situation: 'We feel, as officers, that the arrangement is not conducive to our church and we would like our minister to preach in his own pulpit on the first Sunday of every month.' This was sent to Mr D. Aneurin Hughes, Crosby, Superintendent of the Presbytery Plan, and who had been a member of the chapel in the 1930s.

As the Church had so many talented members, it was fitting for me to invite them to participate in the week-night meetings. Living in the Mossley Hill and Allerton area were some very extraordinary people, who were very willing to visit our fellowship with their expertise in Christian spirituality. In addition, I was soon invited to lecture under the auspices of the Workmen's Educational Association (WEA) and also for the University of

Owen Roberts who left Liverpool for Cricieth with his wife Glenys where he served the community of Dwyfor.

Liverpool's Department of Extra Mural Studies. These public activities became an important aspect of my ministry for the next thirty years.

In 1969 I began organising meetings on themes and topics that would enrich our gatherings. I took the initiative by introducing a number of contemporary Welsh poets and literary figures. The end result was to send a typescript to the National Eisteddfod of Wales when it was held at Flint in 1969, *Portreadau o Bymtheg o Wŷr Llên y Ganrif* (Portraits of Fifteen Literary Men of the Century), a volume that would be suitable for use by students in secondary schools. The portraits sent in were warmly recommended by the adjudicator, R. E. Griffith, Aberystwyth (a former member of the church) and he suggested that the volume be published. I asked O. E. Roberts to read the manuscript and I sent copies of the text to a number of those on whom I had written and I received encouraging replies. Sir T. H. Parry-Williams read two portraits, one on himself, and the other a portrait of his cousin, R. Williams Parry. The novelist Dr Kate Roberts and the poet Gwilym R. Jones also approved of the texts, (these two I had come to know from my visits to the Welsh Presbyterian Chapel of Capel Mawr in Denbigh.) The Reverend L. Haydn Lewis, Tonpentre (a great friend of mine in East Glamorganshire), the Communist T. E. Nicholas, whom I knew well in my student days, and Ffransis G. Payne, who was an expert on the history of the Welsh in Radnor also received copies of the drafts. The short story literary giant, Dr D. J. Williams of Fishguard had died suddenly in the chapel of his boyhood in Carmarthenshire before I could approach him, and J. Saunders Lewis was quite content to leave his portrait in my hands. Saunders Lewis had more faith in me that I had in myself! I appreciated such generosity of spirit and the volume was finally published in 1972, and by the time of the National Eisteddfod of Wales at Ruthin in 1973 it had sold out. On the dust jacket there is a photo of myself in the Presbyterian robes of our chapel, quite a shock to a number of religious nonconformists who bought the volume. By today it is difficult to find a copy in any second hand bookshop!

I decided in 1969 to adopt the Book of Revelation as the syllabus for our Biblical meditations and we had a number who responded – on themes such as John in Patmos and the Glory of Christ in a paper prepared by Ifor Griffiths; Sergeant William Jones provided us with insights into The Church in Laodicea, and Paul's Letter to the Churches of Pergamum and Thyatira was dealt with by Humphrey Wyn Jones. The Message to the Churches of Sardis and Philadelphia was covered by Goronwy Davies, David John Williams, Gateacre, tackled the Vision of the Two Animals and the Lamb; the Seven Angels was the topic given to Glyn Davies, whilst the Reverend D. Hughes Parry gave us a great deal of the eulogy on the Vision of the Heavenly Throne. I remember well the contribution of Mrs Ceridwen Williams, who lived in Woolton, the daughter of a minister, and the widow of Ifor Williams, who had been an elder at Edge Lane Welsh Presbyterian Chapel. She was an extremely able woman. She had been a headmistress in Liverpool and was a great asset to the Sunday School and the *Seiat*. Mrs C. Williams delivered an introduction to the subject on 'The Influence of the *Pilgrim's Progress* by John Bunyan on Welsh hymn writers'. Her theme was so well prepared, that it deserved to be published in *Y Drysorfa*, the monthly denominational journal. We had a large number of similarly inspired addresses: 'Science and Religion' by a lecturer from the School of

Dentistry, in the University of Liverpool, H. Richard Williams (husband of Dr Pat Williams), 'Things to be Reckoned' by O. E. Roberts, 'Religion and Society' by John Edward Jones, 'The Women's Charter' by Meinwen Rees and a joint presentation on 'Heroes of the Faith' by Meinwen and myself. As one would expect, the contributions of the Reverend H. Jones Griffiths on 'Developments in Missionary Works', the Reverend Alun Williams on 'Privilege of the Christian' were extremely useful, as was the address of Gwynfryn Evans on 'Gospel Hymn Singing'.

Gwynfryn Evans

A number of the younger members travelled overseas and we took note of this, inviting Mai Davies to give us a glimpse of Israel and Alwena Davies on the Ancient Civilisation preserved in Egypt. A detailed report was given by Miss Malltwen Griffiths (who lives now in Llanfairfechan) from Garston Welsh Chapel on the Missionary Conference held at Barry. Two doors from the Manse lived Mrs Helen Gray and she was very active in the Presbyterian Church of England at Mather Avenue in Allerton and was one of the founding members of Amnesty International in Liverpool. It was a privilege to invite her to remind us of the witness of Amnesty. Perhaps the most difficult exposition of all was the one presented by Edward Thomas, Pinemore Road, Mossley Hill, on the 'Final Judgement'. I had noticed him in the Sunday School class of William Jones when I first came to Liverpool, many of his views being outlandish to us, in particular on millenarianism. Edward Thomas, a native of Aberystwyth, believed passionately in the Second Coming of Christ and he was an enthusiastic millenarian, as I soon realised when I visited him. After a conversation of ten minutes in the kitchen with his wife and himself, he would lead me to the front room where a large family Bible was open on the table. For the next twenty minutes I would be immersed in theology more conducive to the 'moral majority' that is the followers of Ronald Regan and George W. Bush in the USA than to our religious culture as Welsh people. He strongly believed in the second coming of Christ.

It was very satisfying to welcome 16 new members in 1969, and another minister settled in our midst in the person of the Reverend Alun Wyn Owen, from Glan Conwy. One of the most encouraging aspects of work was to do with the children and young people. It was so satisfying to be involved every Friday in *Y Gorlan* with Miss Alwena Davies, the conscientious secretary. Vincent Roberts shouldered responsibility as a treasurer, and one had the support of a number of young mothers, some of whose children were in *Y Gorlan*.

We rejoiced as a community in the news of John Edward Jones's appointment as a Judge. He was a most dependable elder and always very supportive. We also rejoiced when Dr David Alan Price Evans was awarded his own Personal Chair as Professor in the

Professor T. J. Morgan, the examiner for my M.A. thesis.

Faculty of Medicine at the University of Liverpool. His parents, like us, rejoiced greatly in his genius. Professor Evans has remained with us and we have had more than one contribution from him, especially on the environment, a topic which, in 1969, was hardly discussed publically. I also remember his address on Moral Obligations in Medicine. Another academic from the University of Liverpool who came to us was Professor D. Simon Evans, not as a member, but as a regular attender, with his wife and their son, Dafydd. He was extremely kind to me when I began researching under his supervision for an M.A. research degree in the University of Liverpool. As a result, I was invited to lecture to students who followed the degree course in Welsh in the Celtic Department as well as Dr. Pat Williams and my wife Meinwen, who by then taught part time at the nearby Liverpool Girls' College. Both Pat and Meinwen have been of great help as tutors to our chapel children who have been preparing for GCSE and A level in Welsh under the Welsh Joint Education Board. Dr Simon Evans had considered the call of the Presbyterian ministry and had completed his B.D., which was then as well as in my own day, a postgraduate degree. He had great sympathy with a Minister and he sought to be as encouraging as possible. On 28 April 1969 at our schoolroom, he gave a very outstanding exposition of the Welsh hymn writer of the nineteenth century from Eifionydd, Robert Williams, known as Robert ap Gwilym Ddu.

We suffered a large number of losses through death and we gave a short eulogy to each one in the Sunday service following the funeral; we also sang an appropriate hymn, usually chosen by the deceased's family, to remember the departed. In the nineteen seventies the congregation would stand in memory of the person who had died before singing the memorial hymn.

From 1968 to 1975 the Annual Preaching Service was important in the early period of my ministry. As we had a Saturday night service as well as two services on Sunday, I decided that I would suggest preachers of exceptional ability, not only from north Wales, but much further afield from west and south Wales. In our first year we had two exceptional preachers, the Reverend D. R. Thomas, Aberystwyth, then a lecturer in the Education Department of the University, and the Reverend J. Eirian Davies, a native of Nantgaredig in Carmarthenshire, but then minister at Mold, who took charge of the Seiat on Saturday night. We paid the fee of £15 to the Reverend D. R. Thomas from Aberystwyth and £5 to the poet preacher, the Reverend J. Eirian Davies for Saturday night. The following year we invited the Reverend Richard Williams, Amlwch, a great favourite as a preacher in our community. I had the task

Sir Thomas Parry, guest speaker at our St David's Day celebrations.

of suggesting the guest preachers, and I was able to persuade Richard Williams to come again in 1981 as well as in 1987. In 1971 we had the pleasure of a gospel singer in the person of Miss Beti Mari Owen from London (originally from the Gwendraeth Valley in Carmarthenshire) to sing in all the three services and then to have the Reverend Morgan R. Mainwaring, Cardiff, to preach.

In February 1969, a Young Women's League was formed which would meet monthly, a society which was to do so much cultural and charitable work over the years. This year we took part in a Biblical Quiz, and I took our team with me in the car to compete in the first round at Mold and then in the next round in Betws-yn-Rhos, inland from Abergele. A schoolteacher, Gwilym John Roberts who later became an elder, was our link man and organiser. It was a happy occasion.

There were a number of issues that were dealt with regularly by the elders; one of them concerning the scheme for pew seats. The scheme expected the family who sat in the pew to pay for the privilege! Many of us felt that this scheme which had been in operation since the early days at Webster Road was obsolete by 1969. After all, there were a sizeable number of the congregation who sat in the chapel without thinking of paying and we felt that we should do away with the practice altogether. We asked Judge J. E. Jones to explain to the members in April the possibility of keeping the system going for another period. This was accepted. But in 1971 the practice was finally ended.

In April 1969 the widow of the Reverend Robert Davies died in Llangollen and I sent a letter of sympathy to her daughter, Miss Gwyneth Davies. We received the medal for long term attendance in the Sunday School, the Gee Medal, which was awarded to Mrs Edward Davies, Welbeck Avenue, as a gift to the church and we prepared a special wooden box made for it, by one of our craftsmen, W. T. Jones, Ivydale Road. It is one of the treasures of the church.

Throughout the years the piano has been a problem, as all those that we had were given to us after years of service elsewhere. We received a piano from the Welsh chapel of Walton Park, when the chapel ceased to function in May 1969, and at the time we got rid of two old pianos which were no longer worth keeping. That has been the story from one decade to another, to the frustration of our able pianists. The verdict of the expert who came in 1969 was that these two pianos were worthless; indeed we needed to spend at least £15 to make them worthwhile.

It was sad to hear in July that the English chapel of our denomination, St Columba in Smithdown Road was to cease, the chapel which had the Christian socialist, the Reverend J. H. Howard, as its minister when they worshipped in Catharine Street. We were fortunate in receiving a number of members from that chapel, especially the family of Emrys and Jennie Jones, Garmoyle Road, and Miss Winifred Jones, Bristol Road. The arrival of Emrys Jones, a native of Nantgwynant, was a tremendous asset to us as a chapel. He was a live wire and enthusiastic in everything relating to Welsh culture. You could never find anyone like him to sell tickets for any concert and he made a valuable contribution within the Liverpool Welsh community.

In an Elders' Meeting on 8 September 1969, Glyn Davies raised the matter of those members who lived outside the boundaries of the city and our responsibility to keep in touch with every person in our community. It was considered that a newsletter would be a useful means of communication, and I was asked to prepare it. Ifor Griffiths volunteered to type it and prepare it for distribution, and this was the beginning of a newsletter which has been my responsibility every since, over a period of 37 years. Following Ifor Griffiths came Gwilym Meredydd Jones, who had given assistance with the preparation of the newsletter, and for the last fifteen years. *Y Rhwyd* (The Net) as it is called, has been printed by the County Press at Bala, a printing press which has fulfilled most of our needs.

The leaders of the chapel were supportive of every publication that would be useful for our witness. We purchased twelve copies of epilogues for the youth club, *Epilogau'r Ifanc,* the valuable volume prepared by Dr. Elfed ap Nefydd Roberts. We supported the centenary of the death of the prince of preachers, the Reverend Henry Rees, Chatham Street on 16 October 1969 at Anfield Road Welsh Chapel (which has long been demolished) with a number of our members taking part in a script which I had prepared.

It was sad to have to read on 3 November the report of George Haslam, one of the directors of the J. W. Jones Builder of 158 Allerton Road, on the condition of the wall above the gallery of the chapel, where dampness has been a problem for us every since. It was stated that there was dry rot in some of the wood. This was the first report of many different companies we received over the years, and I reckon that we have spent around £46,000 from 1969 to 2007 without eradicating the problem. The defect is so evident these days and it is one of the reasons why we cannot realistically stay for a much longer period in our sanctuary.

In this period I had the pleasant task of preparing six young people for full membership of the church, and this took place on the first Sunday of the new year. The six that were accepted were Bronwen Davies, Roby; Glenys Wynne Williams, Allerton, Gwyneth Williams, Barndale Road; Elizabeth Thomas, Childwall; Gareth Griffiths, Halewood and Hywel Williams, Karslake Road.

It was a great privilege to administer the sacrament of baptism and I had the opportunity soon after I arrived on 21 July 1968 of baptising Geraint Siôr Roberts, 19 Greenhill Avenue, Allerton and then on November 3 Gwenda Griffith, Woolton was also brought into the fellowship of the Church through the sacrament of baptism. Then in 1969 five baptisms of infants took place in Heathfield Road, namely Cari Garmon Jones, Brendon Road on November 16; Bethan Wyn Jones, Wheatcroft Road, Allerton on May 18 (and little did I realise that morning that Bethan within my ministry at Liverpool would become our daughter-in-law); October 19, Lowri Ann Williams, Menlove Gardens North; also that day I baptised Lynn Sarah Griffiths, Willowdale Road, in her home (with the elder Owen Evans representing the church) and my own son, Hefin Ednyfed Rees on November 2. Of all the baptisms held at the chapel no child cried more than Hefin that morning!

Two of our great friends, Jean and Emrys Edwards, travelled all the way from Abercynon to act as godparents. If we searched the whole length of the world we could never find more genuine believers that Jean and Emrys. It was not a custom in Heathfield Road chapel to have godparents, but the practice grew so by 2008 it has become acceptable and even the service prescribed for the Presbyterian Church of Wales in the *Book of Services* (1991) includes a role for godparents. It is still optional, the rubric in the service states:

> If there are godparents present the minister says to them: 'Do you, as the godparents of this child, confess your faith in God, Father, Son and Holy Spirit, and promise to help these parents to keep the vows they have made to provide for him a Christian upbringing.'

In the beginning of 1970 the BBC came from Cardiff to make television programmes in our chapel and we had to arrange for the large Big Ben Company to build a large stage for the cameras. On January 26 three large vans parked in Auckland Road and two smaller ones in our chapel car park for two TV programmes, one on the history and activities of the Liverpool Welsh and the other Songs of Praise on Monday and Tuesday, 26 and 27 January with the Liverpool Welsh Choral Union. We had a close connection with the Choral Union, for the Chairman of the Executive was Alderman D. J. Lewis, and one of the Vice Presidents was the orthopaedic surgeon, Goronwy E. Thomas, as well as a strong contingent of singers.

A misunderstanding arose as the Liverpool Welsh Choral Union decided to present the whole programme without a congregation. This was made quite clear by Dafydd ap Dafydd Jones, Farady Street, Everton, the Secretary of the Liverpool Welsh Choral Union Executive Committee. In a letter to G. R. Jones, dated 16 January Dafydd ap Dafydd Jones stated emphatically that the only congregation would be the choristers and your reverend minister, who was to announce the Blessing at the conclusion of the broadcast.

The producer was the Reverend Tregelles Williams. It was a privilege to work with him and his visit was a memorable one. This was the beginning of a happy partnership with television producers which has lasted until the present day, and all of it has been a great value to our community and to viewers alike.

I was unable to preside at the Elders' Meeting on June 8 and 13 July 1980 because of distressful pain in my middle ear and were it not for the care of our family doctor, Dr. Yates of Green Lane, an Anglo-Welshman from the Wrexham area, I would have been in serious trouble and my hearing would have been affected. These were the only two Elders' Meeting I missed until my heart operation in the summer of 1999.

In June of that year, a chapter closed in the ministry of the Foreign Mission in Liverpool with the amalgamation of the Forward Movement and the Foreign Mission offices and its centralisation in Cardiff. The work in North-East India had changed when the missionaries had to return home, and two of them came to live near us, Dr R. Arthur Hughes and Mrs Nancy Hughes. The Reverend John Meirion Lloyd and Mrs Joan Lloyd had settled in Liverpool since 1964, and he was appointed as the travelling secretary of the Bible Society for Merseyside and the Isle of Man. He became a member of our chapel and he was very able and supportive till he moved to Prestatyn in 1975.

Dr R. Arthur Hughes and Mrs Nancy Hughes moved to Liverpool in May 1969, and there was a distinct possibility that they would become members of the English speaking Presbyterian church in Mather Avenue. I remember calling on them to discuss this, stating that their contribution would be invaluable to us as a community. I am so glad I took that approach, because they soon won the affection of the community. In 1971 Dr Arthur Hughes was elected an elder together with Vincent Roberts and the Reverend Dafydd Hughes Parry. At that time Dr R. A. Hughes was Adminstrative Sub-Dean of the Faculty of Medicine of the University of Liverpool. He was in this position from 1969 till 1976 but he never missed a devotional meeting on Monday night and took a leading role in the monthly missionary prayer meeting, which was held regularly on the first Monday of every month.

We decided to recognise the service of the Reverend and Mrs H. Jones Griffiths who were retiring to Conwy, and the Reverend Alun Williams had accepted a call to the pastorate of Lixwm in the Flintshire Presbytery. All three were given gifts in accordance with the generous tradition of the chapel and Mrs Griffiths's contribution at the organ had also been a blessing to our services. She was replaced by Gwyneth and Glyn Rowlands, Roby and we were very glad of their commitment for a number of years.

The Reverend Tregelles Williams sought my assistance in October 1970 to arrange another visit by the BBC to record the popular Welsh language version of Songs of

Dr R. Arthur Hughes as moderator of the Presbyterian Church of Wales

Mrs Meinwen Rees being presented to the Queen.

Praise, known as *Dechrau Canu Dechrau Canmol,* for the chapel members. I organised immediately a notice to the Welsh language community paper, *Y Bont*, and with the elders' backing gave permission to use our large schoolroom as a studio to record a programme on the activities of the Liverpool Welsh in the world of religion and society, yesterday and today. The BBC brought all the equipment on 30 and 31 December, and recorded *Dechrau Canu* on the first night and the documentary on the second. We had wonderful programmes and the producer as well as L. A. Stephens, the chief engineer, were very pleased. The singing was of a very high standard, with Gwynfryn Evans as precentor, and Megan Davies as organist, at their best. We were indebted to them.

It was sad to see Griffith R. Jones and his wife Mrs Jennie Jones leaving Liverpool and becoming members of Mynydd Seion Presbyterian Church of Wales in Abergele. Both had given their best to the community over the years. He was succeeded as Secretary of the Elders' Meeting by Ifor Griffiths, and I prepared an entry on his contribution. G. R. Jones also received a gift from us, as Minister and Elders.

The question of arranging joint services for August for the Welsh churches of the district was discussed early in 1971. There were four Presbyterian chapels involved, namely Garston, Princes Road Chapel, known as Eglwys y Drindod, in Toxteth, Edge Lane Chapel and our congregation in Heathfield Road. We felt at an Elders' Meeting that our role as the largest chapel numerically was to listen to the proposals and then express our standpoint after a sensible, constructive discussion. A special meeting was held on 4 April and Eglwys y Drindod in Toxteth, informed us that they did not want to unite in any plan, as they had already booked guest preachers to come to Princes Road for the morning and evening services. As a compromise, the other three churches decided to have a morning service in the Chapel Road in Garston, afternoon in the Edge Lane Chapel and in the evening at Heathfield Road with the same minister or preacher in charge of the services.

More responsibilities came my way in 1971: a period as Moderator of the Presbytery, and a year as Moderator of the Merseyside Free Church Council. The induction took place at our chapel on Monday, 14 June, and this year gave me a wonderful opportunity to meet and acquaint myself with the political, religious and civic leaders of the city of Liverpool. My wife and I were presented to the Queen when she came to open the new Wallasey/Liverpool tunnel, and had dinner with other dignitaries. The Moderator of the Merseyside Free Church Council in those days was on the same level in the arrangements of the Lord Mayor's office as the Anglican Bishop and the Catholic Archbishop for Liverpool. The Secretary of the Merseyside Free Church Council was a Welshman, the Reverend J. D. Williams Richards, who was a pastor with the Welsh Independents, and we became firm friends. After the death of his wife, Mrs Williams Richards, I used to call weekly to see him in Childwall, as he was then failing physically and largely forgotten by those who had known of his distinguished service to the city. By then the Merseyside Free Church Council was a sad reflection of the body which in the 1970s had a centre and bookshop in Tarleton Street in the heart of the city. In addition to religious books it sold books in the Welsh language and it was one of the bookshops I visited regularly. If a hundred ministers had given it the support that I did, it would still be open. We participated in the Liverpool Show in July in Wavertree Park and we had enough volunteers to have our own tent as an evangelistic enterprise.

I also arranged a coach for members and friends of Mrs Mary Jones, 18 Edale Road, Allerton to attend the north Wales Free Church Annual Gathering at Dolgellau so that she could receive the highest accolade given for faithfulness to the Sunday School, the Gee Medal. The cost for the journey from Liverpool to Dolgellau was £1. In view of the fact that we would need two meals we felt that the church should give the minister the sum of £5 to subsidise the bus. We did it without losing money.

On 6 September 1971 we discussed carefully the religious situation in south Liverpool for the Welsh Presbyterian chapels. Although we knew the answer as Minister and Elders, we also felt that we had to tread carefully lest we upset leaders of other chapels. This was the beginning of a long process which came to fruition years later after many long hours of deliberation.

The Praise of God was high on our agenda. We invited two more competent men to serve as organists, namely Ifan Jones, Broadgreen, and David Williams of Woolton. It was a decision that brought joy to us. Ifan Jones was a native of Pwllheli, who had married Enid Hughes Jones, mother of Richard and Helen, and the family had come to us from the Welsh

Methodist Chapel of Oakfield in Anfield. It was a very musical family and Ifan Jones made his mark quietly and was always ready to assist. David Williams was a younger man, a product of Bethany Welsh Chapel in Ammanford, while his wife Greta was from Gwauncaegurwen, and she took part regularly in our prayer meetings, along with many other young people. David Williams, who is now organist in the Welsh Independent Chapel at Sketty, Swansea, told me on the National Eisteddfod of Wales campus at Felindre in 2006 that he had never seen a *Sêt Fawr* with such remarkable occupants as the one he remembers in our chapel in the early seventies. The standard was exceptionally high and his comment deserves to be noted. But the eventual union of Edge Lane, Eglwys y Drindod and Heathfield Road in 1976 brought together more leaders to support the minister in his task.

Another decision that I took in 1971 was to start a Christmas Fayre as one of the activities for all sections of the chapel community. We did well. It was a great success. I felt that we had worked well together and that 1971 had been a year of great promise for our future. The Christmas Fayre became an attractive event for nearly thirty years and we never had one failure. We raised thousands of pounds to relieve the Church's finances and it was a motivation for the Women's Fellowship. Every section of our church did their best to make a clear profit. The bonus was the large number of people who attended who had no connection whatsoever with our community. Many of them used to attend every Christmas Fayre in the locality, but their praise for our goods was encouraging.

We had a very special service on 5 March 1973 – a civic service in the company of the Lord Mayor of Liverpool, Alderman Charles Cowlin, JP, a politician who tried his level best to get me to join the Freemasons, a movement which attracted a large number of our men folk. I was helped in the civic service by three Welsh ministers of religion, J. D. Williams Richards, of the Welsh Independents, Dafydd Hughes Parry and John Meirion Lloyd. The singing was in the capable hands of our precentor, Gwynfryn Evans and our organist for that unique occasion was Megan Davies.

There was a great deal of change in the officers at the beginning of 1972 when Mr and Mrs Goronwy Davies moved to Abergele, and this to me was a huge loss, for Goronwy Davies was a very spiritual person and his public prayers were a means of grace. He brought us near to God and he could be placed in the same company as the luminaries such as Teresa of Avila or Philip Yancey in our generation. He was our lay teacher in spirituality. Glyn Davies was asked to be the Pulpit Secretary, an onerous job at the best of times. He began his task on 1 April 1972.

Another matter which was on our agenda in 1972 was the essential task of decorating the chapel. This was well discussed in the Finance Committee, the Sub-committee of the Organ and in the Elders Meeting. We were not in a position to face such costs ourselves and it meant having a loan from the local Liverpool Presbytery. We needed to spend, from the estimate, the sum of £5,000, which was a huge sum in 1972. We made an application in June for a loan of £4,000 from our Presbytery. Since I had arrived in Liverpool, we had spent £4,500 on the buildings, all necessary work. The task was:

1.   to protect the entrance, the stone stairs from the highway in Smithdown Place to the front door;
2.   to clean the organ as it needed to be overhauled;
3.   to replace the electricity according to need;
4.   to decorate the whole building, the chapel and the schoolroom.

The Appeal Fund was opened and literally within days we received the sum of £93.90 in memory of Mrs Henry Clarke, 42 Childwall Park Avenue. She was a gregarious person, her husband a businessman, and she delighted in playing golf at the Woolton Golf Club. She came to our house early one morning to invite me to join. Naturally I expressed an interest but when I heard the cost of the membership fee, I had to decline. It was beyond my means.

The buildings at Heathfield Road were in constant use by every society and group within our community and in particular *Cylch yr Ifanc* (The Young People's Circle), which was established through the dedication of Dr Idris Owen, Alun Roberts (an elder in Garston), Roderick Owen and a number of other volunteers. We were able to make Friday night an attraction for the children and young people. The Children's gathering was from 6.30 to 7.30 and the Young People's Circle followed till 9 o'clock, a pattern that was followed for years to come.

We also loaned our rooms and schoolrooms to other movements, such as Pastor William Angel and the Christian Evangelical Society among Jews, as well as the Mossley Hill Group of Churches. Thirty five years ago (in May 1972), we also became involved in collecting money in the streets around Allerton Road, for Christian Aid, under the auspices of the Mossley Hill Group of Churches. This meant having a Liaison Officer in our midst and we are grateful to those who acted in this capacity, particularly Judge John Edward Jones, H. Wyn Jones, Dr Ann ap Thomas, the Reverend Eleri Edwards and at present Miss Carys Jones, Wavertree. The amount collected in 2007 was £796.

On Thursday night 28 September we had a special service to re-open and consecrate the chapel on completion of the refurbishing by the firm of W. H. Snow. We expressed our gratitude to the Building Committee in general and in particular to Glyn Rowlands, who oversaw the whole project; he was such a perfectionist. This initiative taken 35 years ago has stood the test of time, but now the buildings are in need of repair. On the invitation of the Mission Board the BBC came to record a special radio service in the company of two well-known Welsh missionaries, Miss Marian Pritchard and Dr R. Arthur Hughes, and this took place on Sunday, 8 October. The Reverend M. R. Mainwaring wrote to thank us on 24 October, stating that he had heard high praise for the service.

In December it was disappointing to receive the resignation of Gwynfryn Evans, Allerton, as a precentor after 5 years' service. He was excellent in his work but I appreciated his decision. The world had changed and to do the job properly and to be fair to his family meant having a team rather than one person at the helm. He did valuable work in those years as conductor of our local chapel concert group called *Parti Maesgrug,* which entertained Welsh communities all over Lancashire and especially Merseyside. Occasionally they would visit mid and north Wales and the practice, as well as the concerts, created a harmonious group. We, as officers, gave them our wholehearted support. On November 6 I asked the Elders' Committee for permission to lead a group of pilgrims to the Holy Land from 11 June to 23 June 1973 and they agreed that it was part of my ministry. By this time, I have led 19 pilgrimages to Israel and hundreds of Christians have been blessed, as we visited the sacred sites in Jerusalem and Galilee. A large number of Welsh people from our own chapel as well as other chapels on Merseyside, in particular Stanley Road Welsh Chapel, Bootle, joined our pilgrimages. They came to the Holy Land as well as to Jordan, Egypt, Italy, Germany (Oberammergau on three occasions), Brittany, Greece, Turkey, most of the countries of Europe such as Hungary, Czechoslovakia, Austria, Estonia, Latvia, Lithuania, Finland, France, seven times to the Welsh settlements in the USA, three visits to Canada, Malaysia, China and Hong Kong, USSR. Many of them were single people or widows and a large number who had never been abroad before and felt safe on our pilgrimages. We had an example of this in 1973 when Mrs Dorah Williams decided to come to the Land of Jesus. She had recently lost her husband, Bob Williams, and wanted to face the future as independently as she could. Mrs D. Williams enjoyed the experience so much that she came on a number of the subsequent pilgrimages. She was one of many who availed themselves of this opportunity to travel. I always succeeded in having a big enough group; however, it entailed organisational skills and advertising, and the majority who came were members of chapels and churches in England and Wales. A large number became bosom friends to us as a family and from 1973 to 2001 these pilgrimages have been a most important factor in the social life of many a community. Indeed a first class book emerged from one of these pilgrimages, written by Eluned Jones from the village of Pwll on the outskirts of Llanelli, under the title *Y Daith* (The Journey) published by Gomer Press in 1993. This is a translation of what is said in Welsh on the blurb:

> In 1989, a fortnight or so before Easter, my sister and I had the unusual opportunity of joining a group led by the Reverend Dr D. Ben Rees, Liverpool, who was visiting Israel. I took advantage of the opportunity, and I must admit that this journey has been an unforgettable experience.

Another of the pilgrims who has lectured extensively on our journeys has been Mrs Brenda James, Elder in Bethany Chapel, Ammanford, while on Merseyside, E. Goronwy Owen, who with his late wife Mrs Marian Owen joined several of these expeditions, has always been ready to share his experiences of these travels and communicate in style the joy we experienced. We cannot forget these experiences which came to us from our pilgrimages to different parts of the world, but this is not the place to do justice to such a varied programme, considering that at least two thirds of the pilgrims from the very beginning came from outside our community as a chapel. But the first choice was always given to our chapel community through our newsletter; it was never announced in a service. Then I would insert an advertisement in the denomination's newspaper, *Y Goleuad*, and circulate friends and acquaintances.

Congratulations were extended to me in 1973 on gaining the degree M.Sc. (Econ) of the University of Wales. I began the research during my period in the Cynon Valley and I did the work under the supervision of Dr George Thomason of the University of Cardiff. The fruit of this research was published in 1975 by the Ffynnon Press in the volume *Chapels in the Valley: A Sociological Study of Welsh Nonconformity.* It received encouraging reviews by sociologists of religion. I would like now, thirty years later, to update the research as the situation in the Cynon Valley has changed dramatically. Time will tell.

A difficult matter arose in spring 1973 when we received a request by the Secretary of the Welsh League of Youth of the branch known as *Aelwyd Llynlleifiad* for the hire of the large schoolroom on 21 March for a visit by the Welsh folk hero Dafydd Iwan. This society, which had been established by a number of young Welsh teachers and students, could not cooperate with the other Urdd branch known as *Aelwyd Lerpwl*. The situation demanded wisdom and we discussed the delicate situation carefully. The conflict between these enthusiastic Welsh people was very upsetting to me as a Minister, as I was on good terms with both groups. In actual fact on Sunday night we had dozens of them in the service and attending the Discussion Group in the small schoolroom. Sometimes the discussion lasted two hours, especially when we had a speaker from Wales to address us. I remember well the psychiatrist, Dr Dafydd Alun Jones flying in his helicopter from Anglesey to Speke to speak to us on a Sunday night. He suggested to the elders that I should have flying lessons as Speke Airport was only three miles down the road!

It was also difficult to decide on the information received from the two branches of the Welsh League of Youth to be announced in our Sunday School and the two services. We decided on a policy and communicated our decision to both branches – *Aelwyd Lerpwl* and *Aelwyd Llynlleifiad* - as both had been accepted by the Welsh League of Youth. 'With regard to the announcements, one has to remember that the chief work of the presiding elder is to announce to the congregation the meetings connected with the Church and the Presbytery. We give the opportunity to disseminate information regarding meetings connected with other churches and societies when they do not clash with the local church's activities and if they have a general appeal to our members, and if time allows, according to the guidance of the officers'. This excellent guideline, prepared by Ifor Griffiths still stands. We do not announce a meeting of another society, if it has been arranged on the same night as the church meeting.

We had a great deal of discussion in the summer of 1975 on the poor workmanship on the entrance to the chapel, and as we had a number of individuals who had been involved in the building industry, it was a valuable asset. Because of illness Howell Vaughan Jones resigned as Treasurer of the church. I was asked to seek a new Treasurer, and I thought of E. Iorwerth Roberts, Welbeck Avenue as one possibility. He was an able person and his wife a devout member. But after a great deal of discussion I failed to persuade him, as they had decided to move to the Machynlleth area. I used to call on Mrs Nan Roberts, especially after she lost Iorwerth, on my journeys to Ceredigion when she lived at Derwenlas and in Machynlleth as well as in Aberystwyth itself, and both my wife and I would receive a warm welcome. The other name I had in mind was F. H. Williams, Bower Road, Woolton, who had been a Director with Morris and Jones, the wholesale grocer firm, and to my relief he accepted the responsibility.

One of the first decisions F. H. Williams took through the Finance Committee, was to purchase three hundred blue chairs for the schoolrooms, but dissatisfaction was immediately expressed by a few of the elders that this was done with insufficient consultation on the financial position of the chapel and also without getting more than one estimate of the cost

Delyth Morris, a member at Bethel, though she lives at Skelmersdale.

involved. The old chairs which were redundant were given to the Richmond English Baptist Chapel in Anfield. Over a hundred of the old chairs were taken away and the Sunday School contributed £10 towards the cost. These chairs have been very useful to us for the last 30 years as they are so easy to handle. We received £15 from Richmond Chapel. A gift was also received from Mrs Anwyl Williams, the mother of Mrs Joyce Lewington and Mrs Delyth Morris, which was used to purchase a microphone and other assets within the chapel.

A Songs of Praise programme for Radio Cymru was organised for 3 June 1974 and the chapel received £21 from the BBC. The producer was James Williams, an able musician who became a friend, and during his time at Bangor the BBC came regularly to our community. 1974 was an extremely busy year as I stood as a Parliamentary Candidate for the Labour Party in the Conwy Constituency in the February and October General Elections. This meant immense physical, mental and spiritual strain and a nucleus of men from the chapel came to assist me in the campaigning. I received immense support though at least two of the elders within the Presbytery, not in our church, behaved quite childishly towards me. But I survived, as I always do, in faith.

In addition to this the General Assembly met in 1974 and the most onerous job fell on my shoulders as Secretary, but R. Glyn Williams was at hand as Secretary of the Hospitality Committe to offer advice, as he had experience of welcoming the General Assembly of the Presbyterian Church of Wales in 1962. I asked Glyn Peters, Avondale Road, to be in charge of the stewards with regard to the meals, the services and the sessions. We had our mid-day meal at Dovedale Towers and I made these arrangements with Glyn Peters. The head of the catering firm, Tom Butler, became a personal friend, and his early death was a great loss to the Welsh community.

It was not an easy task to organise the General Assembly, to arrange with the police with regard to parking (the record in the minutes, says 'the Minister to consult the Chief Constable'), to borrow hymnbooks from other chapels, communion trays and cups from the Communion Service, move the piano from the large Schoolroom to the chapel, arrange the organists, invite the religious and civic leaders to the Welcome Tea and a host of other small matters. Everything was done for the sake of everyone. I was determined to do this as the Moderator was my kind neighbour, the Reverend W. D. Jones of Edge Lane and Garston Chapels. I still remember at the end of the Assembly seeing him and another neighbour, the Reverend J. D. Williams Richards, sitting at the entrance of the large school room, utterly exhausted and W. D. Jones saying to me: 'This man has years of service to this city while I, J. D., have come to the end of my tether.' It was a true prophecy, and by the end of September we were concerned about the illness of the Reverend W. D. Jones. The Reverend Gwilym Evans of Brecon, the Secretary of the General Assembly, sent a detailed letter of thanks dated 25 July 1974 on the contribution of the minister, elders and members of Heathfield Road Chapel. The following remark sums up the general feeling of satisfaction with the event:

> We had a happy and efficient Assembly, and all the arrangements were wonderful to say the least – and this made our work as officers of the Assembly much easier.

At least 250 delegates came to the 1974 Assembly, and most of them were accommodated in the University Halls of Residence at the bottom of Penny Lane, just a mile from the chapel. I made all the arrangements with the University authorities. I was very fortunate in the contribution of the ladies, under the guidance of Miss Doris Thomas, Allerton Road, for the meals in the large schoolroom, and for the cooperation of the English Methodist Chapel of Elm Hall Drive who lent us a large number of tables. I made an appeal to move the tables to our site and we had plenty of volunteers.

At the beginning of October we had a weekend in our buildings under the auspices of the Union of Christian Students in the University of Liverpool. This came through my involvement within the University of Liverpool, and the students gave £10 towards the church funds. I informed the elders on 4 November 1974 that I had no intention of standing again as a Parliamentary candidate for the Conwy constituency; I was the only Welsh Presbyterian minister in full time ministry who stood as a Parliamentary candidate in the last 40 years. I handed to the Treasurer a cheque for £40 to acknowledge the caring way they behaved towards me during the two General Election campaigns. They decided unanimously as elders that the cheque should be returned and they minuted their gratitude for the deed and my service to the community. On 14 November we had a very frank discussion about the situation in the South Liverpool District after the retirement of the Reverend W. D. Jones, and it was decided that we should have a meeting of all the elders of the four chapels on 28 November. Another minister within the Presbytery who left in 1974 was the Reverend G. Tudor Owen, and I have already discussed his contribution in the volume *Alpha and Omega* published in 2006. In a letter from Birmingham, dated 6 November, he expressed his gratitude for our good wishes, saying: 'While I was on Merseyside, I came to think highly of Heathfield Road. Blessing be on you and your minister.' Ifor Griffiths mentioned in his letter the strength of the ministry of G. Tudor Owen, which is to proclaim the Gospel in a tasteful manner. He prepared well for the pulpit.

On the first Sunday in 1975 we had a terrible loss in the sudden passing of Mr R. Glyn Williams, the Finance Secretary of the Chapel, which occurred on his way home from chapel to Garthdale Road after the evening service. He fell on the corner of Allerton Road and Garthdale Road, and one of the stewards of the nearby cinema saw it happen. The police were called, and because the money of Bethel Chapel was in his overcoat they came to our house to ask me to go to inform his wife of his death. It was a most difficult experience, as Mrs Hannah Williams just could not envisage what had happened. I decided to take her to Sefton General Hospital and we were taken to the mortuary. Even then it was impossible for her to realise that the call to the eternal world had come to her husband. It was so difficult for me to leave her that night, but after phoning her niece in Llanbedrgoch, I knew that she would feel a little better the following day. I left her at eleven o'clock, her world changed in a moment, as well as our world as a church, as he was such a dependable, hardworking supporter of his minister. I was like the son he never had. I would go with him regularly on a Saturday afternoon to see Liverpool play football and the following Saturday with Howell Vaughan Jones, his brother W. Glyn Jones and Emyr Jones, Childwall, to watch Everton at Goodison Park. I had lost a good friend, one who had been a friend from the moment I met him at Edge Lane Bus Station on a terrible foggy night.

The matter that took our time and talent in those days was the task of uniting the four Welsh chapels in south Liverpool. On 16 January 1975 we agreed on a number of points that were to be placed before the District Meeting on 29 January. These included:

(a)   the additional responsibilities to be placed on the shoulders of the Minister;

(b)   that arrangements were to be made to sell the buildings of the chapel in Princes Road, Edge Lane and Garston;

(c)   that any money received through the sale be transferred to the fund of the new chapel;

(d)   that we should inform members of the four chapels of our intention for the future and give them the opportunity of expressing their opinions.

The sub-committee of the United Church Committee met under my chairmanship on December with six of us present. The others were Glyn Davies, E. Goronwy Owen from Garston Chapel, Ellis J. Morris, Eglwys y Drindod, E. Emlyn Griffiths (Edge Lane) and F. H. Williams as an observer. The sub-committee was ready to accept that any one of the four chapels could retain its identity and be part of the United Church. Another significant point was added, namely that the officers of the four chapels were to become officers and elders of the new chapel.

In our meeting on 3 February the Reverend D. Hughes Parry and I were of the opinion that we, as officers of Heathfield Road, were acting in the name of our elders whereas a number of elders from the other three churches were expressing their viewpoint as individuals. This meant that there was a great deal of differences amongst us. After a long discussion we passed this resolution: 'We as officers agree with the ideal of one church in principle but we feel that we would like chapels to give fuller consideration to all the obligations involved in this important step.'

The Secretary of the District Committee was the Reverend Dafydd Hughes Parry, one whose roots were deep in the heritage of Heathfield Road, as his mother and father had been members, when, as young people they had lived in the city. He worked conscientiously on behalf of the unity as did others of us, and we had many meetings, one on 4 March, another on 11 March 1975. It was obvious to me that by the end of March that Garston Chapel wanted to stay as a branch, and that is why I insisted on 7 April that the District Secretary should consult with the officers of Garston so that we could have more information about their reasoning. We voted on Sunday night, 19 April, to move forward to unite but the officers of Garston decided:

(a)   to remain as a branch and that membership of the branch be included in the new church;

(b).   that the officers of the branch be included as officers of the new church;

(c)   that the assets and the investments be included in the new church;

(d)   that the tenancy of the chapel caretaker be preserved.

We had a number of meetings in April through to June, and although the majority were in favour of forming a new church there was still a great deal of work to prepare the ground in all the chapels involved. As I was ministering in Edge Lane and in Eglwys y Drindod in that period, I took the opportunity of placing before the two congregations our hopes and aspirations. The vote took place on Sunday 8 June, and the whole procedure was under the chairmanship of the Reverend R. Maurice Williams on behalf of the Presbytery. In his letter dated 13 June we have the details that have never been disclosed till now. These are the details:

Edge Lane Chapel	In favour – 18
	Against – 4
Eglwys y Drindod, Princes Road	In favour – 19
	Against – 10
Garston Chapel	In favour – 9
	Against – 23
Heathfield Road	In favour – 51
	Against – 15

One can make two observations. Firstly, there was an obvious opposition to the idea of uniting the four chapels into one new community of believers. Out of 149 votes, there were 52 against, that is 65% in favour and 35% against. Even in the church which was going to be the host there were fifteen members ready to vote against the union. It would be good to know what troubled these members. Secondly, the vote in itself, like all voting in Britain, in local government elections, referenda of all kinds as well as General Elections was too small. Many more members should have turned out to express their opinion, and this is true, in every kind of election in which I have been involved.

We had a special meeting of the elders on Monday 16 June to decide how to proceed before the matter was discussed in the Liverpool South District Meeting on 24 June. Though disappointed that Garston Chapel had rejected the scheme, we felt that we had ample grounds for moving ahead to unite the three chapels of Edge Lane, Eglwys y Drindod and Heathfield Road, and suggested that this should happen in 1976, subject to the decision of the Presbytery regarding an adequate majority in favour. That is what happened. The Liverpool Presbytery decided that the Minister could serve the new church in 1976 up to 30 Sundays a year, a completely new scheme for Merseyside, but it helped the new church.

We had a long discussion about the name for the new church and in the end we decided on Bethel, a name which has been well received. A new agreement was made with the caretaker of the chapel, R. E. Jones and Elan Jones, and a session was held with them on 17 November.

The last meeting of the officers and elders of Heathfield Road Chapel was held on 1 December 1975, and I expressed my gratitude for the contribution and cooperation of Judge J. E. Jones, Glyn Davies, Owen Evans, Gwilym John Roberts, Howell Vaughan Jones, F. H. Williams, the Reverend D. Hughes Parry and Ifor Griffiths. I made a special note of the work of Ifor Griffiths as General Secretary of the church for 19 years and as Secretary of the Elders' Meeting for five years. He was the Secretary of the Pastoral Committee 1967-68, and his correspondence was always well expressed. Though born and nurtured in Liverpool, he read journals in Welsh and had been well versed in the Welsh Bible, Welsh books and literature. Consequently, he had a vibrant style when he wrote in the Welsh language.

The new year opened its door and we had a unique service on 4 January 1976 under the guidance of the Reverend Griffith Owen, Old Colwyn, and Moderator of the North Wales

Association of the Presbyterian Church of Wales. Nevertheless the months of November and December meant a great deal of work for me, as every member of Edge Lane and Eglwys y Drindod, Princes Road expected me to visit them. It was obvious that four members of Eglwys y Drindod, two of them elders, were not willing to become part of the congregation of Bethel. I persuaded them to join Garston Chapel, and that is what happened. But it was obvious that the visitation helped in keeping everyone on the books for the new church. I felt relieved with the situation, when we had the first service in 1976, but it had taken nearly 12 months and had demanded all the diplomatic skills available to ensure a smooth transfer of resources to the new structure. We had a tremendous amount of energy and enthusiasm as a community, and the couplet by the Reverend H. Elvet Lewis, known as Elfed, expresses my thoughts at that time:

> *Na foed cydweithwyr Duw,*
> *Byth yn eu gwaith yn drist.*
> (May the co-workers of God
> Never be sad in their work.)

We were joyful and optimistic in those days.

Ministers and elders. Back row (left to right), Gwilym J. Roberts, Reverend Dafydd Hughes Parry, T. R. Williams, Vincent Roberts, John Medwyn Jones, R. Ifor Griffith, Glyn Davies, R. Arthur Hughes, F. H. Williams. Front row (left to right), Howell V. Jones, Leah Clement-Evans, Owen Evans, Pierce Roberts, Reverend D. Ben Rees, His Honour J. E. Jones, Miss N. C. Hughes, Mr E. Emlyn Griffith and Miss Mary B. Owen.

At Llanddewi Brefi during a summer vacation. From (left to right) Hefin, Meinwen Rees, Anne Jane Rees, Dafydd and D. B. Rees in the early 80's.

A pilgrimage to the Welsh settlements of the United States of America in 1987.

A group of pilgrims led by Dr D. Ben Rees.

At Liverpool with Selwyns of Runcorn: (left to right) Gwen Owen, Elin Boyd, Eirian Roberts, Enid H. Jones, D. B. Rees, Meinwen Rees and R. Elwyn Wyn Jones, Bootle.

The tour leader in Utica at the site of the home of the anti-slavery reformer, Reverend Robert Everett.

Chapter 12

CO-OPERATION IN BETHEL CHURCH (1976-1985)

In 1976 Bethel's membership was 456 members with 67 children and there was a new spirit amongst us. We had received a number of members from Garston Chapel, who were in favour of unity, and every member of Edge Lane Chapel, as well as everyone from Eglwys y Drindod. The catchment area of Bethel had been enlarged and parts of Liverpool, previously unknown to me, became part of our territory. This was very true for those members from Edge Lane, the majority of whom were living in Fairfield and Kensington. I became well acquainted with the Welsh streets built mostly by R.E. Jones: Adelaide Road, Albert Edward Road, Romer Road; and in Fairfield such streets as Whitefield Road and Elm Vale, to name only two.

I was determined to invite speakers to our community who had a clear and important message. One was the Reverend Jim Pollard, Mossley Hill, an evangelical Baptist in background, whose work also combined two roles: his position as Secretary of the Leprosy Society in our region and his work as a producer of Radio BBC Merseyside programme, *Songs of Praise*. He came to our community wearing both these particular hats,.

Hazel Williams, Eirian Wyn Jones and Bethan Jones at the Welsh Sports Day.

The young ones from Bethel, back row, Dylan Williams, Roy Williams, Dafydd Rees, Alun Jones, Ian Vaughan Jones, David Evans, Gareth Roberts, Sonia Jones, Dr D. Ben Rees. Front row, Iwan Williams, Gwenan Owen, Mair Hughes-Parry, Delyth Rogers, Eirian Hughes Parry, Ceri Rogers and Helen Hughes Jones.

I have been an admirer of The Gideons, the Society that gives copies of the New Testament and the Bible to hotels, hospitals and schools and we, as a chapel, supported the south Liverpool branch of this important Society. In addition, Edward Watkins, a Welshman from south Wales who was a member of Calvary Chapel, Dovecot, came regularly with his team of evangelists to Bethel. We remember them every Christmas. We gave donations to those charities and to movements that came to us, especially those in Wales. We were part of both worlds, Liverpool and Wales.

On my pastoral visits I would come across a great number of people who were neighbours and friends of our members. Frequently, back in 1976, there was one Welshman who was often referred to, namely George Thomas. On 3 February 1976 George Thomas, from Tonypandy in the Rhondda, took the place of Selwyn Lloyd (another descendent of the Liverpool Welsh) as Speaker of the House of Commons. Within three months the voice of George Thomas and his strong Welsh accent was well known throughout Britain. I could inform these people that I knew Mr Thomas and his background in the Rhondda Valley. But I will not forget the admiration, in those days, of English people, as well as a large number of

Eisteddfodic competitors including Hefin Rees, Gwenan and Owain Ellis Roberts.

Welsh people, for George Thomas, even though he was very critical of the Welsh Nationalists and the very active Language Society, *Cymdeithas yr Iaith Gymraeg*.

As a church we remained wedded to missionary endeavours, in particular our overseas witness. We received a visit in 1976 from Miss N. Moxey, one of several unusual women in our city. She lived in Clubmoor and walked on Sunday mornings all the way to Waterloo Welsh Chapel in Crosby Road South. There was holiness in her steps. The Missionary Association for north Wales visited us at Bethel in 1976 and we had services in Elm Hall Drive Methodist Chapel across the road, as well as in St Barnabas, the Anglican Church. The large Bethel Chapel was packed with Presbyterian women from all parts of north and mid Wales. We were delighted to welcome so many Welsh folk; and this has been so true of our community over the decades.

Another important development in 1976 was the establishment of the Merseyside Chair Eisteddfod, a partnership between us and the Welsh students of the University of Liverpool. The young man chiefly involved was Hywel Morris, a native of Uwchaled and a medical student at the University. I well remember him coming to see me to discuss the project and I decided to give him every support. The students were a very enthusiastic group and we in Bethel, in particular, had a number of enthusiastic *eisteddfodwyr* who joined the Executive Committee for this eisteddfod. These included Hugh John Jones, Centreville Road, who was a great asset as he had so much information on the competitions at eisteddfodau back in Wales and he was also willing to design and actually make the bardic chair. Competitors from all over Wales were attracted in the early period between 1976 and 1981; but after the Toxteth Riots the competitors from Wales began to dwindle. The standard was high and the Eisteddfod inspired us as a church to prepare groups to sing, recite and compete. Indeed, our recitation group competed at the National Eisteddfod in Caernarfon in 1979. I cannot overemphasise the importance of the Eisteddfod in Liverpool, to our cultural life as a community in Bethel, and I have continued to serve as Chairman of the Executive Committee ever since. The charity still exists but, in the 1990s, it became an Eisteddfod mainly for Bethel and a platform for Welsh language learners.

During this period, I became fully aware of the importance of a Welsh language class for adults. In 1977 an effort was made to establish one at our chapel on a Friday night, under my tuition. I remained as a tutor for twenty three years, two hours every Friday and hundreds of Liverpool Welsh and English people registered during those years. Many of them had been brought up in our Welsh chapels, others had caravans or second homes in Wales or visited Wales regularly or intended to retire there in a few years time. This was a grand group – enthusiastic and supportive, willing to buy Welsh books and magazines and attend our St David's Day celebrations. I insisted that we should, on those occasions, invite well-known celebrities within Wales as guest speakers. In 1970 the novelist Dr Kate Roberts came to speak to us; in 1971 the playwright, Dr John Gwilym Jones, Y Groeslon; Professor Melville Richards, who had been Head of the Celtic Department of the University came in 1973 and, in 1974 our guest was Councillor Hywel Heulyn Roberts, Synod Inn, Ceredigion, a product of the Liverpool-Welsh community and one who has been supportive of us for years. He and his late wife have attended the festivals of the Liverpool Welsh community regularly. Then, in 1975, we had Emeritus Professor David R. Seaborne Davies, Pwllheli, who had been Head of the Law Department at the University of Liverpool and an accomplished after dinner speaker. In 1976 our guest was the late Ifor Bowen Griffith, a socialist and broadcaster from Caernarfon, and the following year one of the delightful ministers of the Welsh Independents, the Reverend Idwal Jones, Llanrwst. All our guests set high standards as speakers. Indeed we were greatly blessed as Welsh people.

Another important project that I succeeded in launching in 1979, was our community newspaper, *Yr Angor* (The Anchor), which has been published monthly ever since. The previous newsletter, *Y Bont* had ceased a year earlier when the editor, the Reverend R. Maurice Williams, minister of the Welsh chapels at Waterloo and Southport, retired and moved with his wife to reside in Llanrwst. He had been assisted by the short story writer, Gwilym M. Jones, a hard-working member of our congregation, and T. M. Owens, Aigburth, one of the treasurers of Bethel after the amalgamation. T. M. Owens was a bachelor, careful in his measured utterances and opinions. It was quite obvious that there was very little desire amongst *Y Bont's* editorial team to hand over the newsletter to anyone else. So, under these circumstances we needed a new initiative, if we were to contrive to link up the Welsh communities from Southport to Ellesmere Port, Runcorn to West Kirby. I called a public meeting to discuss the possible options. This proved to be a difficult meeting as many of those who had been involved in producing *Y Bont* adopted a critical and negative stance. Fortunately, many others present were fully supportive of my arguments in favour of a new venture. Consequently, I found myself as editor, a post I have filled for the last twenty-nine years, as well as having served as Chairman of the Executive Committee for a period. T.M. Owens accepted the post of treasurer and we had the support of Mr Rolly Pritchard, Broadgreen, a Baptist, as distribution manager. The Reverend B. Ifor Williams suggested the name *Yr Angor,* for our new venture, a very appropriate title, but within a few months we realised that the *papur bro* serving Aberystwyth and District had already adopted the same title.

We had the co-operation of a number of people who were willing to send a monthly account of local activities; and His Honour J. Edward Jones did this for Bethel. As he had the gift of recording every activity in a concise form, his column proved very worthwhile and so has that of his successor, Miss Mair Powell. *Yr Angor* is a newspaper which has attempted to provide a comprehensive account of our activities between 1979 and 2007; and this achievement has been recorded by His Honour J. Edward Jones, in his book on the chapel, *Antur a Menter Cymry Lerpwl,* published in 1987. *Yr Angor* is a useful link for the Welsh of Merseyside and many of those who live in Wales are amongst our generous supporters. It is a paper of standing and fills a huge gap, especially as the Welsh are so dispersed on Merseyside.

In 1987 there was another development. The Reverend Geraint Roberts, who had lived with his family in Kensington, Liverpool, for many years before accepting a call to Manchester, seized the opportunity of bringing the Welsh communities of the two cities nearer by extending the territory served by *Yr Angor.*

Ben Hughes

This has given an excellent boost to the funding of *Yr Angor.* Another lifeline was a financial grant from the Welsh Language Board. We failed to convince the Welsh Office to help us financially but we succeeded, after visiting the office in Cardiff, to persuade the Welsh Language Board that we deserved some financial help, as the only Welsh language community newspaper surviving outside Wales. There are Welsh papers in London, in Patagonia and in the USA but none of these is solely in the Welsh language. *Ninnau,* published in New Jersey, never has more than a page in Welsh, whereas *Yr Angor* has twelve pages of material in the Welsh language. We are unique and from the very beginning we have sold substantial numbers of *Yr Angor* in our Bethel. Most of our flock look forward to its appearance. We have the occasional member who feels that the forty pence we charge is exorbitant and therefore does not buy it, but these are few and far between. You cannot win them all even when their minister is the editor! We have had loyal members from our chapel serving *Yr Angor,* such as T. M. Owens, who was treasurer for years. Others include Gareth Thomas, the barrister who became Labour MP for West Clwyd; the late Gwynfryn Williams, Gateacre, who with his wife Laura retired to Chwilog, and, at present, Roderick Owen. The only ones from outside Bethel who have served as treasurer are Alun Edwards, Blundellsands, an elder in Bethania Waterloo Welsh Chapel, the Reverend Geraint Roberts, Menai Bridge and Ron Gilford, Cheadle who still serves on the Executive of *Yr Angor.* After my stint as chairman, Alun Roberts, Garston, was appointed and was followed for many years by E. Goronwy Owen. We were fortunate in those who have distributed *Yr Angor* on Merseyside: in particular John Alun Hughes, Romer Road, and William Evans, Anfield, and the committee's secretary, Ben Hughes, Childwall. Sterling service for a quarter of a century has also been given by the Reverend Ieuan A. Jenkins, Waterloo, and Ken Williams, Gateacre. Trefor Roberts, Sefton Park, and Arthur Edwards, Aigburth, took charge of *Yr Angor* within our community and on our Editorial Board we also had H. Wyn Jones, Marian Prys Davies and Mair Jones, living near each other in Childwall. The role of *Yr Angor* has been an important one and, for the last eighteen years, we have had excellent photographs from Dr. John G. Williams, an important contribution completely absent from the two former Welsh papers, *Y Glannau* and *Y Bont*, in the period between 1944 and 1979. The title page and banner of *Yr Angor* was designed by the late E. Edmund Clarke, an elder in Garston, who came to love Bethel. His work still flies on *Yr Angor's* front page every month.

The leadership of Bethel in 1976 was exhilarating, a full *sêt fawr* of elders. From Eglwys y Drindod came Pierce S. Roberts, Gateacre, a retired headmaster and an inspiring magnanimous individual; T. R. Williams, Dingle, brother of the poet W. D. Williams, Barmouth, and the preacher, the Reverend Ithel Williams; John Medwyn Jones, Aigburth, the youngest of the elders from Eglwys y Drindod and a member of a family who had been extremely loyal to the cause; Mrs. Leah Clement Evans, Aigburth, born and bred in Liverpool, her parents having contributed immensely to the care of the Welsh people in the city, and Miss Mary B. Owen, Mossley Hill, a retired school teacher. They were five dependable elders. From Edge Lane Chapel we had E. Emlyn Griffiths, Childwall, one of the architects of the amalgamation of the chapels, a very talented individual who was given the responsibility of Church Secretary. The next was R. Conway Roberts, hard-working in his day but who had suffered a severe seizure which denied him his speech. He died in the first year of Bethel's life. His wife, Jane, was everything to him and I visited him regularly. The third leader from Edge Lane was Miss N. C. Hughes, Newsham Park, and she lived in the same house as her sister and brother-in-law, Mr. and Mrs. G. Rees Williams. In retrospect, we could see that the leadership in Edge Lane had been something of a problem before we came together. But, as we review those early years in the life of Bethel, we noticed how everything changed overnight. In 1977 three of the elders decided to move to Wales, namely Pierce S. Roberts and his wife, Eileen, to Betws-yn-Rhos; E. Emlyn Griffith to Bangor and Gwilym J. Roberts, on being appointed to a teaching post in Anglesey, moved to Llanfairpwllgwyngyll. It is no wonder that we decided to consider having more elders. The only one who accepted the responsibility was Edward Goronwy Owen, an elder in Garston from 1952 to 1972, another architect of the union. He, as well as I, was very disappointed that Garston Chapel had voted so overwhelmingly against the proposed union but he and his family, including his brother-in-law, Arthur Edwards, showed great statesmanship by deciding in 1976 to become members of the new chapel community of Bethel. E. Goronwy Owen was a wonderful gift to Bethel, accepting the office of treasurer when F. H. Williams left for Church Stretton. He still remains in this key position, to the delight of his fellow officers.

In 1978, Howell Vaughan Jones died, as well as Owen Evans, Montclair Drive, one who had been an elder at the chapels of Aberfan and Pont Morlais in the Merthyr Tudful area. In 1979 Mr. R. T. Williams died in Australia while on a family visit to that country. One of the lasting losses in 1979 was the death of former Police Sergeant, William Jones, Meldrum Road. He was steeped in Calvinistic Methodism, well versed in his Bible and very knowledgeable about our denomination. His brother-in-law, the Reverend R. Bryn Williams, the foremost authority on the history of the Welsh colony in Patagonia, wrote a memorable poem in Welsh, *Yn Angladd Wil* (At Wil's Funeral). I still remember the day well: the service for him in his beloved Heathfield before we set out for the cemetery of Llan Ffestiniog in the company of his dear wife, Glenys, and their two sons, Dafydd Meirion and John Wynne Jones and their families. Sergeant William Jones had been an example to all of us, but as far as we were concerned, it felt like an exodus with many moving back to live in Wales whilst others were called to their eternal rest. But we were still functioning well in our manifold activities and this concealed the losses. The meetings seemed to be well supported in the week nights as well as on Sundays. For example, on Sunday morning 4 March 1979, a large gathering was seen at Bethel, made up of councillors, civic leaders and guests in addition to our own congregation, for the Civic Service and the visit of the Lord Mayor of Liverpool, Councillor Ruth Dean. She represented the Woolton Ward on the City Council, where many of our members lived. The theme of the service was our Patron Saint, St David. The precentor was John Medwyn Jones (who moved to Colwyn Bay in 1983) and the organist, David Williams, Woolton, who moved to Swansea in 1980. Professor David Alan Price Evans (son of Mr. and Mrs. Owen Evans) read a chapter in Welsh from the scripture and we were led in prayer by His Honour Judge John Edward Jones. One of the hymns was in Welsh to the delight of everyone. It was a service for which we were grateful, the singing coming up to full expectations. In the sermon I emphasized that we, as a Welsh community, were an integral part of the life of the city, although we were naturally proud of our own national language and culture.

We needed to spend money continually on the buildings and during 1980 we had to undertake more repairs on our spiritual and cultural centre. We were making a valiant effort to nurture our children as Welsh citizens, proud of their Welsh Christian heritage, and seven of them were accepted into full membership. The seven who had met for weeks in the Communicants' Class were Robert Clement Evans, Joseph Clitherow, Ian Vaughan Jones, Sonia E. Jones, Mair Hughes Parry, Delyth S. Rogers and Siân Morris (née Hughes), a student at the university. Two of them are still members of our church today. Since 1972 we have been arranging a residential study weekend, usually in early September at the Youth Centre of our Connexion at Bala, and we did this year after year until 2005.

Amongst the members we lost through death in 1980 was Ifor Griffiths, whom I have often mentioned in this account. In 1980 we enjoyed the privilege, as we have since 1970 onwards, of welcoming the elderly and the housebound from the Toxteth area to spend a whole Saturday afternoon under our care, returning for an excellent tea in the large school room and then being entertained by members of our church, in particular, by Gwilym Pritchard, who had long experience as an entertainer. John Wynne Jones suggested the idea, which we adopted as a church. This entailed a great deal of planning and we were fortunate to have Alwena Davies as organiser and then Mrs. Gaenor Gregory who undertook to make all the arrangements. We turned up in our cars, at least a dozen or more of us, as we would have two, sometimes three to a car. One year W. Kyffin Pritchard succeeded in hiring a small mini-bus that carried twelve people: otherwise, we would have had to cancel the day, as we did not have enough volunteers. We used to take the elderly to Otterspool and then on to Calderstones Park for them to enjoy an ice cream each before returning to chapel. This usually occurred on a Saturday in June and it was a deed well-worth doing, as many of the elderly appreciated the care and hospitality.

1980 proved a notable year for marriages. On 12 April, Jean Arwel Dickie, Hornby Lane, married Eurfryn G. Davies, Cwmdare. They met through us as a family. Today, they do excellent work in the village of Llandegfan on Anglesey and in the Welsh Baptist Chapel at Bangor. Then on 26 July, we had two weddings: first, the marriage of Bronwen E. Davies, Court Hey Drive, and the musician Emyr Wynne Jones, well-known as a conductor of hymn-singing festivals. Then I officiated at the wedding of Eleri W. Rowlands, 104 Rose Lane, and Peter Barker, West Derby, both profoundly deaf. This was a service to be cherished. On 4 October Siân Hughes, Eversley Street, married Dr Hywel Morris, 5 Wellbeck Avenue, both of whom had been ardent *eisteddfodwyr* amongst the Welsh students of the University of Liverpool.

From the amalgamation Miss Mary B. Owen had been the Pulpit Secretary, and she was followed by Gwilym M. Jones, who had been involved in similar work during his time as an elder in Anfield Road Welsh Presbyterian Church. Dr R. Arthur Hughes was given a deserved honour in 1980 by being elected Moderator of the Liverpool Presbytery and Chairman of the Elders' Meeting of the North Wales Association of the Welsh Chapel Presbyterian Church of Wales. If anyone deserved those positions it was he, on the basis of his contribution to the local, national and universal church as medical missionary. Amongst the losses in 1980 were a large number of members who had become part of the community four years earlier, including Idwal Thomas, Manton Road, Kensington; Mrs. Kate Thomas, Elm Vale, Fairfield; Mrs. M. Phillips, Ilchester Road, Broadgreen; R. T. Williams, Manton Road, all four of them from the Edge Lane Welsh Chapel and from Eglwys y Drindod; Miss S. Jones, Horringford Road; Mrs. C. Williams, Miller Road; and from Heathfield Road, Robert Jones, the chemist, of Merrion Close; Mrs. M. Hughes, mother of Dilys, Berbice Road, an endearing spiritual person; Arthur Lloyd, Dulas Road, son of the elder and builder John Lloyd; and Ifor Griiffith, Charles

Berrington Road, a stalwart of our community. There were three others, Mrs. Blodwen Thomas, widow of Arthur Thomas, Menlove Avenue, a model treasurer for years at Anfield Road Chapel and also within the Liverpool Welsh Presbytery and Mrs. Letitia Hughes from Marianglas, Anglesey, the mother of Dilys Evans, Sinclair Drive, and John Hughes, Dovedale Road, who had been a precentor and elder at Bethlehem Welsh Chapel in Douglas Road, Anfield. She had come to live with her son and daughter in her failing years and she was steeped in Anglesey Calvinistic Methodism all her life. The third person was J. H. Roddick, Coventry Road, one of the great characters of the Penny Lane area, whom I persuaded to join the fold. An original, down to earth character and an uncle of the well-known barrister, Winston Roddick, QC, who shares in London the same chambers as my son, Hefin. Isn't the world small? Indeed in his younger days, Winston Roddick was a young police constable on the beat in Allerton Road and attended Heathfield Road Chapel.

A detailed analysis of the members who left our community tells a very interesting story. It was back to Wales that most of our members returned before the end of 1980: the medical practitioner, Dr. and Mrs. Ifor Lewis, Aigburth, moved to Rhosneigr; Dr. Norman and Mrs. Betty Jones, moved to Llandegfan; Conway Roberts's widow, Mrs. Jane Roberts moved to Chwilog, where she longed for Liverpool, as she would tell me when I occasionally called on her when preaching in Llŷn or Eifionydd; Roger and Glenys Williams to Llanfihangel Glyn Myfyr to be part of the farming community; David and Greta Williams from Woolton to Swansea; Mrs. Ethel Williams, widow of Professor Owen Herbert Williams (1884-1962), and daughter of the enterprising shipping magnate; William Thomas returned to Rhosneigr on Anglesey, where she celebrated her centenary; Bronwen Jones moved to Bolton on the appointment of her husband, Emyr, as a music teacher. Mr. and Mrs. Iorwerth Roberts moved to Derwenlas near Machynlleth. The sons of Mr. and Mrs. Henry Williams, Cassville Road moved to localities in England, Gareth to Wistanson, near Crewe, and Penri to Gloucestershire. It was a great loss when Arthur and Menna Evans and their children, Elen Angharad and Emyr Wyn, moved to Mold. Their contribution in this city had been an extensive one. Menna was Sergeant William Jones's niece, and Arthur, the son of Mr and Mrs Gwilym Evans, an elder at Bethania Welsh Chapel in Waterloo. Menna Evans was at the 2007 Eisteddfod Society tent at the 2006 National Eisteddfod in Swansea, and both attended a lecture I gave to the Mold Welsh Society with their cousin, Dafydd M. Jones who presided. He is a great Scouser and an authority on the Beatles. He, as well as Bethan Evans (née Thomas), Cardiff (late of Barndale Road, Allerton), were school children at Liverpool's Dovedale Road Primary School with John Lennon. Another of the Welsh who reluctantly left Liverpool was Mrs. Maggie Jones, the widow of the Reverend D. R. Jones and mother of Rhian Mair and Dr. Aled Wyn Jones. She returned to her roots in Pontyates in the Gwendraeth Valley in Carmarthenshire. She, as well as Mrs. M. James, Salisbury Farm, Woolton, always reminded me of my own background in Llanddewibrefi.

The year 1981 brought us a great deal of distress due to the violence experienced in the Parliament Street area of Toxteth. At the end of the day, there was need for us to return to the necessity of a healthy community, discipline amongst children, at home and in school, respect for God and our fellow human beings and a great deal of practical religion. The community at Bethel proved to be a great oasis, even with the stress of Toxteth, and the fellowship we enjoyed at our Youth Weekends at Bala and at the social gatherings we arranged for the disabled of Angers House (whose building was nearly opposite us) was inspiring, to say the least. Three noteworthy events were the providing of tea and entertainment for the elderly of Toxteth, the carol-singing under the leadership of Mrs. Bronwen Rogers and Mrs. Enid Hughes Jones and the efforts of David Evans, Anfield, to raise £81.00 for the needs of the disabled. We remembered a number of other charitable organisations – some of them local, such as Family Link, an organisation that came into existence through the vision of Dafydd Hughes Parry and Channel, others national or international such as Christian Aid or denominational like the Home for the Elderly in Pwllheli.

Our horizons as a community are world-wide and we are reminded of this by the visit of the Khasia Youth Choir from North-East India in May. Our connections go back a long way to the initatives taken at Rose Place, Liverpool, in 1840. That small seed has grown into a large tree. We were highly pleased to have the choir visit us. It was only eighteen strong but their enthusiasm for the furtherance of God's Kingdom was impressive. Our efforts were also communicated in two BBC Wales's programmes of *Songs of Praise*, under the respective batons of Hugh John Jones and R. Ifor Griffith, with Mrs. Margaret Anwyl Williams, Mrs. Glenys Arden and Miss Eirlys Williams, as organists.

We held memorable services, in particular on the Sundays when the Sunday School was involved, the Thanksgiving services and especially the Christmas Nativity play. Although snow was a problem in 1981, the large school-room was packed and the new lights shone bright in the faces of the younger children who brought us to the cradle of our Saviour.

Many more faithful members left us in 1981 – Mrs. Llewelyn Thomas, Barndale Road, moved to Cardiff to be nearer her family and Mrs. Gwladys Lloyd Williams, retired from her long dedicated service as Secretary of the Visitation Committee, as she was moving, to the town of her childhood, Llangefni on Anglesey. 1981 was the last year for Mr. R. E. and Mrs. Elan Jones as caretakers after a period of seventeen years. Since the building of the chapel and the schoolrooms, we have had only four families as caretakers – Mr and Mrs William Owen, Mr and Mrs. J. L. Griffiths, Mr. and Mrs. W. J. Jones and Mr. and Mrs. R. E. Jones. During the spring of 1982 a new caretaker in the person of Elwyn Jones and his wife, Edna, arrived from Bangor. They knew us well for they had been part of our community when they lived in Springwood. Our financial experts, Glyn Davies, E. Goronwy Owen and T. M. Owens had guided us in our stewardship which is part of church involvement.

In 1981 I was still hopeful of achieving more on the Welsh aspect of our ecumenical work in south Liverpool but by now I was asked to extend my ministry to care for the Welsh Presbyterian Chapel in Garston where I had come to know all the members. I had the opportunity of knowing Owen Owen, an elder there since 1937, and a powerful communicator in both languages. I ministered to him in his last illness and the loss of him together with Professor R. Alan Morton, who had been nurtured in Garston Chapel from his christening, made us poorer as a community. I began a Council of Welsh Churches for Liverpool and District. This was to be a means of bringing together congregations of Presbyterians, Independents, Baptists and Anglicans.

The urgent call on our congregation in 1982 was to supply aid for the city of Calcutta and the inhabitants of Rajasthan. We urged our members to respond to our aim to collect £352.00. Through the vision of the Missionary Committee of the Church and the educational aspect prepared by Dr R. Arthur Hughes, who was our Presbytery liaison officer, we succeeded in collecting the huge sum of £861.00. We rejoiced in this effort and we thanked everyone who had responded, as this was not our only missionary effort. We welcomed, once more, the elderly from the Dingle and from Toxteth; and we also held a special event for the inhabitants from Angers House, many of them severely disabled.

The social aspect of our community was always well appreciated. We held a Civic Service on the first Sunday in March, our Sunday School went on a trip to Alton Towers in July, and the Maesgrug Concert Party was invited to hold a number of concerts throughout the year. We looked forward to the pleasure of having a cup of tea after the evening services and it was sad to lose Emrys Jones (Garmoyle Road) quite suddenly in September, as it was he who organised this pleasurable fellowship. We found ourselves in a difficult position: could we still carry on with the post- service cup of tea? The Literary Society, with Mrs. Eirlys Lloyd Williams as convenor, decided to carry on in memory of all the members, sixteen of them whom we had lost, some very suddenly, like Mrs. Lena Jones, 23 Centreville Road, on her doorstep on 22 January, 1982. We lost Alderman David John Lewis, who had been so supportive, as well as the organist, Gwen Griffiths, Fallowfield Road, who taught generations of children to play the piano. There were three more weddings during the years: W. Trevor Williams, Fairfield, and Lora Malltwen Griffiths on 21 August; Miss Eryl Lloyd Jones, Grassington Crescent, and Michael Raymond Chitty, a good friend to the Liverpool Welsh and the historian of Wavertree and then on 23 October, Eirlys Nancy Williams, Rokesmith Avenue, married John Gwyndaf Richards, Paradise Street, who in 2007 began as a Nonconformist minister in north Montgomeryshire, serving twenty four chapels belonging to three denominations: Welsh Independents, Methodists and Presbyterian.

We have to mention two other significant events. First, the task of instructing and accepting eight young people as members of our Christian community, namely Jennifer Clitherow, Alun Edwin Jones, Gwenan Wyn Jones, Helen Hughes Jones, Gwenan Haf Owen, Eirian Hughes Parry, Dafydd Llywelyn Rees and Ceri Annwen Rogers. Of the eight, only three remain as members in Bethel today. Another exodus took place among our people. Today they are to be found in Norwich, Edinburgh, Cardiff, London and Worcester, and two in Liverpool. Then on Sunday, 28 November, 1982 the church decided to elect nine more elders. Only six of them accepted the invitation, namely W. Elwyn Hughes, Calderstones (who had been an elder in Anfield 1947-1979), Hugh John Jones, H. Wyn Jones, J. Gwyndaf Richards, Mrs. D. Bronwen Rogers and Dr. John G. Williams. The other three – Gwilym M. Jones, John Bain and William Evans – felt unable to accept the congregation's invitation at that particular time. I cannot recall so many being elected as elders in a Welsh-speaking

Young people group.

chapel in Liverpool, but the church felt the need for younger leaders such as Dr. John G. Williams and John Gwyndaf Richards.

As a church, we were delighted when Gwilym Meredydd Jones gained the highest accolade of the National Eisteddfod of Wales in 1982 at Swansea. He won the Prose Medal for his volume of short stories, *Ochr Arall y Geiniog*. We arranged a meeting to honour him on his achievement.

Nine of our members moved to Wales – Siân and Dr. Hywel Morris to Blaenau Ffestiniog; Nesta Rushton to Llandudno; Trevor and Malltwen Williams to Llanfairfechan, and five to different places in England. The following year we lost the contribution and leadership of three of our elders from the inner circle – Miss N. C. Hughes and John Medwyn Jones, who moved to the north Wales coast and Dafydd Hughes Parry who had given nine valuable years as an elder. There was another exodus from us in 1983. We lost Mrs. Hefina Turner to Helensburgh and Mrs. Muriel Owen to Caernarfon, two persons whom I see occasionally, in London and in north Wales. After all these members had left us, we were conscious of the decline in numbers at the services of Sunday and on week nights, in the cultural life as well as at the Merseyside Chair Eisteddfod.

An event, which became another memorable experience was the visit of the North Wales Association in September 1982. We received invaluable co-operation from the women's societies, which ensured great success. Also, we enjoyed working closely with members of

St David's Dinner and officers of the Literary Society (left to right), Gwynfryn Williams, Vaughan Hughes (Guest speaker), Dr D. Ben Rees, J. Gwyndaf Richards, Menna Owen, Enid Hughes Jones and Nan Hughes Parry.

the Manchester Welsh Presbytery. The Oaker Avenue Welsh Chapel Drama Group from Manchester came to entertain us whilst our Maesgrug Concert Party made a reciprocal visit to them in West Didsbury.

Other events that entailed a great deal of preparation were the services arranged by BBC Radio Cymru. We presented three services in Welsh and two others in English. I was extremely grateful to Hugh John Jones, Gwynfryn Evans and R. Ifor Griffith who were the precentors and to the organists Mrs. Margaret A. Williams, Arthur Edwards and Ifan Jones, for their splendid contribution to those broadcasted events.

The Sunday and week-night services were not the only highlights of our witness. There were many Welsh cultural activities, which took place using our splendid facilities. These were arranged by *Y Gorlan*, the Women's Fellowship, Young Wives' Circle and the Literary Society. All these events were very well supported. When the Reverend Harri Parri of Caernarfon visited us in November 1983, an audience of sixty turned up to his lecture. At our St David's Day Supper, when the Reverend W. Eifion Powell, Wrexham, was the guest speaker, we had 140 around the tables in the large schoolroom. At concerts or the children's meetings (for example, the Nativity at Christmas) or our Christmas Fayre, we had large and much valued support. The secret or our success had been due to the enthusiasm of the officers and members of the committee, the effectiveness of the secretaries, the policy of advertising through our newsletter, *Y Rhwyd*, our community newspapers, *Yr Angor* and *Mersey Mart,* and the use of posters which always bring Welsh people in from outside our own community, in particular, adults who are learning the language.

In 1983 our Church enjoyed the fellowship of two medical men from Assam at our services, namely Dr. Pherlock Lamare from the Welsh Mission Hospital in Shillong (where the Reverend Dr H. Gordon Roberts and Dr R. Arthur Hughes had served as missionary surgeons), and Dr. Ryngad from Jowai Hospital in North-East India.

We rejoiced in the One-Day Missionary School that I organised on Saturday 19 November at the Welsh Methodist Chapel in Renshaw Street, in the heart of Liverpool, when we received a great deal of very interesting details of his experience there from the Reverend John H. Tudor (who had been a missionary in Taiwan) and Dr. R. Arthur Hughes on the theme of 'Politics on the Mission Field.'

I was deeply involved in the events celebrating the five-hundredth centenary of the birth of the Protestant Reformer Martin Luther (1483-1546). This resulted in an exhibition on his life and work, as well as three lectures on his influential witness in our very well-attended One-Day School at Bethel. In June I was asked to lead a delegation of ministers and priests, who were well known for their emphasis on the social gospel, from Britain to the German Democratic Republic (GDR). We were welcomed by the Mayor of Wittenberg and other leaders in all the towns associated with Luther. In August 1983 I arranged a journey to Italy, when a good number from Bethel joined the group. This was another means of understanding the great revolution instigated by Martin Luther and his theology, as well as other Protestant Reformers, in particular John Calvin in Geneva.

The continuing needs of Uganda and Sudan, the elderly of Toxteth and the disabled from Angers House, came to disturb our comfortable living and encourage us, as people of faith, into action. Again we had to spend a great deal of money on our buildings. A new central heating boiler was installed to heat the whole building at the total cost of £8,000. This was made possible by a loan from the Liverpool Presbytery. But the Presbytery, through death, lost its dedicated Moderator on Tuesday 22 November. It had been a privilege to work with the late Reverend Idwal Jones, Birkenhead. His ministry on Merseyside has been chronicled in the bilingual volume, *Alpha and Omega: Presbyterian Witness in Laird Street, Birkenhead (1906-2006)*.

Our witness as a church in 1984 was threefold. First, we remained conscious of our historical achievements as a cause, which has given the Connexion and the denomination, its splendid heritage from the Methodist Revival of the eighteenth century. It was a privilege to welcome my friend, the Reverend Rhys ab Ogwen Jones, Chester, to remind us of our roots in Trefeca, Breconshire and the work of Howell Harris; the significance of Bala and the founding contributions of Thomas Charles, architect of the Sunday School movement; Llangeitho and the pulpit orator, Daniel Rowland. The climax of all this was the service held on 12 July with the Liverpool Welsh Choral Union, when we launched the bilingual volume *Liverpool Welsh and Their Religion*. This contained three lengthy articles, one prepared by Dr. R. Merfyn Jones, then at the University of Liverpool, and two by myself. Today, Dr. R. Merfyn

Jones is Vice-Chancellor of the University of Bangor, and one of the most important figures in higher education in Wales. We worked closely together, and his article on the origins of the Liverpool Welsh is one of the best pieces ever written on our past. It is a splendid original study and a substantial contribution. This volume has been used often by scholars and students and frequently quoted. It is now out of print and should be republished.

Secondly, in 1984, we decided to place a great deal of emphasis on the world in which we live. We decided to cater for the children as an integral part of the morning worship, which has been a very successful arrangement and has given an added impetus to the morning service as well as to the Sunday School. In 1984 we had the opportunity to acknowledge the many services of Mrs Nan Hughes Parry as a Sunday School teacher for twenty-two years. Today, two of her daughters, Mair Thompson and Eirian See, have followed her example and continue to contribute to the work of the Sunday School. We rejoiced in accepting ten young people from the Sunday School as full members of the Church. The Communicants' Class was made up of Bethan Wyn Jones, Gareth Llewelyn Owen, Hefin Ednyfed Rees, Geraint Siôr Rogers, Lowri Ann Williams, Dylan and Iwan Williams and Roy, Pamela and Hazel Williams. The cultural and religious opportunities we have given to our young people and the activities for them are an example that other Welsh chapels could follow. These activities included our Eisteddfod, the Sunday School work, the successful concerts that we arranged in co-operation with the local Jewish community, as well as for our own community and the Mossley Hill Group of Churches. All these activities provided considerable organisational experiences for our young people and it is not surprising that they succeeded so well in the worlds of medicine, law, civil service, media and education. Nevertheless, probably because of other demands in building their careers, they have not involved themselves as fully as they might have done in the life of the Christian church. But those that have, are today, students of the Word of God, involved in the faith of the church, its worship, its teaching in Bible Studies and Sunday School. It seems as a church that we cannot retain the commitment of all our young members. They have chosen a different option, but one prays that they might return in days to come. That is our hope.

Our Church very much remains a missionary-minded church. Thus, it was natural for us to seek ways to say farewell to the two young medical men, Dr. Pherlock Lamare and Dr. Gordon M. Rangad. We received inspiring messages from them and opportunities to listen to the Team of Good News from Mizoram, in North-East India. It was a thrill to present two cheques to them, amounting to a total of £670.00 to help them to continue with their work in Jowai and Shillong Hospitals. Also, in 1984, Dr. R. Arthur Hughes, OBE, and Mrs. Nancy Hughes, visited Shillong to advise on problems that had risen in the hospital where Dr. Hughes himself had given thirty years of valuable service. Dr. Hughes decided that he would like to be relieved of his duties as Secretary of the Church but we were fortunate in having a worthy successor in H. Wyn Jones, who has by now been longer in that post than anyone else, except Owen Hughes, our first secretary of the Church.

Concern for the present-day needs of the chapel inspired the Women's Fellowship, under the leadership of Mrs. Jane Mathias, Woolton, Mrs. Gwyneth Hemingway, Wavertree, and Mrs. Gwerfyl Jones, Mossley Hill, to work so hard, along with members of the Executive Committee. These included, in particular, Mrs. Ann Hughes, Wynnstay Street, Toxteth, Mrs. Muriel Edwards, Fallowfield Road, Wavertree, Mrs. Megan Jones and Mrs. Glenys Jones, both of Woolton, Mrs. Olwen Jones, Allerton, Miss Winnie Jones, Calderstones Road; Mrs. Meinwen Rees and Miss Eunice Thomas, Miss Mary B. Owen, an elder, and Mrs. Edna Jones, Chapel House. All these women members worked together to make the annual Christmas Fayre so successful. They arranged, discussed and inspired others to work and, in the end, transferred £481.00 to the chapel funds. The Estates' Committee, with H. Wyn Jones as chairman, and Myron G. Jones, Calderstones, as secretary, was also very active. And we established an effective Executive Committee with craftsmen and business-people caring for the Heathfield Road site. The sum of £8,147.00 was spent on re-painting the chapel and tackling the dampness in the large section above the gallery (once more). I stated in my address for 1984: 'I hope that we, at last, have had the last word on this obvious weakness.' But to our distress, we have not solved the problem in twenty years of effort.

In 1983-1984 it was an honour for me, in the name of Bethel, to lead as Chairman, the nine churches that formed the Mossley Hill Council of Churches. Another scheme that now came into existence was the Merseyside Welsh Chaplaincy. The need was tremendous, as I was the only full-time Welsh speaking minister in Liverpool in 1984, and I had never-ending calls to visit people in the hospitals, and sometimes Welsh people in Walton Prison. It was impossible to respond to all these calls without some assistance, and I saw this as an important step to proclaim the Gospel. The scheme was discussed in detail, presented locally and then through the courts of the Connexion right up to the Mission Board who decided to advertise for a Chaplain to the Merseyside Welsh Community, an appointment for which eight candidates applied. The National Committee selected John Sam Jones, a native of Barmouth, who had been educated at the University of Wales, Aberystwyth, and California, USA. He was welcomed by us in his post as Chaplain and he became a member of our church. John Sam Jones, who served as Chaplain between 1984 and 1986, did a great deal of valuable visiting and comforting hospital patients. After he left, we decided to extend the scope of his work and involve other denominations, including the Welsh Independents, the Baptists, the Anglican Church, the Methodist Church as well as the Presbyterian Church of Wales. We had a short but well worthwhile contribution from our eldest son, Dafydd Llywelyn Rees, at the end of his stay at Oxford. He was followed by Ms. Rachel Gooding, a native of Stalybridge, who had learnt Welsh at Ceredigion as a student, the missionary Eleri Edwards and then, on a part-time basis the Reverend Nan Wyn Powell Davies, Mold, whose grandmother, Mrs. M Jones, Sudbury Road, Anfield, was a member of our congregation and one of the great characters of the Liverpool Welsh community from the first day she arrived here in 1919 from her native Trawsfynydd. One cannot over-emphasise the personal contribution of every one of the chaplains and their ecumenical initiatives. As secretary of the local Chaplain's Committee from the beginning, my admiration for those from the other denominations mentioned, has been sincere: in particular, those that have been involved for the last twenty-three years. The loss of two of these members in 2007, namely the Reverend

Eleri Edwards and Rachel Gooding who served as chaplains to the Liverpool Welsh.

R. J. Môn Hughes, Birkenhead, from the Welsh Independents, and Hugh T. Williams of the Welsh Anglican Church of Sheil Road, has made us very appreciative of their involvement since 1986.

In view of the shortage of ministers, I was asked by the Presbytery to prepare a theological Biblical course of lectures for elders and lay people within our chapel. This was the beginning of what became known as *Y Cwrs Byr* (Short Course). This was extremely useful, in as much as it offerred a well-supported training for sermon preparation and practical suggestions for conducting a religious service. This initiative helped to maintain the high standards of our pulpits on Merseyside.

We congratulated Dr. John G. Williams, M.D., M.R.C.P. on his appointment as medical specialist at Runcorn Hospital (now known as Halton Hospital). He has become a renowned chest specialist in the Warrington/Widnes/Runcorn area, as I know from personal experience of visiting the hospitals where Dr. Williams is involved. On 23 June 1984, Goronwy Evan Thomas, Mossley Hill Road, died. He was another notable Welsh medical surgeon based at Broadgreen Hospital and Alder Hey, who had been extremely kind to us as a family. He and his gracious wife, Morfudd, always gave us a warm *croeso* on our regular visits to their home at Eastfield, Mossley Hill. Another great loss to the Welsh community was the sudden passing of Griffith J. Williams, 23 Kylemore Avenue, Mossley Hill, a pharmacist by profession, but a caring and helpful Christian in his way of life.

We heard in 1985, that the Welsh Baptist Chapel in Earlsfield Road, was being sold, so we decided to extend a warm welcome to the remaining members to use one of our schoolrooms as a centre for worship. Nothing came of our invitation, but after the closure of the chapel we welcomed three faithful members to our Church, the two sisters, Myfanwy Hughes and Gwen Kennedy, Deepfield Road, and the retired schoolmaster, William Owen, a native of Amlwch, Anglesey.

In 1985, we arranged a sponsored walk and raised £504.00 for our Charities. The chapel community celebrated many events in 1985. The Presbyterian Church of Wales marked the beginning of the Methodist Revival in 1735 and we enjoyed excellent lectures based on the diaries of Howell Harris, the hymns of William Williams, Pantycelyn, and the sermons of Daniel Rowland. A One-Day School, under the auspices of the Department of Continuing Studies of the University of Liverpool, was held

Dr John G. Williams.

and we invited Dr. Derec Llwyd Morgan to our midst at the Centre in Mount Pleasant. A service of thanksgiving was held at Bethel. The celebration of two hundred years in the life of the Sunday School was another important event for our church.

Special arrangements were made which enabled us, as a family, to spend six weeks in a Presbyterian Manse belonging to Oak Hill Chapel in Akron, Ohio in the summer of 1985. Dr. Harold Kelly, the minister of Oak Hill, brought his family to Liverpool and stayed in our Manse. Our six weeks there included my month's holiday, whereby in the middle of July, the four of us travelled to Akron whilst Dr. Kelly and his family came to Allerton. A special meeting was held at Bethel to welcome them and, likewise, we also had a similar sincere, warm welcome at Akron. As far as I can gather, much more was expected of me in Akron than was expected of Dr. Harold Kelly in south Liverpool, and there were

Miss Myfanwy Hughes

reasons for this. The situation was quite different. Bethel Chapel in Liverpool was a Welsh-speaking church, whereas Oak Hill was English-speaking. I could see increasing numbers in the congregation as the weeks went by. Oak Hill Chapel had a second full-time minister who carried out all the pastoral work. Thus the minister's main task was to prepare for the Sunday morning service.

Members of my family who have settled in the United States of America came to visit us, and we were invited to a number of homes in Akron and the surrounding area. We came to know the religious scene within the city where we were welcomed in large churches with thousands of members. It was an experience that we will never forget. Back in Liverpool Bethel Elders' Meeting's minutes on 9 September 1985 records: 'With regard to the visit of the Reverend Dr. Hal Kelly and his family, the general opinion was that everything had been a huge success.'

W. Gratton Thomas, Teilia, Woolton Road, the senior elder of the Presbytery, died on 1 October. He had spent most of his long life as an elder at Anfield Road Welsh Chapel and he believed, implicitly, that there was no other chapel community that was even comparable. After the closure of Anfield Road, Mr. Gratton Thomas and his wife, along with others, became members at Bethel. W. Gratton Thomas was highly opinionated and, at times, difficult. Neverthless he had been extremely supportive of the Anfield Chapel, where he had been reared in the chapel house. His ideal preacher was the Reverend E. Gwyn Evans, for years minister at Charing Cross Welsh Chapel in the heart of London. One observer said of E. Gwyn Evans, 'God's last great preacher'. During the year, the people of Bethel experienced a variety of different talents amongst the preachers, ranging from the psychiatrist Dr. David Enoch, to that of the Welsh poet, Eirian Davies, Rhydymwyn, near Mold, the humorous novelist, the Reverend Harri Parri, Caernarfon, to the biblical exponent of great style, the Reverend Dr. Elfed ap Nefydd Roberts from the United Theological College in Aberystwyth (now closed).

In December 1985 membership at Bethel stood at 337, with 43 children. As we have seen, during that year many of the members moved back to Wales, twelve died and six moved away from Liverpool. But, on the other hand, we received seventeen new members, ten from the young people of the chapel, three through transfer and four through our own missionary endeavours. As a chapel we remained extremely aware of our cultural identity and background due to the effectiveness of our own missionary outreach in a large English-dominated but cosmopolitan city.

Chapter 13

GOD'S FAMILY AT BETHEL CHURCH (1986-1995)

A festival, which we supported at the end of May 1986, took place on the premises of the Royal Welsh Agricultural site at Llanelwedd, Builth Wells, in Powys. A coach, as well as a minibus, travelled to this festival, which was held under the title of 'God's Family'. Here we all had the opportunity of meeting fellow Christians from every part of Wales to see and hear the charismatic Anglican leader from South Africa, Archbishop Desmond Tutu, addressing us with gospel joy. All of us, of every age, were extremely happy with the arrangements, although those of us in the large coach were extremely annoyed with our driver, when he did not appreciate our desire to stop for fish and chips at Newtown on our return journey! His Honour Judge J. E. Jones had to use his persuasion to make the driver realise that he had very little option but to follow our wishes!

In 1986 we all understood that we were participating in the year of God's Family when we invited fifteen preachers from Wales to visit us. Some of them, such as Reverends Arthur Jones, Llanrhaeadr, in the Vale of Clwyd; T. Leonard Williams, Gellifor; Richard Jones, Trefnant (he had been an elder for years at Anfield Road Chapel); Emlyn Richards, Cemaes, and Huw Jones, Rhuddlan, came regularly to preach at our chapel. The latter, the Reverend Huw Jones, Rhuddlan, had been encouraged to consider the call to the ministry by the Reverend E. Watkin Jones. Others were visiting for the first time – Wayne Roberts from the Theological College in Aberystwyth and the Reverend G. Edryd Jones, Wrexham. The only layman amongst them was my old college friend, Geraint Jones, from Trefor in Caernarfonshire, who had served as columnist in Y Cymro for a short period of twelve months. The Reverend J. Eirian Davies travelled all the way from Carmarthen and stayed with us over the weekend. Our boys liked him immensely, and when Dafydd had an opportunity to offer a name for a guest speaker at the centenary of the Dafydd ap Gwilym Society in the University of Oxford, he nominated Eirian Davies. Eirian, himself, had never been a student at Oxford and yet he had known personally one of the most remarkable philosophers of the twentieth century, Ludwig Witgenstein. Also it was good for the chapel to have a minister to preach on a Sunday from other Free Churches, such as the Reverend J. Haines Davies, Old Colwyn, a dynamo belonging to the Methodist Church and the Reverend Tecwyn Parry, Nantwich, who had not been at our chapel since 1940. Amongst the members' favourites, was the Reverend Dewi Wyn Williams, Dollgellau, the minister who had officiated at the wedding of Beryl and John G. Williams, and the Reverend Trefor Jones, Engedi, Caernarfon, who came as our guest preacher of the Preaching Festival.

But, as a Church, we had an interest in and concern for all members of the family of God at Bethel. Every member is called a shepherd of the family and this reminds us of the

(left to right) John Alun Hughes, D. B. Rees, W. Kyffin Pritchard, Goronwy Owen, H. John Jones, Trefor Rees, Eluned and D. Emlyn Davies and Elfed Williams with the BBC van that visited Liverpool to invite us to express our views on Welsh broadcasting.

sick and of those unable to attend the chapel. During 1986, we lost through death, eleven members, some who had been members of the chapel since they were christened, such as Eleanor Williams, 87 Herondale Road, she and her brother, T. Lloyd Williams, Greenhill Road, and also, others who had become part of the family in 1976, including Eirwen M. Davies, Lyttleton Road, from Eglwys y Drindod. Others had been with us longer, like Norman Charles Williams, Long Lane, nurtured in Newsham Park Welsh Chapel, Liverpool, where his father had been an elder, and Mrs. Margaret Pugh, Druids Cross Gardens, who as a young child had attended the Welsh Presbyterian Chapel in Warrington. William John Howarth, Thingwall Lane, was an Englishman, but after marrying a Welsh girl, he felt that he should be part of her God's family, because in his words they were 'so friendly and welcoming'. He experienced this fellowship for years at Edge Lane Welsh Presbyterian Chapel. The kind Mrs. Elen Jones, Bartlett Street, Wavertree, had been a member of the chapel for years and had brought her daughter, Mrs. Mona McEvoy, Mossley Hill, to be within the family at Heathfield Road. She has been a very endearing and supportive member. We are grateful that we have in Bethel a large number of committed visitors who comfort the sick in Liverpool's hospitals; and, in particular, visit Welsh men and women who have to spend periods at these hospitals, far from their homes. They, also, like our own members, are part of God's family.

Mair Powell, Enid P. Hughes and Olwen Jones.

We welcomed new members to our Church family in 1986, among them eight young people who had been faithful as attenders at our Friday night meetings and the Sunday School. These eight were Heather E. Bain, Huw and Peryn Clement-Evans, the three of them highly talented musicians; Gwenan and Owain Ellis Roberts, both working in the television and radio environment; Carys E. Williams, Gaynor Clitherow and Eirian W. Jones. Two of these three still live in the city and the three of them are members of our chapel community.

Like all families, we have our relatives, many of them in Wales and others who come to us on visits to the hospitals or become students at Liverpool's universities. Some, especially Welsh-language activists are sent to spend periods at Walton Prison. I visited Walton Prison on a number of occasions in 1986, as well as the hospitals all over the city, to dispense comfort to the Welsh. In 1986 we continued to welcome a large number of friends from other Christian traditions. We learnt a great deal in the company of that saintly scholar, one of the great exponents of the New Testament Scriptures, Professor Barnabas Lindars from the University of Manchester. We received a visit, also, from Alwyn Rice Jones, Bishop of St. Asaph, who gave us a glimpse of the spirituality within the Anglican Communion. We were disturbed, humbled and deeply impressed at Bethel when we listened to Father Gherogohe Calciu, who had suffered for his faith in the dismal prisons of Romania. In 1986, we enjoyed an impressive address by one of our own missionaries, Mrs. Nansi Mary Thomas (1910-1988). In 1985, she and her youngest son, Arwyn, returned to the mission field in Shillong where she and her husband, the Reverend Trebor Mai Thomas, had ministered for years. They

Young People of Bethel before a sponsored walk.

came when the Association arrived in May 1986 when Bethel, which holds 750, was full to hear an account of her visit. In 1986, conversely, it was a thrill to welcome hundreds of ladies from north and mid Wales. The north Wales Women's Association has never been back to Liverpool. I doubt if it will ever come again, because, except for the two cathedrals, we do not have any chapel, besides Bethel, which can hold more than 550 people.

The BBC was involved with us on more than one occasion in 1986. To the BBC in Wales, Bethel, as well as our home, is the embassy for the Welsh life of Liverpool! Indeed, our schoolrooms and rooms were used by a number of societies during the year, everyone commenting favourably on the excellent condition of our buildings. We spent £30,400 to preserve them in 1986. The continuing work of our caretakers, Elwyn and Edna Jones, and the Building and Finance Committee, ensured that we were operating responsibly.

In looking back over 1987, there emerge three aspects that need to be emphasised in this volume. The first was the great losses that were experienced in 1987; it was a year of much distress throughout the United Kingdom. These are the names, which linger in the mind: Zeebrugge, Hungerford, Enniskillen, King's Cross. Each disaster brought distress and tears to numerous families.

Closer to home, we at Bethel experienced tears and *hiraeth* after the deaths of several members. These included the university lecturer, H. Richard Williams; the Reverend Dafydd Hughes Parry, who gave of his best to all the Welsh Presbyterian Chapels on Merseyside; Michael Williams, Old Colwyn; Glyn Peters, Avondale Road, an outstanding singer with a powerful voice; and Ernest Ellis, Old Swan, who spent most of his life in a mental hospital; Mrs Mair Hooson Court, Bundoran Road, from a notable family of Welsh Presbyterians, originally at Liverpool's Princes Road Chapel and John Morgan Davies, Stoneycroft, a somewhat eccentric bachelor who was very much a distinctive character of our chapel. Other losses included Mrs. Enid M. Pryce, who had been a member for years at Edge Lane; and Mrs. Catherine Leong, Sundale, who had spent years with the Society of Friends, but missed the warmth and deep concerns of Welsh Presbyterianism. When she was over ninety years of age she came on one of my pilgrimages to Italy and, like Gracie Fields, the popular singer, she really did enjoy Capri. We have already mentioned Mrs. Enidwen Bowden, Hunt's Cross, and one of the members of Eglwys y Drindod was Mrs. Ann Taylor, Sefton Drive. We also suffered losses when some of our members decided to move away from Liverpool. The grand-daughter of the pioneer, John Jones, Drinkwater, Mrs. Mair Hughes Parry, moved to Anglesey, while Dilys Ward (née Hughes), Berbice Road, Allerton, moved to Shrewsbury after her marriage. She had been extremely active in our Church along with Mrs. Rhiannon Williams, Karslake Road. Another loss was Mrs. Dilys Jones (daughter of the elder, John Lloyd) and her husband, Emyr G. Jones, who moved to Birkenhead and enrolled in Salem, Laird Street; Mrs. Megan Hughes, Aigburth, ceased to attend our services as her grasp of the Welsh language was extremely limited, quite different from her eldest sister, Mrs. Olwen Owen, Llanbedrog, whose articles in *Yr Angor*, on her memories of the Liverpool Welsh, have been greatly appreciated. Hugh Rowlands, Albert Edward Road, Kensington, a loyal member at Edge Lane Chapel, as well as

One of the earliest Adult Welsh Learner's Class at Bethel.

in Bethel, returned to his roots on Anglesey. No chapel, anywhere, has had a more sincere Christian adherent than Hugh Rowlands. From the leadership we lost Mrs. D. Bronwen Rogers when she and her family moved to Deganwy. This was an obvious loss for us as the family filled a whole pew – father, son and two daughters and their mother. Since moving to Deganwy, Mrs. Bronwen Rogers has been made an elder at the United Chapel of Gloddaeth in Llandudno and has become a Moderator of the north Wales Presbytery of the Presbyterian Church of Wales.

In 1987 we held a very special service to celebrate the opening of the first Welsh Presbyterian Chapel in Liverpool in 1787 at Pall Mall, the centenary of the cause at Webster Road, Heathfield Road and at Bethel as well as the sixty years since the large Bethel Chapel was completed in 1927. We celebrated through our services, our singing festivals, a lecture, an exhibition and a special supper. Glynne Jones, Dowlais, the conductor of Pendyrus Male Voice Choir in the Rhondda Valley, led the *Cymanfa Ganu* in great style. The Melody Group and Gaenor Howells, daughter of Geraint and Olwen Howells, Ponterwyd, in Ceredigion also visited us. Her father had been the Liberal MP for Ceredigion since 1974. Another great joy was to have the Ruthin and District Choir and the Reverend W. J. Gruffydd of Tregaron, known in eisteddfodic circles as Elerydd, came as an adjudicator and as a preacher, spending the weekend in our home. We also invited the Missionary, the Reverend Mair Bowen, Llanfairfechan, who, after having been brought up in our chapel, has spent a lifetime with the Welsh Baptists. We also had the company of Glenys Roberts, Harrow; H. R. Williams,

Enid Jones and Ann Roberts

Roderick Owen, E. Goronwy Owen, D. Ben Rees and Reverend H. G. Parri, Caernarfon.

Waterloo, and the Reverend R. E. Hughes, Moderator of the Liverpool Welsh Presbytery, to assist us in our celebrations.

For many of us, the climax of these celebrations was the launching of the volume, *Antur a Menter Cymry Lerpwl (*Adventure and Endeavours of the Liverpool Welsh), by Judge J. E. Jones, who was honoured by the National Eisteddfod of Wales's Gorsedd of Bards, adopting the title 'Ioan Maesgrug' [John Heathfield]. He was also honoured by the Liverpool Presbytery after serving forty years as an elder together with W. Elwyn Hughes, Calderstones. Mr Hughes is a link with those men who had built our city, the Welsh builders of Liverpool.

Thirdly, during 1987, we continued to conduct a faithful witness. That was true with regard to the missionary witness, our musical tradition, Biblical teaching from the Book of Genesis, the training of lay preachers, the enjoyment of Welsh culture through the Literary Society and regular worship together on Sunday mornings and evenings. We raised money for the special Christian Aid Appeal of the Presbyterians, and, were enlightened to this particular need by Dr. R. Arthur Hughes, Gwilym M. Jones and the Reverend Dewi Lloyd Lewis at Bethel, and during the weekend spent together in September at the Presbyterian Church of Wales Centre in Bala. We raised money by preparing envelopes on behalf of the newsletter, *Peacelinks,* produced by the Fellowship of Reconciliation (England). The total amount collected for Christian Aid came to £850.00, an excellent response. The Women's Fellowship handed over to the church and other good causes the sum of £670.00, primarily raised by our Christmas Fayre. Our caretaker, D. Elwyn Jones, took the precaution of placing a defensive sheet over the windows facing Auckland Road when some unknown, irresponsible persons were tempted to break the windows, when there was light in the schoolrooms. Sometimes, we were visited by distinguished preachers on a Sunday, including some who had strong links with the chapel, including the Reverend Trefor Davies Jones and the Reverend Richard Kilgour, grandson of Mrs. E. Kilgour, Arranmore Road. She used to fly regularly to spend some months with her son, Len, in New Zealand. Clearly, she was enjoying a full and active life. We wished a number of members, who had left us in 1988, every blessing.

I can summarise the witness of the year under seven headings.

1.   The trainers in our community

We appreciated the contribution of Mrs. Enid Hughes Jones with *Y Gorlan* and the Sunday School for a period of eighteen years, and also those who were guiding the young in the 1980s, Beryl Williams, Helen Wyn Jones, Eirlys Evans and Meinwen Rees. R. Ifor Griffith was thoroughly enjoying the task of conducting his mixed choir at Bethel, which made a valuable contribution to two Welsh television programmes of hymn singing – known as *Dechrau Canu, Dechrau Canmol*. Hugh John Jones, Centreville Road, was very willing, as usual, to prepare us in hymn singing on a week night for those television programmes and, also, the annual singing festival which we welcomed to Bethel in 1988.

2.   The location of our Church

Situated just twenty yards from Penny Lane, Allerton Road, Church Road and Smithdown Road at the bottom of Heathfield Road, Bethel is a convenient location for the whole of Liverpool. This is one of the main reasons why so many meetings were held in our buildings from the 1960s onwards.

3.   Our tradition as Celtic people

We belong to a specific nation – one that preserved its language mainly through the publication of the Welsh Bible in 1588. As Protestants, we naturally place a great deal of emphasis on the word of God in every service. The end result of this was two wonderful services in September 1988 to celebrate the first publication of the Welsh Bible four hundred years earlier. In the morning we held a singing festival with T. Gwynn Jones as the guest conductor. He is the composer of remarkable tunes such as *Tregarth* and *Diolch i'r Iôr* . We had a thrilling time and then, in the afternoon, we had an excellent appraisal of the life and work of Bishop William Morgan, who translated the Bible into Welsh, by Dr. R. Geraint Gruffydd of Aberystwyth. We also held a singing festival to welcome the publication of a new translation of the Welsh Bible at Liverpool's Anglican Cathedral. In our chapel we sold a large number of copies and accepted a special edition of the pulpit Bible in memory of John Morgan Davies, Stoneycroft, given by three of his friends.

4.   The generosity of the Church

One of our most important events of the year was our support for the Nairobi Appeal Project in Kenya through the efforts of Hefin Rees, who had spent some months of his gap year amongst the poorest of the poor in a shanty town outside that capital city.   Through Bethel, we collected £2103.51 and through other movements £1100.00, making a total of £3203.51.   A centre was built in Kokarkocho in 1989 and we established a charity called *Gobaith Mewn Gweithrediad*, and in English, 'Hope in Action', to be responsible for sustaining the school, paying the salaries of the teachers, and feeding the poor undernourished children.   A number of us in Bethel supported Hefin personally in his work, including the chairman, E. Goronwy Owen, our treasurer Gareth James, Aintree, and from the Executive Committee, H. Wyn Jones, Dafydd LL. Rees, Meinwen Rees and

Lord Reverend Roger Roberts and Euryn Roberts at Bethel.

myself as secretary.   The charity is still in existence, and two of our endearing members, Misses Adelaide and Mary Jones, Kingsdale Road, Allerton, as well as others in the Presbytery, have made generous contributions to the work.   Often, any donation I receive from my lecturing activities, are passed to the charity.   Now, we are on the verge of beginning another involvement on the continent of Africa, this time in Uganda, again in the field of education.

5.   The variety of gifts within our community

Our members contributed some excellent interviews on the S4C hymn singing programmes and distinguished themselves by the high standards of performance by our children and young people.   We were well served by our concert groups, known as 'Parti'r Bwthyn' and 'Parti'r Werin'.   We took the opportunity of giving a sincere thank you to Glyn Davies for all his service as Finance Secretary of our chapel since 1975.   He undertook these duties very effectively.   We also voiced our appreciation of the services of his wife, Megan, as one of our organists.   Dr. Glyn Roberts, Aigburth, a retired lecturer, was approached to succeed him, and he worked in partnership with E. Goronwy Owen and T. M. Owen.

Glenys Johnson and Wena Evans.

6. The glorious *koinonia* in our witness

Koinonia is the New Testament Greek work for 'fellowship'; and, in a world where there is so much pain, strife and violence, truly we have been blessed with harmony and fellowship. This was evident on 2 January at the wedding of Mair Hughes Parry and John G. Thompson. Their involvement as a family in our Church has been chronicled in the volume *Welsh Routes*, published by Liverpool Community Spirit in 2006. On 5 November we rejoiced with Gwenan Wyn Jones, Wheatcroft Road on her marriage to Brian Howard Wiley. The family now live in Edinburgh.

7. Rejoicing in the Lord

This is a key to any Christian grouping. We rejoiced in the Lord, in praising God, in proclaiming and listening to the word being part of our life.

We remember with affection, all those called into higher service who deserve to be in our minds, namely the Liverpool builder, W. Glyn Jones, Quarry Street, who followed in the same business footsteps of his father, J. W. Jones; Mrs. Gwenno Bouch, Cassville Road. Her conversation and her accent reminded us of her native Blaenau Ffestiniog, although she had worked at T.J. Hughes, the large store in London Road, and had lived in Liverpool for seventy years; Morgan Jones, a joiner by trade, who lodged with Mr. and Mrs. William Roberts in

16 Winchfield Road, Wavertree, throughout the years, all three hailing from Anglesey; and, also, Trevor Roberts, Aigburth Drive, born and brought up in the City of Liverpool, who had been so kind in bringing members to our chapel from the Dingle area in his car; Owen Henry Williams, Adelaide Road, Kensington, the loving father of Ann Clitherow, her brothers and sister, and Mrs. Elizabeth Jones Parry, Hollytree Road, mother of the Reverend Dafydd Hughes Parry, who remembered the chapel in its early days in the 1920s. It was sad, also, to eventually lose Gwilym J. Pritchard, Moor Lane, Crosby, who had been a valuable member in Princes Road. He had survived, after being knocked down by a speeding car on a pedestrian crossing in Aigburth Road when the traffic lights were in his favour.

By 1990, we began to see the fruits of the lay training and the support we now received. During the year we had Dr. Gareth Lloyd Jones, of the University of Wales in Bangor, and Professor Barnabas Lindars, from the University of Manchester, assisting us in our Biblical studies. Historically, the University of Liverpool has never had a Theological Department, because of the influence of the University's founding Unitarian merchants who were against the teaching of religious doctrines. But neither has the federal University of Wales any provision for teaching doctrine, which had to be done in associated denominational colleges. Consequently, we had to depend on Manchester and Bangor for our expertise.

We made valiant efforts to respond to the cry of the city. Whilst the tragedy of Hillsborough still lingered in our minds, we also collected money for the Lockerbie Fund. I was invited to lecture in a Liberal Arts College in Caldwell, Idaho, USA, and had the honour of delivering three public lectures for town and college. As I was leaving the College Hall

(left to right), R. Ifor Griffith, Dr D. Ben Rees, H. Wyn Jones, Rhiannon Liddell and Rhys Williams at a Sunday School Festival.

after delivering my second lecture on Sunday night, one of the men who had been in the lecture turned to me and said, 'I feel sorry for your city'. I had no idea what he meant but when I telephoned home that night I heard of the tragedy that had happened to so many Liverpool supporters in Sheffield. It was a great experience to visit Idaho but I was given a warm welcome when I returned home within the week.

In 1989 we had an opportunity of welcoming a number of young people to the Communicants' Class. These included the brothers Dylan and Alan Evans, William Williams, David Hughes, all from Allerton, and Gareth Carr, a young student from Port Talbot, who became one of the most loyal of our members until he moved, after his marriage, back to Wales.

Another important occasion, on behalf of the Liverpool, as well as the Manchester Presbytery, was to welcome the North Wales Association of the Presbyterian Church of Wales, to our chapel. I acted, once more, as the secretary of the local committee and everything went well. We had a memorable address from Gareth James, Aintree, on behalf of Hope in Action, at one of the public meetings. As usual, the ladies, under the guidance of Gwyneth Hemingway, with Olwen Jones and the members of the Executive Committee as helpers, prepared all the meals for members of the Association in our large schoolroom.

We had another opportunity, in the summer of 1989, to welcome the elderly of Toxteth and Dingle. This had now occurred every summer for twenty one years. The birthday cake looked well and was delicious to eat and the event was recorded as a video programme. We also welcomed BBC (Radio Cymru) on three occasions. The television producers, both

The fifth Dr Arthur Memorial Lecture, from left to right, Reverend Dr John Hughes, Dr D. Ben Rees, Mrs John Hughes, John Lyons, Mrs Nancy Hughes and Professor Aled G. Jones of Aberystwyth

Welsh and English, came to us at least a dozen times. This was the time that we began to consider adapting our chapel building to suit the needs of a new period. I wrote in our Annual Church Report for 1989 these words:

> There are difficult times on the horizon and we have met as elders to analyse the situation and to prepare a report on the history of the cause, which, in my opinion, should be published. We feel that we should publish as much as we can, of our Christian witness, and up until now we have realised that we need to adapt, venture and make our vision a reality.

As we shall see in the next chapter, ever since that time, we as leaders of the chapel, have been discussing these proposals, but until 2008 we have not yet succeeded in starting to develop our site along new lines.

In 1989, we received a visit from Pastor Ephraim M. Muthuri, an evangelist from Nairobi, Kenya, as we were supporting the 'Generating Hope in Action' project of a school and community centre. He stayed with our family for a week when he addressed meetings in Bethel and Birkenhead, but sad to say, we were disappointed in him. This came as a bitter blow as eventually we decided to break off all contact with the project. This was due to the fact that we now realised that we could not co-operate with any institution without complete honesty and with full confidence in those with whom we dealt. Instead, we took on another missionary challenge, this time to raise money for the Nurses' Project in Shillong Hospital, raising the generous total sum of £2336.15. This was just part of our generosity but along with others this placed Bethel Chapel, Heathfield Road, in the front rank of outgoing and responsive communities.

We lost a number of committed members during 1989, including Miss Winifred Ann Jones, 14 Calderstones Road, on 24 March; one of our treasurers, Thomas Meilir Owens, 12 Honiton Road, Aigburth, on 6 October; the quiet but kind Miss Mabel Williams, 34 Heydale Road, on 14 December; Miss Adeline Jones, 27 Kingsdale Road, one of the most devout of our members who had been brought up in the Chapel House of Chatham Street Chapel; and on 21 December, Evan Philip Price, Caldway Manor, one of the flock that came to us from Edge Lane Welsh Chapel. We valued the special Fund set up to commemorate all these good people; receiving £650.00 in memory of Winifred Jones; £775.00 in memory of Trevor Roberts, Belem Tower; £85.00 after the death of Miss Adeline Jones, and £4809.37 after Gwilym Arthur Jones, Trinidad, had died. In his earlier days he had been a member at Princes Road Chapel. Our membership at the end of the 1980s stood at 279 adults and 39 children. We had received five new members, but lost seven.

It was now literally impossible to hold our own as a chapel, as the decline in our membership was so evident year after year. We repaid £1000.00 to the Liverpool Presbytery but our debt remained at £4000.00. The payments for the year came to £34,390.35 and a large nucleus of our members were willing to work hard to raise the monies.

In 1990, for the first time in our history, we took the opportunity to welcome those of our own members who were disabled or confined by age and infirmity to their homes.

The broadcaster, Dei Thomas and Eryl Dooling of Bethel.

We brought them all together in the large schoolroom for a special dinner prepared by our ladies. The idea came from the Women's Fellowship and as a result £575.00 was transferred to chapel funds.

Among our losses in 1990 was Miss Doris Thomas, Allerton Road, one who laboured in our vineyard for decades. She died on 17 January and left £1000.00 to our Memorial Fund. On 24 May, Mrs. Elizabeth Bennion, Woolton, a native of the Llŷn Peninsula, died. Although she was unable to attend regularly, her interest in our chapel was fully evident. Mrs Olwen Williams, St. Michael's-in-the-Hamlet, was nearly blind and yet she coped remarkably well. She recognised my knock and would throw down the keys from her flat to me, when I visited her in Sandhurst Street. Another kind-hearted person was Mrs. Gwyneth Anne Evans, Woolton, and through my pastoral work, she became a member. For years she was a faithful attender of the Sunday night evening service until she started to fail physically. On 18 August we mourned the death of Miss Mary Jones, Kingsdale Road. She, also, left £1000.00 in her will to Bethel and a larger sum for the charity 'Generating Hope in Action'. I remember taking two of our elders to her home, when she was dying. They were all surprised to see that the only photograph in her room was that of her minister and the elders of Bethel. Literally we were her family on earth. It was a great privilege for me to place her ashes in Nercwys cemetery, near Mold, from where her family hailed. On 4 December, we lost John Alun Hughes, Romer Road, one of the great characters of the Liverpool Welsh community; and then on Christmas Day, Miss Hannah Jones, Parkfield Road, passed into glory. She had come

Carol singers from Bethel at the home of our eldest member, Miss Laura Jones, in Calderstones Road.

A record of a faithful family.

to Liverpool as a domestic maid but she remained in the City for the rest of her life, as did her sister Miss Mary Jones. She had been a maid in the home of Sir Douglas Crawford and his sisters, in Fernlea, Mossley Hill. She was well cared for by them to the end of her days, as was Miss Hannah Jones.

On 16 June, Mrs. Mary Boyle, Denman Drive, Newsham Park, only daughter of the Reverend Dr. Thomas Williams, Gwalchmai and Holyhead, died. Dr. Thomas Williams was a preacher of remarkable originality with a style all his own. His daughter, Mary Boyle, had been unfortunate in her marriage and she came to Liverpool from London after suffering abuse. For seventeen years she lodged in the Salvation Army Hostel in an old Welsh Independent Chapel in Netherfield Road. The Reverend E. Watkin Jones was in regular contact with her and, in time, she began to attend our Sunday morning services. This is where we met and she became part of our lives. A great deal of her father's originality and sincerity was to be found in his daughter. After seventeen years she had to seek another refuge and I well remember her asking for my assistance. The only place I could suggest for her was at Abbeyfield House, where there is care, at least one good meal a day prepared, and a warden to keep an eye on all the inhabitants of this home. I knew of a number of Abbeyfield Homes on Merseyside and I decided on the one in Denman Drive, Newsham Park. Her application for admission was successful. This was in 1982. The next problem was to find furniture for her room. Mrs. Mary Boyle had nothing except a large brown bag, which she always carried to chapel and everywhere else, and the clothes she wore. I asked my wife to have a word with our ladies in Bethel so that we could provide spoons and knives for her, the things we take for granted.

On 23 January, 1982, Mrs. Edith Evans, 41 Valescourt Road, Liverpool 12, died. She had been brought up in Douglas Road Welsh Chapel and lived at her home in West Derby. I had a word with her family, mentioned the circumstances and, in this way, I was able to arrange for Mary Boyle to have a bed at Abbeyfield Home, an armchair and other furniture to

Another gathering of Bethel members.

make her new home more comfortable than she had experienced since leaving her parents' home on Anglesey. She refused any extra help from social services besides her old age pension, and she contributed generously to our chapel. When she died at Sefton Hospital, I did not have any means to meet the cost of her funeral, but I need not have been concerned. I received a telephone call from the warden asking me to go to Abbeyfield Home in Denman Drive to go through her familiar big brown holder. We came across a bundle of notes, enough to clear the costs of her funeral. Mary Boyle, mentioned earlier, was one of the most humble, poverty-stricken Christians that I have ever met. Yet she was quite content with her world. When we speak of poverty in society, normally we think of relative poverty. But in the case of Mary Boyle, she had experienced real poverty as she did not think or expect the state to care for her at all. In actual fact, she had refused housing benefit, as she believed that the old age pension was sufficient for her needs. Mary Boyle had inherited quite different standards from those of some of her contemporaries.

1990 proved to be a very fruitful year. We had a large number of enriching meetings that emphasised our heritage, such as the address of the poet and academic, Jâms Niclas, who was a great speaker at our St. David's Dinner. Also, we enjoyed a remarkable lecture from an old school friend of mine at Tregaron, Dr. John Davies, Aberystwyth, author of the huge volume published in Welsh by Penguin on the history of our country and people. I sold ten copies of *Hanes Cymru* within the chapel community, and it still provides much insight, and since then there has been an English language edition.

For the first time, ever, we had the opportunity on 1 July to broadcast live on Radio 4, a morning service in English. We included one Welsh language hymn. The producer was Rhodri Prys Jones from the BBC at Bangor. He had produced a large number of services from our chapel and had given our chapel community wonderful opportunities. Rhodri was not at all well that morning in July and was very concerned that our members and the Liverpool Welsh Community might not turn out in sufficient numbers; and I understood his concern, as most of the service was to be through the medium of the English language. A Welsh language service is an attraction and encourages Welsh people to travel a long distance to attend for their enrichment. Nonetheless, a large congregation came along and we had a superb response. I received 120 letters, including one from a woman from Wallasey who had listened to the service in the heart of the French countryside. It was obviously an attraction that the service was broadcast immediately before the regular 'Letter from America' by the late Alistair Cook from New York.

A charming individual, Rhodri Prys Jones had a strong personal Christian faith. It was this that supported him when he was told in October 1990 that he was suffering from cancer. He died quietly on 15 February, 1991, at the early age of 43, leaving a widow and three sons.

It was good to have other opportunities. These included the special service that I prepared in memory of the first Welsh missionary, Thomas Jones (1810-1849), who left Liverpool for Khasia Hill on 25 November, 1840. Over one hundred years later, this was an opportunity to celebrate his missionary outset. A number of us recreated the saga in the parish Church of Our Lady and St Nicholas, Liverpool, which had been home-from-home for many of the early Welsh migrants. We also had the opportunity to give thanks for the life and work of Miss Laura Myfanwy Jones, Calderstones Road, who had reached her centenary – the first from the Welsh community of Bethel to do so. We praised God for her valuable contribution to the city. Two new persons were elected as elders, namely Mrs Nan Hughes Parry, Woolton, and W. Meiron Evans, Allerton; both had come to Liverpool from Caernarfonshire. Earlier, W. Meiron Evans had served as an elder in Garston Chapel.

The call to adapt the buildings came high on our agenda as elders. It was in 1990 that we decided to initiate new important discussions as to the future, when we invited an expert on this topic, David Kitton from Surrey, to join our discussions. He prepared a comprehensive report for us. This asked for creative decisions as he suggested that Bethel Chapel should be kept as a place of worship in partnership with the English Methodist Church of Elm Hall Drive across the busy Allerton Road; and that we should make greater use of the joint facilities. But Elm Hall Drive Methodist Church felt unable to accept David Kitton's recommendations.

Since three of our officers were members of the Rotary Club of Toxteth, in 1990 we decided to hold a carol concert in our chapel. With the co-operation of our organist, Margaret Anwyl Williams, I introduced the carols while one of the Toxteth Rotarians, John Thornton or the Reverend Bob Metcalfe, led the singing. I contacted the local schools in the area and invited them to participate and this new event proved to be a refreshing success.

We saw horrible scenes on our television screens in 1991: violence from continuing conflicts, in particular the Gulf War in Iraq, the abuse suffered by ordinary people in Albania and Romania, and the decision of our Government to allow supermarkets and stores to desecrate the uniqueness of Sunday. The positive aspects include the break up of the Soviet Empire and that, we as a Christian community, were still witnessing and welcoming people among us as speakers and preachers.

Many of our members supported the National Eisteddfod of Wales when it came to Mold in the summer of 1991. As a result of that occasion, we set up a Welsh Library in co-operation with the Clwyd County Library, mainly through the vision of Dr. Pat Williams. We were delighted with the outcome and this new venture has served the Sunday School and the Literary Society.

The General Assembly of the Presbyterian Church of Wales was convened in Liverpool in 1991, all the arrangements being the responsibility of the Lancashire and Cheshire Presbytery. All the meetings were held near us at St. Catherine's College, Childwall, part of what is now the Liverpool Hope University. We welcomed the Young People's Assembly to our own premises for a dinner on the Sunday before the proceedings began and this met with a great response. In this Assembly it was decided not to vote on candidates to be the next Moderator but instead to invite Dr. R. Arthur Hughes, OBE, to become the Moderator for 1992-1993. He and his supportive wife, Nancy Hughes, carried out a large number of engagements during his year of office, but some of the long journeys that he made to south Wales and to London brought on angina attacks which concerned all of us.

The elders and members of Garston Welsh Chapel decided to unite with us on the first Sunday in 1992, after I had served as a minister with them for fifteen years. This meant

Dr D. Ben Rees and Mrs M. Rees and their two sons at the celebration.

The celebration of 25 years as Minister in Heathfield Road and Bethel, (left to right) Dafydd Rees, Meinwen Rees, D. Ben Rees and His Honour John Edward Jones.

Celebrating with the Sunday School.

Mrs Beryl Williams thanking the Minister and his wife on behalf of the Sunday School.

that I now conducted morning and evening services every first and third Sunday in the month at Bethel and the service at Garston in the afternoon. We succeeded in getting most of the members to become members at Bethel but it was necessary for me to make regular visits to Garston during 1991 before this took place. Some were considering joining other Welsh Chapels in south Liverpool but I succeeded in ensuring that all those who wanted Welsh services should come to Bethel. A few, including one elder from Garston opted for English language services.

But unity, I thought, should be unity for all members. This is a difficult concept. On the same Sunday, union also took place between the chapels of Stanley Road, Bootle, and Crosby Road South, Waterloo. Within a year, at the beginning of 1993, I was inducted minister of that united church at Bethania and Bethel, which entailed visits to Welsh people throughout the whole of the city of Liverpool and Sefton Council area, extending from Southport to Widnes.

Throughout my ministry I have always arranged pilgrimages. During 1991, I arranged one to the cradle of our Connexion, to the Lay Centre at Trefeca, near Talgarth, and then on to Pantycelyn, near Llandovery, on the road to Brecon, the farmhouse, which was the home of our greatest hymn writer, William Williams. We stayed the night in Trefeca, then visited Pantycelyn, and on the way home we stayed for tea at Gregynog Hall near Newtown. As we stood in the cemetery of the Parish Church of Talgarth on a fine Saturday morning listening to Trefeca Lay Centre's Warden describing the life of Howell Harris preaching in 1735 and how William Williams, the student from Pantycelyn had been brought to full salvation, I felt that the hymn writer had been very near the mark when he said that there is no more time to rest for long as we have a glorious responsibility to proclaim the good news of the New Testament to our generation.

Among the christenings in 1991, we had the opportunity of presenting Hannah Mair Thompson and Aimee Fay Johnson, Tuebrook, who have been loyal to the Sunday School and our community ever since. Also christened were Hannah Parsons of Aigburth, Cicely Catrin Blacklow-Jones, the daughter of Mr. and Mrs. Richard Blacklow-Jones, Hereford, and later Haverfordwest.

The funerals held during the year brought a great deal of *hiraeth*. We lost Harold Owen, Llanddeusant, Anglesey, a stockbroker by profession, who had been a member at Princes Road Chapel before he came to our community: R. Goronwy Jones, Cleveley Park, Allerton, who thought that no chapel in the world was like the chapel of his childhood in Anfield, namely Bethlehem, Douglas Road; and

A willing hand.

Trevor Rees, Orrell, who used to visit every hospital in Liverpool to see Welsh patients and who had strong connections with Barmouth, a place he visited regularly. We lost David Tegid Griffith's wife, Gwendoline Kate Griffiths, and her funeral was held in Barmouth. She was quiet and charming as was Miss D. Jones, Llandudno Junction, and Mrs. Olwen Batty, Heswall. Losing all these members weakened our community and, at the end of 1991, we had 259 members at Bethel and 47 children. Then, on Saturday 5 January, we welcomed eleven new members from Garston Chapel, which included Eiluned and D. Emlyn Davies, Riverbank Road, who had enjoyed real fellowship at Bethel for years before they became members. She had been a nursing sister, extremely popular for her kindness and care for others, especially for her friend from the Welsh Independent Chapel at Woolton Road, Mrs. Myfanwy Diggory, Wavertree. Eiluned and Emlyn Davies were kind to many of us and they were delighted at the union of Bethel and Garston.

An enthusiastic elder in Garston was Trefor W. Griffith and his wife, Mrs. Mari Griffith, as well as his sister-in-law, Miss Megan Jones, who had been nurtured from childhood in the fellowship of the Welsh Chapel. They all retained perfect command of their spoken Welsh. At Basing Street in Garston lived G. R. Jones and his wife, Mrs. M. Jones, both natives of Anglesey. Eric H. Thomas, Goleufryn, was the son of an elder, and a builder and I well remember his mother Mrs. Thomas celebrating her centenary. She lived for another four years. Her daughter-in-law, Mrs. Margaret Thomas, cared for her diligently and, until failing health,

Ieuan Care and Elin Roberts.

attended regularly our morning service. Miss Gwladys Williams and her late brother, Robert P Williams, of Booker Avenue, Allerton, were always proud of their roots in Garston Chapel but very willing to adapt to the new situation when their chapel amalgamated with Bethel.

In 1993 I celebrated twenty-five years as minister in Liverpool, and I compared the situation then with that which I had experienced when I first came to Liverpool in 1968. What was still common in 1968 and 1993? What were the activities associated with the children and their teachers in the Sunday School and *Y Gorlan*? Back in 1968 one could never have envisaged that we would have made so much effort on behalf of Welsh children in 1992. In some respects more was done for our children in 1992 than in 1968.

I had argued constantly that Siôn Corn should give out Welsh books at our annual party. This suggestion was never given any support until the 1990s when this policy was finally adopted under the guidance of a team which included

Beryl Williams, Siân Hartley, Helen Wyn Jones and Mair Roberts, some of our young mothers. The support to 'Hope in Action' confirmed the quality of the new generation and their support for the school in Nairobi, Kenya was admirable.

In 1968 we offered opportunities to put service before self in our effort to entertain the elderly from the underprivileged areas of Toxteth and Dingle. Another example was to revive our carol singing traditions that had ceased in 1960. Significant changes occurred amongst the chapel's officers between 1968 and 1992. Out of the forty names on the list of chapel officers and the personnel of the societies in 1968, only seven were still listed in 1992 but several new faces were now included.

1992 proved to be another year of losses in our ranks. We were very disturbed on 2 February with the news of the sudden death of one of our most enthusiastic members, Gwilym M. Jones, at Ness, near Neston. We felt deep sympathy for his wife, Mrs. Gwerfyl Jones, and their sons, Gwyn and Huw. Gwyn had been a faithful member of my Welsh Adult Learning Class. We also lost Ifan Jones, Broadgreen, an organist at Bethel. Another loss was that of the chapel caretaker, W. J. Jones, Queensdale Road, who had been wounded in the Second World War and who had served with a battalion of the Liverpool Welsh Regiment. Another loss was that of Miss Mary Jones, Park Avenue, mentioned earlier, when I referred to her sister, Hannah Jones; another was Mrs. M. Roberts, the widow of Morus O. Roberts who had moved from Barndale Road, Allerton, to Arnold, in Nottinghamshire, to be near her daughter. Another death was that of Mrs. N. C. Williams, Quarry Street, Woolton, who had been so welcoming in her lifetime and so courageous in her suffering at the end. She was related to

Rhys Jones, Prestatyn and his concert party.

*Dannie Absie who came to Bethel
to read his poetry.*

the musician T. Gwynn Jones of Llanfairfechan, who came regularly to adjudicate in our eisteddfodau.

Another big change concerns the falling number of students attending our chapel. Back in 1969 there were dozens of them: the back seats of the chapel were full of students every Sunday evening. The numbers of students attending have not ceased altogether and we welcomed Ms. Rachel Gooding as an Ecumenical Chaplain to the Liverpool Welsh. She has had the difficult task of recruiting Welsh language students to our ranks. This seems to have been one of our most disappointing changes in the 1990s compared to the 1960s. It seems that Welsh-speaking students now prefer to enrol in the colleges of the University of Wales rather than in Liverpool University.

Our leaders have been determined to meet all our responsibilities. His Honour Judge John Edward Jones became Moderator of the Merseyside Free Church Federal Council while I accepted, for the third time, the task of being chairman of the Mossley Hill Group of Churches. We had an induction service followed by six meetings dealing with training, cultural events, as well as a service of thanksgiving for the effective stewardship of Edward Goronwy Owen, Calderstones, as an elder in our district since 1952.

In 1992 the family of John and Margaret Clement-Evans, Ullet Road, left for Flintshire and we also expressed our gratitude to the Reverend Robin Wyn Griffith, Stand Park Road, Childwall, and his wife Joyce, when they moved to live at Llangybi, near Pwllheli.

The summer of 1993 was an unforgettable experience when I celebrated twenty-five years in the ministry in south Liverpool. We celebrated on Sunday morning, 4 July, in the company of the children and the young people. We enjoyed a dinner at the Anchorage, near the Holiday Inn in the centre of Liverpool on Saturday 10 July. The celebratory service on Sunday 11 July was inspiring, followed by refreshments, prepared in the schoolroom. My wife, Meinwen, was desperately ill for fourteen weeks in Broadgreen Hospital during the year but she gradually recovered her strength after her operation. I was so grateful to the hospital and the prayers of our people for her recovery and for the kindness that we received from our friends in the churches and in Liverpool and Wales.

On 13 July 1993, I arranged a bus from Liverpool to the General Assembly held in Birmingham to hear the Valedictory Address of the Moderator, Dr. R. Arthur Hughes. Our secretary, H. Wyn Jones, was elected Moderator of the Presbytery for 1994 and I had the honour of being made Moderator of the North Wales Association in May 1994. In 1993 we established a Strategy and Stewardship Committee which has been extremely valuable. Four years had gone by since we first began discussing our strategy for the future at Bethel, back in September 1989.

We had severe losses in our ranks as a chapel in 1993. Dr. Idris Owen, Menlove Avenue, died after had just retired as a medical practitioner in the Edge Lane/Kensington area. He had been our family doctor and he felt a great concern for all members of our family. One of our members, Mrs. Cissie Lewis, Green Lane, used to tell me that she would never have lived to a grand old age without the caring ministry of Dr. Owen. Miss Megan Jones, Garston, died on 2 December 1993, and we had happy memories of her commitment to the Welsh Church in Chapel Road. Laura Geshen, Reedale Road, was one of the children of Heathfield Road, but Mrs. E. Gratton Thomas, Woolton Road, came to us from Anfield Welsh Chapel. She was so likeable and always invited us to sing carols at her home. One of the effective workers in our chapel was Mrs. Rhiannon Williams, Karslake Road, who was extremely popular with everyone. She nurtured two sons and a daughter, while at the same time caring for students who lodged in her home.

There were seven christenings during the year but only one, Lucy Ann Thompson, became a member of our Sunday School. This happens sometimes; circumstances and legitimate reasons prevent the children who have been christened from following in the footsteps that we hoped they would follow. On 11 September, Gaynor Clitherow, Kensington, married Steven Hunt at Bethel, and they came to live in Allerton; we are fortunate that they have stayed in the city.

At the end of this period (1986-1995) we were still involved with developing our strategy for the future. The Development Committee, as it was called at that time, met at least three times with Dr. John

Mr J. H. Thomas, Heswall, Mrs Nan Lewis, Litherland and Mr Arthur Edwards, Bethel being acknowledged for their contribution to the Songs of Praise.

Jane Jones, Evelyn Griffiths, Megan Lewis, Nan H. Parry and Dr Pat Williams.

G. Williams as its convenor. A sub-committee was established to meet a company of architects to clarify objectives and prepare a report. I also established a research unit called North-East India Wales Trust, with the project of preparing two dictionaries of biographies with entries on all those Welsh men and women who had served our Church in India. We welcomed the initiative that arose from within the Welsh Council of Churches for Liverpool and District. It was suggested that we at Bethel, and the Welsh Methodists of Central Hall, Liverpool, should worship together from January 1995 onwards. The Welsh Methodist Church under its minister, the Reverend E. Gwyn Hughes, came to our chapel from Renshaw Street. The two chapels kept their own identities but we now began to worship together on a Sunday and on week nights. A number of items were moved from Central Hall. These included a wooden cross, which bound us together as Christians and this was set up on the wall of our small schoolroom. It was a pleasure to work with the Reverend E. Gwyn Hughes, until he left the city. During his time in Liverpool he gave ten Sundays a year to our joint congregations.

Towards the end of this period, we acknowledged the massive contributions of Dr. R. Arthur Hughes, over a period of fifty years, to the Presbyterian family in Shillong and as a conscientious elder in Liverpool. One of our young people, Helen Hughes Jones, Broadgreen was married on 16 April 1994, to Richard Charles Tait, and the family now live in the Cardiff area, with their children learning the Welsh language at school to the delight of their grandmother in Liverpool. We again lost faithful members of our community including the

*Gravestone of
Mr John Davies and
Mrs Pugh Davies*

Mrs Janet Green and Edna Jones, Chapel House

medical practitioner, Dr. Tudur Glyn Thomas, Gateacre, who did so much good work in the inner city. Dr. Thomas passed to glory on 27 March 1994. Then, on 23 April, 1994, Mrs. Mary Margaret Powell, the widow of the late Reverend R. J. Powell, minister of the Welsh Chapel in Garston died, followed by D. Emlyn Davies, Riverbank Road, Grassendale, on 24 November, a benefactor of the first order. We also lost Hugh C. Hughes, Aigburth, a pharmacist and brother of Miss Olwen Hughes, Edge Lane and later Bootle. Katie Lloyd Davies, Broadgreen, originally from Edge Lane Chapel had been great friends with Olwen Hughes, Ceridwen Williams and, that most remarkable person of all, Elsie Grace Parry, West Allerton. The three used to meet every week in the city. Elsie Parry's brother was in the ministry. He was the Reverend Meic Parry. Amongst our members no-one was more faithful, until she had to enter a residential old people's home in Mossley Hill. She lived to see her hundredth birthday and her family honoured her memory by making a generous donation to our chapel. We lost, through death, Mrs. Gwen Garner, Cleveley Road, Allerton, who had a great affection for her childhood chapel of Fitzclarence Street in Everton. Mrs. Meira Howell Hughes was the wife of the surgeon, John Howell Hughes, and had suffered a long and difficult illness. Mrs. Hughes had been very heavily involved with the missionary work of the Welsh Presbyterians in India. She and Doris Thomas, of Allerton, had been the leaders in these endeavours. It was sad, also, to lose Mrs Mair Parry, Score Lane, Childwall, who knew a great deal about the saga of the Liverpool Welsh. Mrs. Jane Mathias, Allerton, had always been in Princes Road Chapel, as well as Bethel, from 1976 and was one of the most efficient organisers we ever had in our annual Christmas Fayres. In her last year as organiser, we made a profit of £825.00. It was an excellent boost to our funds. Mrs. Jane Mathias had been a very effective infant and primary headmistress for years in the private sector of education. I always admired Mrs. Hannah Williams, mother of Glenys Daniels who, in her professional life as a nurse in Liverpool, had a deep concern for all her patients. She hailed from Rhosesmor in Flintshire, and it was always a delight to visit her and her family in Centreville Rod. This was true of Mrs. Margaret Kilgour in Arranmore Road, for she had brought up a family that honoured the Saviour. She left the village of Trefor in Caernarfonshire to work in Birmingham at the age of thirten; then she moved to Liverpool three years later and stayed with us until her death in her early nineties. The funeral was in her home village and I travelled there with thanksgiving in my heart for her long and useful service. Our last member to be mourned in 1994 was Miss Dilys Hughes, who lived very near to our chapel, in a comfortable flat at 12 Heathfield Road. She loved attending the Sunday morning services. These were the members of the family of faith who died in 1994 and as a result we had in our Memorial Fund a total of £1500.00.

Contributions also came in remembrance of Laura Myfanwy Jones, Mary M. Powell, Hannah Williams, Gwen Garner and David Emlyn Davies. All these donations have help ed safeguard and sustain the cause in the 21st century. A number of friends, besides our members have been kind to the chapel. One of them was Mrs. Laura Edwards, Roby. Ever since I officiated at the funeral of her husband, a Welshman, this lady of German-Jewish background has been generous in her donations to our chapel. I used to visit her in Wyndham Avenue every Christmas, after seeing one of our members, Mrs. Ceridwen Jones, in Trent Avenue, who lived nearby. For a quarter of a century she never forgot us at Bethel and she used to express her gratitude for the pastoral concern that she had received from me personally.

Margaret and Hywel Heulyn Roberts.

Also, during this period, Huw Thomas, of the John Moores University was a regular attender who never forgot our chapel. The son of a remarkable Welsh Independent minister, he never forgot his roots and was an excellent ecumenicalist. Another academic, who is still a faithful attender, is Professor Huw Rees, of the University of Liverpool, President of the Liverpool Welsh Choral Union.

Two faithful families left us at the end of 1994: namely Dr. Glyn Roberts, Aigburth, and his wife Mrs. Ceinwen Roberts, on moving to Llangefni and Gwynfryn and Laura Williams, who moved from Gateacre to Chwilog near Pwllheli. We enjoyed many years of service, co-operation and fellowship from these two families.

Nevertheless, even after considering all these losses, we remained active in every way – locally, in our own area, in the life of the city and in meeting the needs of Welsh people generally, including those within the Connexion. Our premises continued to be used for the needs of the local community on Saturdays and on week nights. However, the behaviour of some children and young people in the area, whose behaviour leaves much to be desired, has remained a continuing problem. During a half term week in 1995, eighteen of our windows were broken. A number of these windows were in the main chapel, and this has disturbed us because it seemed to be a form of persecution of our faith. We had to insert protective covers over the windows in the small schoolroom. During this period we were in discussion with a company of developers concerning the site and buildings.

During 1995, we retained our strong bond with the Merseyside Free Church Federal Council and with the Council of Christians and Jews. It was good to see our large schoolroom full on a beautiful evening in June, when we welcomed to our midst Rabbi Hugo Greyn from London, who reminded us of his awful experiences in the concentration camp at Auschwitz and how he was able to survive the Holocaust. We continued to support a large number of charities and organisations including 'Hope in Action', The Samaritans, Family Link, the Gideons and the Whitechapel Project (which helps homeless people on Merseyside during the Christmas period). Also, throughout 1995 we supported, through the initiative of the Sunday School, the Zoe Centre in West Derby. This was the first centre of its kind in Britain to care for seriously ill babies in the first two years of their life. It gave us pleasure to make a donation of £210 to this worthy cause.

In addition, our buildings were in constant use to accommodate Welsh classes for adults, as well as children. We revived the Welsh Kindergarten on Monday mornings, we welcomed the cameras of S4C on a number of occasions and it was here that the TV programme *Grawnsypiau Canaan,* was filmed. This singing festival occurred on 24 October and it was very much an inspiring event. Messages from viewers came from near and far. During that broadcast I made good use of the booklet, the first hymn book published in Liverpool in 1795 that I have compiled and edited.

As far as the Connexion was concerned, we carried out everything that had been recommended to us by the General Assembly. In September, we again extended a warm welcome, in the name of the Liverpool Welsh and Manchester Presbyteries, to the North Wales Association to convene its Synod in our buildings.

There were two weddings in Bethel in 1995. On 14 January, Dr. Bethan Wyn Jones and Hefin Ednyfed Rees, both christened and accepted from the Communicants' Class as members in the same year, were married. This is a somewhat rare event these days. It was a memorable day and the Liverpool Welsh Choral Union (the Welsh section of the Liverpool Choral Union) attended the service and added an extra dimension to the happiness of the occasion. On 15 April, 1995, Jennifer Ann Clitherow and David Michael Hughes were married at Bethel, but, during the reception, David was taken ill and rushed to hospital where he remained in a poor condition for some days. We prayed, fervently, for them both, and their families; and we all rejoiced when he finally recovered.

We lost six members during 1995. These included Mrs. Ann Hughes, who had been living for some years in Thorburn Road, New Ferry, from where she had a splendid view of Liverpool across the River Mersey. Mrs. Catherine Ellen Jones, Granard Road, the mother of Aerwyn, who took such great care of her, also died. Her roots were in a slate quarrying family in the Llanberis area. Another person who passed away was David Tegid Griffiths, Alexandra Green. He had a Liverpool-Welsh background, but he was without any family and I made all the arrangements for his funeral. Tegid who was laid to rest in the cemetery of Barmouth, remembered Bethel Chapel, as well as Tegid Chapel at Bala, in his will. Why Capel Tegid, Bala? Tegid's father had worked on the building of this chapel, and this is how he met the woman who became his wife, a lass from Llangywair, and mother of David Tegid. Tegid had a remarkable memory for recalling particular sermons, as well as preachers. In some regards he was similar in outlook to Sergeant William Jones, mentioned earlier in this book. On 28

(left to right) Joyce Lewington, Glenys Johnson, Meinwen Rees, Elan Jones and Beryl Williams.

November, 1995, William Kyffin Pritchard, died. He was a native of Amlwch and a staunch Anglican until he became a member of our church, together with his daughter, Glenys. He was extremely supportive, always ready with his wit and comments, but grateful to Welsh Presbyterianism, which he praised at all times. Hywel Roberts, Hunts Cross, was another who died in 1995. During his long illness he received much loving care from his wife, Blodwen, who still remains faithful to our services. At the end of the year, on 28 December, we heard of the passing away of Mrs. Agnes Mary Davies, a native of Ammanford. She came to Liverpool when her husband joined the Liverpool Police Force. She never lost her Amman Valley accent and our conversations often talked about her home town that I know so well.

At the end of 1996, our membership stood at 227 with 48 children in our community. Only two new members had joined us during the year and we lost nine. The usual support, from Welsh speaking people moving into Liverpool, that we have depended upon, was slowly disappearing, after two hundred years of continuous immigration. Our members were being weakened on two fronts: many young people, nurtured in our community, moved away from Liverpool after completing their higher education. Examples include John Cenrick Clement-Evans who moved to Cardiff in 1995, to be a solicitor and he is now active with the United Reformed Church. He was only one of many. Others include Mrs. Gwyneth Struthers, daughter of Mr. and Mrs. John Williams, Barndale Road, who moved away, after the passing of her parents, to Kelsall in Cheshire, and Mrs, M.B. Ward, Chapel house, who moved to Astley in Manchester. The second front on which losses occurred was the inevitable death of our members, which occurs unremittingly year by year. But God, who foresees all things, is aware that a 'remnant will survive', a penitent few like the living stump or a fallen tree. I have been very much aware of this the longer I have stayed as minister of Bethel Chapel, Heathfield Road in Liverpool.

Dr Rees at Bodffordd, Anglessey. The photo also includes Ceinwen and Dr Glyn Roberts (late of Bethel) ¸ Llangefni.

Elin, Aimée, Aled, Dewi, Lisa and Ieuan.

Siôn Morris

Outside Bethel, (left to right) Miss Dilys Griffith, Mrs Edna Jones, Miss Megan Lewis, Mrs Eirlys Williams and Mrs Nan Evans (of Garston Welsh Chapel).

Ramilies Road Schoolroom after its first adaptation.

The entrance to Bethel Chapel.

Glory be to God the giver.

Bethel Chapel with its pulpit and organ.

The splendid wood of the pews.

Away with our fears! The wall above the gallery which has given us distress for 40 years and we still have not eradicated the dampness.

Reverend W. Bryn Williams, Rhys and Genni Williams and the minister.

Olwen Jones and the Welsh paper that used to be printed in her native town of Caernarfon.

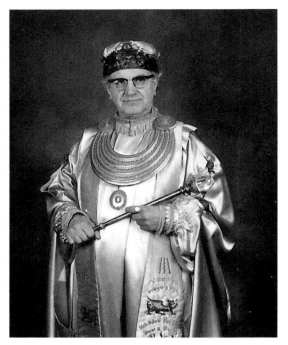

W. R. P. George, Cricieth (nephew of David Lloyd George) Guest Speaker at our St David's Supper at Bethel.

Reverend W. J. Gruffydd, Tregaron, who preached at Bethel. A poet and an Archdruid.

Hefin Rees evangelising in a slum town near Nairobi, Kenya.

Glenys Johnson with her daughter Aimée and her friends after a service where Aimée, as a candidate for membership was accepted into the fellowship of the Church.

Alun Hartley, Hywel Care, Sara Williams, Angharad Care and Ffion Evans with the Minister who prepared them for membership at Bethel.

Chapter 14

EXPECTATIONS OF A NEW CHAPEL BUILDING (1996-2007)

The idea of a new building for our church has been one of our greatest desires over the years. We need a smaller building to welcome the new millennium and a new century. After persuading the General Assembly at Lampeter in July 1996 that the denomination needed a full time Estates Manager for the Connexion, we co-operated with E. James and Mark Davies, the newly appointed officer to this post, as we considered all the options.

In the summer of 1996, we heard that the developers saw no hope of adapting our present buildings and thus it was important for us to take a new initiative. So, in co-operation with the Properties Board, we invited two architects to discuss, with us, possibilities for the future. Both gave clear guidelines on which to proceed. We discussed their suggestion with the Development Committee and subsequently H. Wyn Jones and Dr. J. G. Williams outlined the developing situation to our congregation on Sunday night, 8 December 1996. Unanimous support was given for us to move forward, and so we instructed the architects to prepare a report by April 1997. We also explored possible avenues for financial help. Our aim was to complete the whole project by the middle of 2000.

R. Ifor Griffith and the Bethel Mixed Choir.

The Côr Adrodd of Bethel at the National Eisteddfod of Wales in Caernarfon, 1979.
Always competitors at the Merseyside Eisteddfod.

Arthur Edwards

In the meantime, as a community, we were heavily involved in charitable projects and we reached the goal of collecting £1627.00 for the hospitals of North-East India. We handed over this sum to Mrs. Menna Green, Y Bala, in a meeting at our chapel in June 1977. Also, at this meeting, we thanked Ms. Rachel Gooding for four years' ministry as Chaplain to the Merseyside Welsh. In her place we were fortunate to appoint, as her successor Miss Eleri Edwards, who had been a Missionary in Madagascar for nineteen years. Within a short period of time, she became an integral part of our community and fulfilled her ministry with zeal and dedication.

The community remained enthusiastic on behalf of the Welsh language, organising the Liverpool and District Eisteddfod, all of it a labour of love by the young mothers and fathers of our chapel in supervising outdoor activities, as well

The deterioration of the wall in the gallery.

as the Young People's Circles in our large schoolroom. For these purposes we revived a committee, which had been redundant since the inter-war years, including a specialist music panel, which was a good move. So much of our life focuses on music: the choir, conducted by R. Ifor Griffith: the annual singing festival, the Sunday School Festival, carol singing at Christmas time, hymns in the Sunday services and on week nights. We fully appreciate the commitment of our music experts and we are well served by Arthur Edwards, Aigburth, who for years was an organist at the Welsh Chapel in Garston. Others involved included Mrs. Rhiannon Liddell, daughter of the Manse, whose father, the Reverend David Poole, had close connections with the Welsh on the Wirral; Mrs. Margaret Anwyl Williams and Mrs. Eryl Dooling, Rainhill, both schoolteachers, and the young schoolboy, Rhys Williams. In 1996, he and his friend, Gareth Roberts, became full members of our church, fruit of the Sunday School and homes where the life of the chapel has had a priority. In many respects, the Sunday School remains something of a handmaiden to the chapel. The promise is still there, and at the chapel's 1997 Christmas party, I counted 48 babies, children, and young Welsh people there that particular evening. We were grateful for the co-operation of those who had joined us from the Methodist chapel and their faith in me by inviting me to be their pastor.

On a personal note, I appreciated the strong support evident at the meeting held at Bethel to present me with a volume that I had written which had been published by Gwasg Gee of Denbigh under the title *Pregethu a Phregethwyr [Preaching and Preachers]*. Emlyn

The Minister's Room.

Evans and Alun Williams from Gwasg Gee came to Liverpool and the meeting was an enjoyable and widely appreciated event.

During the year we lost very well known spiritual leaders, Dr. R. Arthur Hughes and Hugh John Jones, two of our elders. We valued all their advice and leadership and their conversations with us were inspiring.

Our strategy for a new chapel building remained high on the agenda of our Elders' Meetings every month during 1997 when we created a Steering Committee as a backing to the architect, John Hughes from Rhosllanerchrugog. This steering Committee met to discuss, exchange ideas, and propose schemes and we were extremely grateful to it for supporting us as trustees. The long-awaited report eventually came into our hands and both churches met in July. The report was an exciting one, ambitious but costly to implement. We expressed our gratitude to John Hughes, but, at the same time, we were concerned about likely reactions, within a denomination well known for its conservatism. Indeed, we felt overwhelmed by the task of collecting adequate finance to ensure that we could adapt the site and the arrangement to link us to different centres throughout Wales. In our meeting with them in September 1997, the scheme was welcomed by Eurfyl James, the Estates Manager, and by the Reverend Dafydd H. Owen from Cardiff, the General Secretary of the Presbyterian Church of Wales. Following this, we had more meetings in which we reconsidered the whole scheme.

We made a superb contribution with Hand in Hand Appeal, the fund in the name of Christian Aid. We doubled our initial goal when the final sum collected came to £2,222.00. Within our chapel, Rhys Williams was extremely effective as secretary of the appeal, as was Mrs. Nan Hughes Parry, the liaison officer for the Merseyside Welsh Chapels.

Another important event was the publication of two volumes, one in Welsh, *Cymry Lerpwl a'r Cyffiniau,* and the other in English, *The Welsh of Merseyside,* both written by myself. They sold well.

We received three young people as full members of the Church from the Communicants' Class, namely Bethan Evans, Allerton; Jennie Hartley and Alun Roberts. Conversely, we lost seven members from our community, Hamlet Hughes, Allerton, the pharmacist; Wallace Price Jones, Woolton, the cultured teacher from Llangoed, Anglesey; Oswald Thomas, Speke, one of the children of Heathfield Road Chapel, and John Trevor Jones, at Dartington near Totnes in Devon, the son of a remarkable Welsh builder; Herbert Evans who kept a bicycle shop in Anfield, and two mothers, Mrs. Sylvia Jones Williams, Montclair Drive, who brought Roy, Hazel, Pamela and William into full fellowship of our chapel, and Mrs. Leah Kenrick Clement-Evans, Woolton, who came from a notable family in the Liverpool Welsh community and had been an elder in Eglwys y Drindod, as well as Bethel. Her three sons, John, Edward and Basil meant so much to her.

Two members who had been supportive and friendly also left our chapel, John Lyn Jones, Hoylake, and John Gwyndaf Richards, Wavertree. John Lyn Jones travelled frequently from Hoylake to our services when he was Deputy Director of Education for Liverpool and we never had anyone more grateful for the services and the preaching. John Gwyndaf Richards, who by now was living in his native area of Montgomeryshire, requested that he should be relieved of the responsibilities of being an elder. On 19 October, 2006, he was ordained as a minister with the Welsh Congregationalists in Llanfyllin and in 2007 he began serving as a minister in north Montgomeryshire, caring for twenty three chapels belonging to the Presbyterian Church of Wales, Welsh Methodists and the Congregationalists. We held a special meeting in 1996 to wish his wife Eirlys, and their children, Anwen, Angharad and John Alwyn, every blessing. We also felt the loss of Miss Meirwen Hughes and Miss Margaret (Maxi) Roberts, when they both moved from Allerton to live at Rhosmeirch, near Llangefni.

As a church in 1998, we remained mindful of our heritage and our determination to consider every aspect of our community. We collected towards the Alder Hey Children's Hospital, £364.00 towards the floods in Bangladesh and £800.00 for the needs of Nicaragua and Honduras in Central America, a great deal of it having been received in memory of one of our most committed members, Mrs. Marian Owen, Tegfan, Calderstones. We received a contribution of £1,000.00 in memory of Marian from her husband, E. Goronwy Owen, and her sons, Hywel, Robert and Aled. We thanked them for taking this opportunity of commemorating Marian, in a way that she, as one of our most enthusiastic communicants, would have desired.

Having the company of Euryn Roberts, Childwall, one of the leaders of the Welsh Methodist community, in our monthly meetings of the elders and minister was indeed, encouraging and useful. The future of our chapel building remained one of the priorities on our agenda in our last meeting of 1998. We were still considering future possibilities and spent time in the company of the architect, Jonathan Pritchard, whose office was in Merton Road, Bootle. Time waits on none of us and that is a fact which we realised during that year. Four of those, whose support had been consistent and wholehearted for the new chapel, died during the year. I have named one already, Mrs. Eunice Marian Owen, Calderstones. The others were Mrs. Gwen Owen, the widow of Dr. Idris Owen and the mother of Siân Barker; and His Honour John Edward Jones, an elder since 1947 and a most influential person within our community. Death struck again when we lost our caretaker, D. Elwyn Jones, Chapel House. He had many ideas as to possible future developments for us. It was only he, and his wife, Edna, who were fully aware of all the hours that I spent within the walls of Bethel meeting various people to discuss what could be done to have a brand new home for God's people which would serve for decades.

1998 was an interesting year. We had the opportunity of welcoming coaches from Wales on Saturdays, and sometimes on Sundays, to visit the interesting places associated with the Welsh in the City of Liverpool. Visitors came from Anglesey, from the Conwy Valley and from Clwyd, as well as from the Chester Welsh community. I reckoned that over five hundred people visited our buildings at Bethel, the majority to join in fellowship over a meal prepared by a small group of our ladies and then to receive the blessing of a Welsh religious service in the land of *hiraeth* and exile. These visits have increased over the last ten years and have provided interesting experiences for many and enhanced love of our city. This aspect of our Welshness needs to be mentioned at the end of the twentieth century.

In the last year of the century I had to face two experiences that have never left me: my health and strength deteriorated and my mother died. As one who had been blessed with great physical strength throughout my ministry, it was a dismal experience to be unable to walk to a service or to concentrate on a piece of academic work week after week. Losing my health was an experience that will remain with me for ever. I found our Sunday School trip to York on the Saturday hard going. The following day I had to travel over a hundred miles one way to preach at Seilo Chapel in Caernarfon at the 10.00 a.m. service. The following Wednesday was a day of rejoicing as we celebrated my mother's hundredth birthday at home in Llanddewibrefi. A week later the doctor at the Cardiothoracic Hospital in Liverpool told me that I had three months to live, at the most, if I did not have a heart by-pass operation. The National Health Service was at its best. The operation was undertaken and a quadruple heart by-pass operation was carried out within three days of the decision taken. Afterwards, I spent two full days in intensive care at the hospital but I have no recollection of that. I shared my experiences with my chapel members and it was good to do so, as my experience might be of help to other Welsh speakers:

1.   The need for spirituality, which comes from our heritage. When the individual is too weak to read, the only alternative he has is to recite to himself the Lord's Prayer, the prayer of the heart, and the prayers of love and faith, most of them derived from the hymns of

William Williams, Pantycelyn; Robert ap Gwilym Ddu; Pedr Fardd (Peter Jones, Liverpool) and W. Rhys Nicholas.

2.　　I greatly valued my family and friends; the human family of kith and kin and God's family of fellow members.

3.　　I finally appreciated the concerns experienced by others in their letters and cards. A simple ministry but effective and the letters and cards (over twelve hundred of them) were a great comfort to me during heart by-pass surgery and during the period of losing my mother on 14 October. I thank the leaders and members of our chapel who travelled from Liverpool to be at her funeral on a stormy, wet Saturday in Llanddewibrefi. It was 23 October 1999, a day when I was almost too weak to leave the Chapel Vestry for my childhood home of Nythfa, Llanddewibrefi.

4.　　I experienced many deeds of love and good community care. All of it proved to be just as good a tonic as the perfume that was spread in the home at Bethany in the days of Jesus.

5.　　I fully appreciated the solid support that I received during my weeks of physical weakness, with our chapel elders and others removing any obstacle that might create distress or worry for me.

I had to put aside a great number of schemes, during my period of convalescence when I restarted my ministerial duties on 1 December. On the second day I officiated at the funeral of the grand-daughter of the late Reverend J. O. Williams (known as Pedrog), the poet-preacher who had ministered with the Welsh Congregationalists at Kensington in Liverpool.

One of our new schemes was to give permission for a talented woman to start a new private school in our schoolrooms. In a very short period of time, this became a success story. The school was known as Auckland College. Our schoolrooms would have been unused for most of the time, so this partnership was appropriate. The venture was clinched when we made an agreement with her to rent the school accommodation for three years. Despite a few teething problems, this new school grew, until there were 150 children being taught by dedicated staff and an enterprising warden. It was always a pleasure to visit the premises when the Auckland College was in session, as it was a hive of activity.

In 1999 our Chaplain, Eleri Edwards, was ordained as a minister at an Association held at Glyn Ceiriog; and a coach load of our members and friends travelled to the service in the Ceiriog Valley. W. Meirion Evans also asked us to relieve him from being an elder and we thanked him for his kindness over the years. Rhys Williams, Gwydryn Road, Calderstones, decided to spend a year working at the Youth Centre in Y Bala before attending university. This proved to be an excellent experience for him, especially when he became the Chairman of the Youth Assembly of the General Assembly.

To mark our passage from the twentieth to the twenty first century, we established a Millennium Committee. The year 2000 started well with an ecumenical service in the Welsh Methodist Chapel in Bebington. During the year we received a report from the company of E. G. Harris on the condition of our building and we convened an important meeting

Sports Day for Rhys Williams and Gareth Roberts.

Hywel Davies of Allerton.

at Bethel on Monday morning, 27 November to discuss the issues it raised.

As part of the millennium celebrations we produced two more volumes about the Liverpool Welsh community, one in Welsh, the other in English. These were *Cymry Lerpwl a'r Cyffiniau yn yr Ugeinfed Ganrif* (The Liverpool Welsh and their boundaries in the Twentieth Century) and *The Welsh of Merseyside in the Twentieth Century*. Both volumes were launched at a special event on Saturday, 7 July 2001, in Bethel schoolroom and there was a good response as far as sales are concerned. So in four years I had been responsible for four volumes on the history of the Liverpool Welsh community.

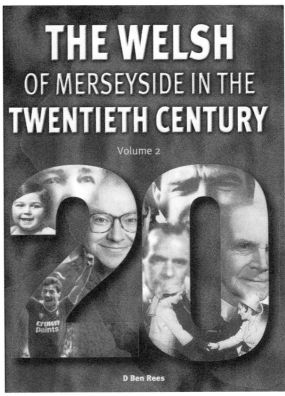

A copy of the volume which has been well received.

During 2000 on Merseyside, we lost John Caradog Hughes, Formby, one who, from 1941 to 1951, had been a valuable member of Heathfield Road Chapel. Later he became a leader at Peniel Welsh Chapel, Portland Street, Southport, and occasionally, he came to Bethel as a guest lay preacher.

We also lost a number of supportive members from our community: Mrs. Harold Owen in Anglesey; John Williams in Porthmadog, brother of W. R. Williams, the Presbytery's solicitor. Another person who died was Mrs. Muriel Edwards, Fallowfield Road. She suffered a painful illness but for years she attended my local history class for disabled people, which met in Islington, Liverpool. She really enjoyed meeting fellow sufferers, and they shared their problems as well as their love of Liverpool. W. Hywel Davies, Wheatcroft Road, Allerton, was another great loss. He had come to the city from the small village of Betws, near Ammanford. He had had a remarkable career and became Head of the CID in Liverpool. He solved nearly sixty murders that happened during his time as Head of the Liverpool CID. In his old age he became a committed Welshman, listening from early morning until late at night to Welsh language radio. After the funeral service, I scattered his ashes on Betws Mountain on a Saturday afternoon in the company of his daughter and son and their families. His contribution to the police service in the City of Liverpool was immense. Another friend who died was Elwyn Hughes, Yew Tree Road. He had been an elder in our midst, as mentioned earlier and his social life was focused in our community. He had inherited a building company from John Hughes, his father, but it was his Welsh language activities that gave him sustenance and deep interests. This was true, also, of the kind and compassionate late Eiluned Davies, a native of Blaenau Ffestiniog, mentioned earlier.

During 2000 we were enthralled at the number and company of children participating in our services. Five of them, Angharad and her brother Hywel Care, Ffion Evans, Alun Hartley and Sara Williams, were received, as communicants, into full Church membership of Sunday 4 February 2001.

On Saturdays and Sundays on at least five occasions during the summer months, we offered hospitality to crowds of visitors from Wales, when I took each party on a tour of Liverpool lasting a few hours every time. The aim was to bring to the notice of these Welsh men and women, our heritage as the Liverpool Welsh community. In 2000 we welcomed the Llanelli Male Voice Choir and the chapel was filled to capacity again for the first time since 1986; it was packed and we made use of the gallery. A choir from Lampeter also visited us as part of the Literary Society's programme in conjunction with the Millennium Committee. The North-East India-Wales Trust was able to publish, under my editorship, a splendid large volume on the Welsh missionaries who had served in India, under the title of *Llestri Gras a Gobaith: Cymry a'r Cenhadon yn India*. This was a huge task, as I prepared and wrote most of the entries myself, 225 of them, for the volume. The volume is now out of print.

At the end of the year we took the opportunity of inviting members of different faiths to our premises. I was invited by the Merseyside Council of Faiths to open a discussion on the subject 'Give Peace a Chance', a very appropriate message after what the world witnessed on 11 September. The massive crime committed in New York, Washington and

Acknowledging the contribution of Morfudd and Euryn Roberts as they left Liverpool for Abergele.

Pennsylvania was way beyond our comprehension, as was the response by the Free World in Iraq and Afghanistan. This has been reinforced by the theologian, Hans Küng, who has argued that we will never have peace in the world until the world's religions accept each other and reconcile with each other in humility. Without peace among religions there will be no peace in the world. How will this happen?: Through the simple way of every believer of every religion accepting each other, acknowledging different viewpoints but ready to be tolerant and kind-hearted towards each other.

It was a privilege to welcome every remaining member of the Welsh Methodist Chapel, who lived in the City of Liverpool as members of our chapel in October. We were glad that every one of them had decided to join our chapel and we valued their support. That Church transferred the sum of £5,000 to the Memorial Fund of Bethel. It was not easy to see Morfudd and Euryn Roberts and family leaving for Abergele, for they had kept the Welsh Methodist Chapel together for a number

Mrs Anne M. Jones, author of a number of contemporary carols.

Dr D. Ben Rees and Emrys Williams, Llangefni who has been a friend to the Liverpool Welsh

of years, and with their departure a decision had to be taken as to the future of the Methodist Chapel. In a letter, dated 19 October 2001 they both wrote:

> We thank you personally for every kindness that we have both experienced during the last five years as we worshipped at Bethel. I also feel that you gave full equality to the Welsh Methodists at all times. We were not swallowed up or ignored at any time.

That is a tribute well worth recording here, for it is testimony to the co-operation that existed during that period between the two churches.

We also believe, as we have seen, in every chapter since the beginning of the cause in Liverpool, that there is need for a social witness under the influence of Christ's teaching. The author of the Epistle of James is quite sure in his mind that 'faith without works is dead'. (James 2:26), and this was our belief in Bethel. As a result, in 2001, we sent an encouraging sum of money to the Rural Church Appeal in Madagascar, raised as a result of letters translated into Welsh by the Reverend Eleri Edwards and published in our community newspaper, *Yr Angor*. We responded generously to this cry for help for the poor in Afghanistan. Our children and the young people, as well as their parents, were involved in the Connexion Appeal for Bangladesh before the end of 2001, but the main effort was geared for 2002. One of our elders, Mrs. Nan Hughes Parry, again accepted the challenge of acting as our liaison offer. In reflecting on the splendid achievement, the words of the Swiss theologian,

Archdruid Dic Jones and his wife and Henry Pearson near the grave of Gwilym Deudraeth

Emil Brunner, immediately come to mind: 'If the church does not create loving deeds for the community around it there is great fear that it is sick unto death.'

During 2002, we received a number of letters thanking us for our response to so many missionary, charitable, cultural, peace, ecological and Welsh-based movements during the year. This list is long and the Literary Society, as well as the Women's Society, was also generous. It was encouraging to see so many people, again, at our Christmas Fayre, and that we were still attracting so many of our English-speaking neighbours into our fellowship. This was a golden opportunity for us and we also issued further initiatives during Advent, and as a result welcomed, for the first time, a group of hand-bell ringers from the Parish Church of Maghull, at our Sunday evening service on 16 December. The music that the hand-bells created was so evocative, as we sang carols from different nations, as well as Welsh carols from our hymn book, *Caneuon Ffydd* [The Songs of Faith]. The following night we were enriched by readings from Welsh literature on the threshold of Christmas – an anthology specially prepared for us by Nan Hughes Parry, who has done this for the last decade. On the Sunday before Christmas, we enjoyed and cherished the traditional carols sang as solos and duets by Mrs. Anne M. Jones and Mr. R. Ifor Griffith. Some of these had been written specially by Anne for this occasion, which put us all in the Christmas mood for the nativity play and the Christmas messages. The Sunday School teachers, under the superintendent, Siân Hartley, had prepared another surprise for us, a celebration at Christmas in a grand style.

We decided to publish our bilingual document, *The Strategy of Bethel, Heathfield Road,* and a copy of it was sent to every member with our Annual Report for 2001. This is an important document and we are grateful to H. Wyn Jones for preparing it in both languages. In addition, this report was presented to the *North Wales Association Properties and Finance Committee* so that we could contemplate moving ahead with our strategy. At the end of 2001, there were 188 names on the membership list, with 34 children. Seven left without asking for the transfer privilege of becoming members elsewhere, six died and two left for other chapels. Although we received twelve new members, in numerical terms, we were still losing ground. The miracle was that so much had been achieved at Bethel and that

The College which became a part of our buildings.

in comparison with our efforts, so many other chapels and churches that we knew of were offering so little new provision for their members.

In 2002 we had very enriching services in the company of the children and the young people. The Missionary Committee, in collaboration with Merseyside Welsh Heritage Society, decided to place a commemorative stone on the grave of the Liverpool Welsh poet, William Thomas Edwards (Gwilym Deudraeth, 1863-1940), in Allerton Cemetery. Occasionally, he came to Heathfield Road Chapel in the 1920s and 1930s, where he had a large number of friends and admirers, such as Isaac Roberts (Ap Carog) and O. C. Roberts, Bryntirion, Menlove Avenue. I do not have any evidence that any of the Chapel elders were within his circle of friends and he never wrote an *englyn* to anyone within Heathfield Road except for O.C. Roberts, when he lived in Birkenhead. We also placed a plaque on the wall of Chatham Street Welsh Chapel to commemorate its first minister, the Reverend Henry Rees, who, with others, was responsible for establishing the roots of our community. We also placed a plaque to commemorate his brother, the remarkable Reverend William Rees (Gwilym Hiraethog) on the wall of the present-day Robert Robinson Laboratories, which is the site, where the Welsh Congregational Chapel of Grove Street once stood. The two brothers were from the parish of Llansannan in Denbighshire. Côr Meibion Bro Aled, the Welsh male voice choir drawn from the Llansannan area, under the baton of Mair Selway, were invited to our midst on the last day of the festival, commemorating the two brothers, held on Sunday 10 November 2002. It was

Auckland College

A classroom of the College.

Modern technology.

a strange experience to see such a large gathering by the grave of the gifted William Rees in Toxteth Cemetery, as we sang his best-known hymn, *Dyma Gariad fel y Moroedd.* Memories of that experience will remain with me for years to come. Then, on Sunday afternoon, 10 November, we held a singing festival, one of the best that I have attended in Liverpool, under the conductorship of R. Ifor Griffith, from the ranks of our own Chapel, who was completely in charge of us all.

R. Ifor Griffith was the only new member that joined us in 2002 after the closure of his childhood chapel in Bontddu near Barmouth in Merioneth, and we were delighted. It was good to have a number of preparatory rehearsals and also to have at least half a dozen services a year, with everything (hymns, prayers, and meditations) specially printed as a leaflet for every participant in the service. This gave us the scope to include prayers for the congregation so that they could participate fully in the service and feel part of the worship. It was at that time I read Bishop Stancliffe's book, *God's Pattern,* where he writes:

> How do worshippers manage to keep on going to church faithfully when the way worship is prepared and offered is often so dire, when it is frequently confused with entertainment and when it is led by those who apparently have no idea about what they are doing or professional competence in doing it.

Another Auckland College classroom from our small schoolroom at Bethel.

Morfudd Peters who kept faithful to all activities at Bethel.

Glynwen Griffiths, Mary A. Williams and Iola Daniel in Edeyrnion in 1986. Glynwen and Iola came to Bethel from Edge Lane Welsh Chapel.

Griff J. Williams, Mossley Hill with his son Gareth Wyn Williams at the Degree Ceremony of the University of Wales, Bangor in the summer of 1980.

Ceinwen Lewis (née Roberts) of Wembley Road, Allerton and Mary A. Williams (née Owen) together in Pwllheli.

Auckland College ready to move to St Michael-in-the-Hamlet.

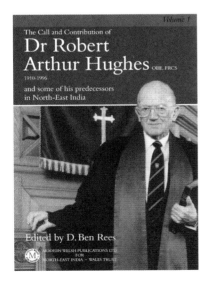

A publication which preserves the first three of the Dr R. Arthur Hughes Memorial Lectures

The Sunday services are at the heart of our community and the pattern on Sunday mornings (four hymns, scripture reading, prayers and sermon) is regarded as the sustaining glory of Welsh Presbyterianism. We made a valiant effort to be contemporary as well as traditional, and we try to avoid including tedious and embarrassing items.

We also enjoy an excellent relationship with Bethania, our sister church, at Waterloo. This, we consider to be very important, as we hope to unite with them at the end of 2010. Initially, we hoped to do this by the spring of 2004 but this was unrealistic. To make the union viable, we decided, in 2002, to invite two members/elders, from Bethania, Mona Bowen and John P. Lyons, to become part of our Strategy Committee. At the same time, four members of our chapel joined this Committee, namely Joyce Lewington, Wavertree; Mair Powell, West Derby; Dr. Pat Williams, Calderstones, and Roderick Owen, Springwood, and they gave the minister and the ruling elders a great deal of support. We were able, as a church, to collect, not only the sum of £1,000 expected for the Connexional Christian Aid Bangladesh Appeal, but also to increase the total to £1,600.00. Our treasurer, E. Goronwy Owen, was honoured for completing fifty years' service as a dependable elder at Garston in south Liverpool and then at Bethel. Another elder, Dr. John G. Williams, and his son, Rhys, gave a personal example of Christian service by collecting £8,000 towards the Macmillan Fund at Halton Hospital, where he is a chest specialist.

We were so happy on Monday night, 2 December, when Mr. Terry Radcliffe, architect for the developers, TRB Estates, explained the new scheme for a new home, the development of our chapel buildings. As a Church with a large active membership, he expected that the work would start in the summer of 2003 and would have been completed by spring 2004. We were full of expectation as we faced 2003 to see the work completed but, as we shall see, we were sorely disappointed. The year 2003 did not bring much change. We decided, as trustees, to invite a deputation from the Refurnishing Committee, made up of Myron Jones, Roderick Owen, John Bain, William Evans, Mrs. Norma Owen and myself, to visit a number of Welsh chapels that had been built recently or renovated. On Tuesday April 15 2003, we saw three new buildings in Gwynedd, all Welsh Presbyterian churches: Berea Newydd in Bangor, Y Groes at Pen-y-Groes, in the Nantlle Valley, and two that had been adapted for modern times, Bethania at Y Felinheli, and Capel y Traeth in Porthmadog. The end result of this visit was a determination not to adapt our small schoolroom as a new chapel. This was discussed with the Connexional authorities and with our congregation on 18 May. Also, this decision had been agreed with the trustees and Mark Davies on behalf of the Properties Board by the middle of June. We received advice and guidance from Robert Owen, the architect for Owen Ellis Partnership, and from W. Raymond Williams of Bremner, the Presbytery's solicitor.

We worked hard that summer. The Music Committee travelled to Oldham to see a collection of musical instruments and we were grateful to Margaret Anwyl Williams, Rhiannon Liddell and Arthur Edwards for their detailed report and recommendations concerning a new organ. We also organised two meetings to discuss the newly introduced Child Protection legislation and our involvement with children and young people. These meetings were conducted under the capable guidance of two ministers, the Reverend Trefor Jones-Morris, Wrexham, and the Reverend Meirion Morris, Llansannan.

It was a privilege to welcome a number of articulate speakers into our community: Emeritus Professor Hywel Teifi Edwards, Llangennech; Canon William Price, Wern (E. Goronwy Owen's nephew), and Hafina Clwyd of Ruthin. During 2003, we mourned the loss of Miss E. May Hughes, who had been a stalwart of Trinity Road Welsh Methodist Chapel in Bootle in her younger days; Miss Dorothy Williams, Kensington, who had moved in 2002 to Llanelltyd near Dolgellau; Mr. Eric Thomas, Goleufryn, Aigburth, whose father, R. J. Thomas, had been an elder at Garston; and the elderly Mrs. Morfudd Peters, Greenbank Road, widow of Glyn and mother of Gwynfor Peters, Cricieth. When I first came to Liverpool, there were three sisters from Bwlchgwyn, near Coedpoeth, Wrexham, who supported the Welsh witness in the city, namely Mrs. Annie Roberts, widow of Arthur Roberts (Alaw Maelor), mother of

Miss Nansi Pugh and Elan Jones

Gareth and Gaenor; Mrs. B. Pritchard, Seaforth, was the second sister and she attended Waterloo Welsh Chapel. The third was Morfudd Peters. In 2003, Trefor Griffiths of Garston was congratulated for celebrating forty years as an elder in the Connexion. His loyalty to our cause is exemplary.

We received a great deal of inspiration from the visit of the Reverend Dr. Elfed ap Nefydd Roberts, Wrexham, who came to deliver the third Dr. R. Arthur Hughes Memorial Lecture. I, myself, had delivered the fist commemorative lecture at the Liverpool Medical Institution in Mount Pleasant, when the Moderator of the General Assembly, the Reverend Harri Owain Jones, Llanfairpwll, presided. The second was delivered at Bethel by the diligent Secretary of the Mission Board, the Reverend D. Andrew Jones of Cardiff. I gathered together the three lectures and edited them for publication in English, under the title, *The Call and Contribution of Dr. Robert Arthur Hughes, OBE, FRCS, 1910-1996 and Some of his Predecessors in North-East India* (Liverpool, 2004). This volume was well received and subsequently we have enjoyed another three lectures from Professor Aled Jones, Aberystwyth University, Dr Gwyn Aman Evans of Gobowen Orthopaedic Hospital and the Reverend Dr. Alwyn Roberts, Tregarth.

The Association in the North came to us again on 1 September, and it was good to be able to use the Roman Catholic Centre, known as 'LACE', for our deliberations, morning and afternoon. In the evening we arranged the Ordination Service for Eirlys Gruffydd of Mold, a daughter of the Manse, to the part time ministry of the Presbyterian Church of Wales in the Llanarmon-yn-lâl area. John Lyons, an elder at Bethania Chapel, prepared a detailed historical account of the Welsh Presbyterian presence on Merseyside and this included a number of interesting observations with regard to Bethel. Bethel, he stated, was 'a dynamic Church, which has an active agenda for weekday inputs as well as on Sundays'.

For reasons one can understand, our caretaker, Mrs. Edna Jones moved from our Chapel House to live near her youngest daughter, Glenys and husband Philip Davies, at Wrexham. She has been an integral part of our community for twenty two years, accepting several Church responsibilities, since the death of her husband. In recognition of all these contributions we presented her with gifts on Sunday morning, 2 November. During the five years that she had been solely in charge as caretaker of the chapel, we had the presence of Auckland College in our schoolrooms. The school left us for Aigburth in March 2004. When Edna Jones moved to Wrexham and the school had departed, we were left with something of a vacuum. Fortunately Blodwen and Sam Prowting were willing to assist with the needs of our church on a Sunday.

The worst aspect of an empty chapel house is that a number of youngsters on drugs and binge drinkers broke in and occupied the premises. Although we often asked for police assistance, they would not appear on the scene, despite the inevitable damage to much of the property. In the end we were forced to board up the house, the windows as well as the doors. We have had to spend hundreds of pounds to try to safeguard ourselves against the vandals. This was a continual stress on all of us. Moreover, the developers' failure to convince the Corporation Planning Committee, and the subsequent Planning Application, made the situation more disastrous. Despite all these problems we insisted on continuing to testify the gospel and to hold our services and meetings in both the schoolroom and in the main chapel. Many of the young people who had entered our premises have no respect for the buildings and feel they have a right to be there, even though, in reality, they are trespassers. Moreover, they often refused to move when asked to vacate our garden and premises.

We still continued to celebrate our Welsh heritage. A festival was organised and held to celebrate the contribution of two brothers from Toxteth; the poet and Celtic scholar, John Glyn Davies, and the pacifist, George M. Ll. Davies. We were reminded of the Welsh Religious Revival of 1904-05 by Miss Nansi Pugh, Aigburth, daughter of the Reverend E. Cynolwyn Pugh, who had been involved in the Revival as a young coalminer in the Rhondda Valley. On 5 December, we held another Civic Service in the company of the Lord Mayor of Liverpool, Councillor Frank Roderick. Everything went well.

I organised a coach to take us to the Sunday Festival, under the auspices of the Fellowship of the Lord's Day in Wales, at Adfa Chapel, near Llanfair Cereinion in Montgomeryshire. It was an eye-opener to see the chapel so full for the singing festival, with R. Ifor Griffith as the conductor and Margaret Anwyl Williams, as the organist.

During 2004 the Reverend Eleri Edwards received a call to care for the Welsh Presbyterians in the Manchester Presbytery and her induction service was held at Oaker Avenue Chapel in West Disbury on 30 October. Eleri Edwards had been a splendid Merseyside

Councillor Warren Bradley, leader of the Liverpool City Council with his wife and daughter at the Welsh Civic Service of 2007 at Bethel.

Welsh Chaplain for nearly eight years, and we missed her at Bethel, along with her mother, Angharad Edwards, who was another daughter of the Manse.

We continued to witness faithfully for peace and justice in a world that is getting smaller and smaller. The tsunami that occurred around the coasts of Indonesia, India, Sri Lanka and other countries in the Far East brought sadness to our souls. As a community, we at Bethel responded immediately with a substantial donation towards helping the families who were suffering there. The total result of our effort amounted to £1,800.00.

I cannot say that 2005 was an easy year for us as we faced so much distress from illnesses, disappointments and our plans for the development of our buildings continued to be frustrated. We experienced a real loss in the death of W. Raymond Williams, the chapel's solicitor from the Liverpool firm of Bremners, and we decided to ask his son, Nigel, from the same company to represent us. We cannot enter into a detailed appraisal of the situation since the end of 2005 as it is now in the hands of solicitors. But the whole future of the site will be settled, hopefully, before the end of 2008.

Of the societies within our chapel, the Literary Society must be regarded as one of the most successful. This group works hard and prepares a comprehensive programme with Miss Mair Powell as an ideal secretary. The deaths of our treasurers, Berwyn Morris and his wife, Margaret (a native of Carno in Montgomeryshire) left us in a void that was difficult to cope with, but we were successful in appointing a new treasurer, Mrs Lillian Coulthard, a personal friend of Margaret Morris. We had changes to our arrangements for our St. David's Day Dinners in 2005, 2006 and 2007 by holding the event at the Adelphi Hotel. In 2005 we invited the Plaid Cymru doyen Dafydd Wigley, and his wife, Elinor Bennett, the harpist, to be our guests. Huw Edwards of London, the TV newsreader, came in 2006; and then, in 2007, a star of Welsh radio and television, Dai Jones of Llanilar near Aberystwyth came as the guest speaker for our celebration of the day of our patron saint. Seventy six attended the dinner in 2005, 114 in 2006 and 104 in 2007. Each event was a huge success thanks to Mrs. Gwerfyl Bain, Mrs. Lillian Coulthard and Mrs. Enid Pierce Hughes, the organisers from our Literary Society.

Nevertheless, in our joy, often we had to face losses from our ranks. In 2005 as a result of death, we lost Herbert Davies, a native of Llanelli, who had been an elder in Carmel Welsh Chapel, Ashton-in-Makerfield; Mrs. Margaret Morris, Aigburth, a charismatic schoolteacher; Hywel Lloyd, Rainhill, a native of the Denbigh area; John L. Williams, Wellington Road, an Anglesey man who had a deep interest in photography; Mrs. Dora Williams, Wavertree, late of Kingsdale Road, whom I have already mentioned earlier in the context of the pilgrimage that I organised in 1973, and Mrs. E. A. Williams, Caldwell Road, Springwood, a native of Blaenau Ffestiniog. All of them, except Mrs. Dora Williams, who had spent her childhood holidays in the Tanat Valley, were natives of Wales.

It was a joy to participate in the wedding of Gareth Rhys Williams and Genni Mary Allen of Caernarfon, on Saturday 27 August 2005. This was a day for us to remember. Both have now settled in Coedpoeth and are part of the Street Pastors in Wrexham.

The Lord Mayor's Civic Service has been held at the beginning of December at Bethel every year since 2004. On this occasion in 2005, Dr. John G. Williams prepared an exhibition on the walls leading to the schoolroom, which

Mr D. Berwyn Morris.

Huw Edwards

The Minister's Family at the Retirement Service.

revealed all the vitality, energy and the efforts that have been shown within our community. All the contents have been retained.

We remain heavily involved in the gospel witness, serving the Welsh community of Liverpool. We are glad when we are strengthened by new members arriving, especially those who come as students. Sophie Dark of Pontarddulais, a student at John Moores University, between 2004-2007, appreciated our concern, culture and the ethos in our chapel that re-connected her with the Welsh Congregationalist chapel at her home in south Wales. We have a strong sense of Welshness and of a common purpose, especially for those who value worship in our native tongue. For nearly forty years, we have maintained a belief in continuous learning, sharing of experiences, a strong sense of interdependence and a broadminded approach to our faith, built around the scriptures and the prayers and sacraments of the Free Church. Since 1896, we have been a community united under a supportive leader, the Reverend, often known in a Catholic city like Liverpool as 'the father in God.' When I wear my clerical collar, which I often do, I am referred to as 'Father'.

We believe in preaching as a priority and our emphasis is Calvinistic evangelicalism. Our aim is to 'promote evangelical unity' between churches and 'change society' for good. With the exception of Henry Rees, none of the leaders in our community have ever been what might be regarded as high Calvinists, but we have understood the value of Calvinism as a theological system that has done so much good for the western world. After all, we are still widely known as Calvinistic Methodists but the term 'Presbyterianism' has become a more official title since the 1930s.

Our praise to the Lord, at its best, is enthralling, as our friends and guests who attend the civic service often testify. Praise is always loud, upbeat and completely triumphant. The spirit of God when it moves in a service or *Cymanfa Ganu,* make the morning, afternoon or evening a completely unique experience.

We have inherited Nonconformist spirituality, which has deep Celtic roots in the 18th century. Our spirituality exudes a gracious and enriching confidence in the life and work of Jesus Christ. Our Faith is uncomplicated and is derived from the all-sufficiency of the scriptures, from the Psalms of the *Old Testament* to the Epistle to the Romans in the *New Testament.* This egalitarian spirit is evident in all our gatherings as we claim that the fullness of God's grace is available to all our members without distinction. Moreover, it has special meaning in the context of the Liverpool Welsh community, in the abolition of slavery, home rule or devolution for Wales, disestablishment of the Anglican State Church in Wales, the establishment of the Welfare State, the establishment of the National Health Service, the progressive nature of the Liberal Party and the origins of the Labour movement.

Our future as a chapel has always been in the hands of the Presbyterian Church of Wales's Properties Board, the developers that will gain the contract, and our determination as a community to safeguard this rich cultural traditional history. We have to remain confident, but at the same time, realise that at Bethel we have a congregation that has been in decline since the Second World War. Attendances at English-speaking, as well as Welsh-speaking chapels have been falling for some six decades. Moreover, the number of working ministers are becoming fewer. In the denomination as a whole, in 2007 only one individual expressed a desire to work in the full time ministry. Just one Welsh Presbyterian Church in ten, bucks this declining trend when average attendances at Sunday mornings are over 100. In my experience, these congregations are to be found in Bangor, Carmarthen, Caernarfon, Aberystwyth, Wrexham and Cardiff. You do not find them anywhere else, not amongst the Welsh of Los Angeles, Toronto, London, Birmingham, Manchester, Liverpool, Swansea, Merthyr, Haverfordwest or Newport. Two-thirds of our chapels have fewer than fifty attending services regularly. On a Sunday morning, when there are no school holidays, there can be around seventy worshippers at Bethel, when the minister is in his own pulpit. But in all other Welsh chapels on Merseyside the situation is entirely different. In 2007 two of the last Welsh-speaking Anglican Churches on Merseyside decided to close. Although we celebrated a hundred years of Welsh Presbyterianism in Ellesmere Port on 3 June 2007, the question remains, for how long? One third of our Welsh Presbyterian Chapels in Wales have, on average, fewer than twenty attending Sunday worship. These dwindling congregations are called upon, not only to maintain buildings, which are getting older, often dating from the Victorian era, but also to meet all the other expenses of heating and lighting, insurance, to conform with health and safety regulations and to meet the subsistence and travelling expenses of visiting preachers.

Buildings do differ, but Bethel Chapel has a bleak future without a smaller building. The final demolition of Bethel Chapel, Heathfield Road, will be truly devastating for me personally. This is the place where I have preached conscientiously and with passion for forty years. It has been my second home and now we are contemplating its demolition. This is the last thing I want to see and yet what choice do we have? There is no one in the

City of Liverpool willing to give us sufficient financial support to preserve a unique building, no evangelical celebrity pop star or rich Welsh Christian who will hand us a cheque for one million pounds, and none of those who have worshipped within its precincts in eighty years have left a sufficiently huge sum of money to us in their last will and testament. All the gifts and donations that have been given to us have all been valuable, but, elsewhere, in some parts of Wales, members have left £100,000 to their chapels; and this will ensure a long period of existence for that particular cause. We praise their example.

When the building at Bethel needs any extensive renovations on its roof, then it is necessary to erect scaffolding and employ steeplejacks. Because thieves strip away the lead, our chapel has to have a new roof from time to time. If we remain in this building until, say, 2010, there will be need for repointing the fabric, repainting (sorely needed), and for rewiring. Even, when all this has been done, at a huge expense, devouring our capital, then the wonderful Welsh Temple, our *Capel Mawr* [large chapel], will not be suitable for regular use by seventy plus adults and children in 2008. Our pipe organ, though carefully maintained through the expertise of Arthur Edwards, will not necessarily be the musical choice for our children. When they have their opportunity they will want to bring their drums, guitars and other instruments to play in the services. Definitely, neither the pews, as hard as nails to sit on; nor the *sêt fawr* [elders' pew] would be the seating of choice in the future by the majority of our members or elders. But, at present, they put up with these out-of-date facilities as there are no alternatives. Our chapel is very well-heated so, when the boiler has been working for twelve hours before the Sunday morning service, we feel really at home and comfortable. We would like to have new lighting in the minister's room, in the large schoolroom and in the chapel sanctuary. Also, we could do with new plumbing for the heaters and pipes have been there since 1927 – yes, over eighty years. Our congregation meets in a huge sanctuary, the largest of any Free Church building on Merseyside, with uncomfortable pews; there could be better lighting and, at times, the microphone in the pulpit, as well as in the *sêt fawr*, is somewhat temperamental. Currently we have a useful stage inside the chapel for our children's services and the choir, where we also place our internal and external literature as well as the offertory collecting plates.

Changes to the building and, in particular, its demolition are controlled by the local authority and the developers. We, also, have a number of individuals, not amongst chapel members, representing organisations that will oppose any adaptations, as we have noted. Fortunately, we have a loyal nucleus of attending members, Sunday by Sunday, and we do not allow fundraising events, as other chapels often do, to dominate our newsletter, *Y Rhwyd*. Last week's collection is never reported until the total is published in our Annual Report. We do not follow some of the Anglican Churches who prepare graphs (although our Church Secretary could produce excellent ones) of parish income and expenditure to be placed on prominent pillars for fund-raising! Envelope schemes for every Sunday, standing orders and Gift Aid (a Gordon Brown Presbyterian initiative) are promoted, but not overdone. The minister, elders and lay people who attend regularly accept their responsibilities for maintaining the chapel building, while those members who never attend do not seem too bothered. Our best-attended Sunday services are the Family, Christmas and Civic ones.

The church will have to look for a new leader as my successor in 2008, and in the next few years Bethel and Bethania Chapels in Liverpool will be united under a new minister. As I retire, I will be on the threshold of having ministered for nearly forty years throughout a very busy period, and, I hope, a spiritually enriching one for everyone within the fold of Bethel Chapel, Heathfield Road. I pray that I will be able to pass on the torch to another minister to cater for the needs of the Liverpool Welsh. Their loyalty to our Christian Cause deserves another committed leader, with ecumenical and social skills, a gospel evangelical who will lead a full and useful life for Christ. We must remember at all times the words of Jesus: 'Judge not that you be not judged'. We hold on to the very heart of the gospel which states that Jesus, our Saviour, died for our sins and that he has called us to be his faithful disciples. We actually know and experience God to be generous and loving and merciful. That is, believe it or not, the basis of our salvation. Our Presbyterian Church of Wales is derived from the early Dissenters of the Christian Church, those brave souls, long before the Reformation, who pleaded for the Scriptures in their own language; for freedom to be wandering evangelists and to visualise the Kingdom of God as a reality in our own land. Following the Reformation, our origins lie with Calvinism, inspired by none other than John Calvin of Geneva, and, through the Puritans and the Methodists, we have brought hope and salvation to an entire Celtic nation. Indeed, we were responsible, with other committed Puritans, for a whole new civilisation in North America and in northern Europe.

Our forefathers, who came to Liverpool in the eighteenth century, were, in the main, the 'hotter sort of Protestants': Welsh Congregationalists, Baptists, Wesleyan Methodists and Calvinistic Methodists. Most of these, our forefathers, were poor and young and had been persecuted for their faith. But they had great passion to serve Christ and to improve their material situation and standards of living. But, it was the spirit of Christ, the spirit of love for language, for country and distinctive culture, the Bible and preaching, which knit them all together in a truly Christian society. They would have heartily agreed with the puritan sailor, John Winthrop, when he preached on his boat, 'Arabella,' in the middle of the Atlantic Ocean, as he took his fellow Puritans from Southampton to New England in the spring of 1603:

> For this end we must be knit together in this work as one man; we must entertain each other in brotherly affection; we must be willing to rid ourselves of our superfluities for the supply of other's necessities; we must uphold a familiar commerce together in all meekness, gentleness, patience and liberality; we must delight in each other, make others' conditions our own, rejoice together, mourn together, labour and suffer together, always having before our eyes our commission and community in the work, our community as members of the same body, so shall we keep the unity of the spirit in the bond of peace.

Something of this kind happened amongst the Welsh who came to Liverpool, and these ideas still remain an important part of our belief as Welsh Christians in 2008.

GREETINGS ON BEHALF OF BETHEL CHURCH

During the fellowship meeting following the evening service one Sunday more than forty years ago – there are but a few members left who were present on that occasion – the then minister, the late Reverend E. Watkin Jones, to the surprise of all present, announced his retirement. He'd probably informed the Elders beforehand, but to us the ordinary members – shock and trepidation. Who would replace him? Who would come to minister this corner of God's acre?

Eventually, having bid farewell to the late Reverend and Mrs Watkin Jones – peace be with them, both – the process of appointing a successor was initiated. A Pastoral Committee – consisting of the Elders and delegates, both male and female, representing all aspects of church life – was appointed to undertake the task. There are only two members of this committee left here in Bethel – Professor David Price Evans and myself (I note that one other, Mr Glyn Davies of Ruthin, is present in the congregation) – but I would claim on their behalf that they did a very good day's work. A number of meetings were held, and all aspects of the ongoing debate were considered and deliberated upon. Who was known to be currently 'mobile'? Who was likely to accept the invitation? Who was likely to 'fit the bill'? Who would

H. Wyn Jones

be acceptable to the members? What might be a new minister's expectations and demands – a young minister, hopefully? So on and so forth. There was complete unanimity on one requisite – we needed a young minister. But who?

Four or five individuals were named – so and so was disregarded as he'd only recently accepted a new pastorate; another named could be eliminated as he was unlikely to move across Offa's Dyke. Who does that leave? Well, there's A, B, C and that young man from south Wales; now what is his name – "D. Ben Rees". Does anyone know anything about him? "I've heard he's a very good preacher." "A bit of a commy, so I've heard!" "No, no, a member of the Labour Party, I believe." "Same thing!" "I've heard he's very hard working." "He made quite an impression at the Gym-Gyff (*General Assembly*), apparently." "Has anyone seen him, or met him?" "No!" "Well, obviously we shall have to do some research."

That meant going to the very source. And so it was, very early one Sunday morning – having made certain the minister would 'playing at home' – representatives undertook a journey to South Wales, aiming for the Cynon Valley.

We shall never know what crossed the minds of those who formed the congregation at Abercynon that fateful Sunday evening on seeing three strangers sitting in a rear pew: especially when they emerged from the service to see a large Rover parked the other side of the road, with the three visitors making a hasty departure.

Sadly, none of those who undertook that journey are with us today, but on the strength of their report an invitation was sent to the Reverend D. Ben Rees inviting him to Liverpool for approval.

Some of us have heard the tale of that first visit to Liverpool; and we have the Almighty to thank for ensuring the fog had lifted by Sunday morning, otherwise he might not have returned to Merseyside – I refer to the young minister, of course, not the Almighty! But, back he came, accompanied by his family; consequently, we are today celebrating and giving thanks for almost forty years' of service and ministration by the Reverend Dr D. Ben Rees. And that is what we have received from him – service and ministration, particularly ministration.

Firstly the ministry of the Word of God – firm and robust preaching based on a strongly held conviction in belief and faith in the Lord Jesus Christ. His sermons display extensive knowledge and scholarship, particularly of the Bible and Welsh hymns. Complete devotion and unyielding attachment to the basic tenets of Christianity. Throughout this period of forty years we have been privileged as a Church and congregation to hear preaching based on the Crucified and Risen Christ – our comforter and consoler, our saviour and salvation.

Secondly we received the ministry of the Sacraments. Who amongst us failed to experience, at times, an emotional thrill whilst partaking of the bread and drinking the wine? Under the leadership of our minister the Communion is Holy. More than once we have been touched when present at a service of baptism. The gentle kiss pierces one's heart; particularly if we happen to be the parents, or the grandparents! He has always insisted that a Service of Baptism be a public event; that it is a service of commitment by all who take part – as individuals and Church. The one like the other undertaking a vow before God. A number of us have personal experience of the manner in which he conducts a Marriage Ceremony, and can testify to the dignity and particular distinctiveness that permeates the proceedings when the Reverend Dr D. Ben Rees unites a couple in the holy estate of matrimony.

Thirdly we have received unstinting pastoral ministration. There can hardly be a sole present this afternoon who hasn't received a word of comfort and commiseration in an hour of anguish and sorrow, or tribulation and suffering: his has been a shoulder to lean upon, and a welcome embrace when in the throes of bereavement. We all know, through personal experience or as observers, of his innate sensitivity and poignancy when conducting a Funeral Service.

As for those welcome visits; benefactions, large and small; and acts of kindness and assistance – they are countless. We who are fit and healthy, and secure in the company of our friends and family, will never know the extent of his commitment to the lonely and needy. At all times he has been a friend and comforter when in need.

Fourthly we saw his commitment to the ministration of the children and young people, as well as to the fellowship meetings, prayer meetings, the literary society, the short (ministerial) course, the one-day courses and the Welsh Language courses in their day, the Nine Churches and the exchanging of pulpits – and I'm bound to have left something unmentioned. For many years it's our minister who has edited 'The Net' our monthly newsletter, as well as the 'Anchor' the monthly local publication for the Merseyside Welsh community. How many churches, I wonder, have managed to arrange over so many years such a plethora of activities for its children and young people? Performances of the Nativity Play, the Bala Weekends, Thanksgiving Services, Flower Sunday Services. Ah well, you might say, it's the generation after generation of Sunday School teachers, parents and others who have been responsible for those events. Indeed so, but it all calls for leadership; to be honest now, how many of us have become involved in these events because 'he' has asked us, and how difficult it is 'to say no'.

"Leadership", that's what it's about!

In this context, I have become an aficionado of Peter Drucker, the American business guru, who said somewhere: *"Management is doing things right, leadership is doing the right things."* And we have seen plenty of the *"right things"* being done over the years.

Latterly, possibly over a period of some twelve years even, we have enjoyed special Commemorative Festivals, such as 'The Davies' Brothers Festival' (John Glyn and George M. Ll. Davies), 'Gwilym Deudraeth Festival', The Mimosa Festival', 'The Alun Owen Festival', and so on. Also, under the auspices of the Merseyside Welsh Heritage Society and The Society of Ex-Students of Welsh Colleges (a branch of the Guild of Welsh Graduates) – societies where his leadership has been crucial – we have enjoyed numerous lectures delivered by noted Welsh scholars and men of letters. We have also enjoyed the company of numerous noted Welshmen and Welshwomen as Honoured Guests at St David's Day Celebrations over many years. Who but Ben could have persuaded Huw Edwards to be our guest two years ago? This year, due to his leadership and perseverance, we shall enjoy a feast of events during the first week in March as part of our contribution to this special year in the city's history. It would appear that Liverpool has been a centre for pilgrimages from Wales. And who escorts these pilgrims around the city? That's right, no less a person!

Writing, that's another of the minister's interests; we've seen numerous books relating to Liverpool published under his name, such as V*ehicles of Grace and Hope: Welsh Missionaries in India 1800-1970* and *The Welsh of Merseyside in the Twentieth Century*, to name but two. We look forward to a new book that is to be released within months *Labour of Love in Liverpool: The Welsh Presence in Smithdown Lane, Webster Road and Heathfield Road*; English and Welsh editions will be published.

As intimated, when that young man left South Wales in 1968 he didn't come empty-handed – in one hand was Meinwen and in the other (on his arm more than likely) Dafydd; they were accompanied by Mrs Llywelyn. These days, when appointing someone to important positions in business, as an MP even, the partner falls under scrutiny. As far as I can remember, this did not happen in 1968. We were aware that she was a teacher and would, more than likely, want to pursue her chosen profession here in Liverpool. Which would have been no different to others of our young wives at the time, so that was that.

Have you noticed how sometimes you receive a bonus if you are prepared to invest money in a bank or a building society? Well, this is what you call a bonus! A talented and gifted young wife who, even more importantly perhaps, was prepared to involve herself in church activities side by side with her contemporaries – Sunday School teacher, the Young Wives' Society, and so on. But more important still, one who was prepared to support her husband one hundred per cent.

Within the year, well less than twelve months to be exact, we saw, in the arrival of Hefin, an addition to the family at Garth Drive. Henceforth we were to enjoy the privilege of seeing the sons of the manse developing and maturing. Today we take pride in their achievements, their lives and careers, as we do with all our young people – after all, we regard them as much ours as they are their parents'. Of course, some of us have an invested interest in their wellbeing!

I referred to Mrs Llewelyn – Mrs Rees's mother – as another member of the family at the manse. We pay tribute to her memory, and give thanks for her quiet and treasured contribution, her tender care and unyielding support.

So far, I have portrayed and presented an ideal account, but two very dark clouds were seen hovering above the manse this past decade.

The minister had to undergo serious and intricate surgery. Fortunately, we saw him recovering his health. Due to the skills and professionalism of the surgeons and the nursing staff, together with the loving care he received from Meinwen when back home – and, it must be admitted, a healthy dose of wisdom on his own part – we saw him back in harness, much to the delight of all and sundry.

The second dark cloud arose as a consequence of the measures undertaken in order to ensure our future on this site – a threat to take the minister to the High Court in civil proceedings. We were all convinced that the allegations were completely groundless, and indeed the matter was eventually withdrawn. Nevertheless, those were months of pain and

MINISTERS OF THE CHAPELS THAT HAVE THEIR WITNESS TODAY IN THE CHAPEL OF BETHEL, HEATHFIELD ROAD, LIVERPOOL

BEDFORD STREET AND PRINCES ROAD

1862-1868 David Saunders

1871-1891 Owen Thomas
1894-1906 John Williams
1904-1906 John Hughes
1909-1927 H. Harris Hughes

1928-1939 Griffith Rees

1944-1949 R. Howell Williams

DRINDOD

1950-1964 Ifor Oswy Davies
1965-1971 Emyr Owen

MULBERRY STREET AND CHATHAM STREET

1865-1869 Henry Rees

1872-1892 Owen Jones
1893-1901 W. O. Jones
1903-1911 Richard Humphreys

1913-1922 R. R. Hughes
1923-1925 T. Arthur Jones
1925-1930 W. Llewelyn Lloyd
1931-1934 T. M. Perkins
1935-1943 Enoch Rogers

DAVID STREET AND BELVIDERE ROAD	HOLT ROAD AND EDGE LANE	WEBSTER ROAD AND HEATHFIELD ROAD
	1894-1936 David Jones	1896-1915 William Owen
	1937-1949 Llewelyn Evans	1916-1923 Daniel Davies
1886-1905 William Jones		
		1923-1939 Robert Davies
1906-1913 John Roberts		1942-1948 R. Glynne Lloyd
1915-1937 D. D. Williams		
	1950-1974 W. D. Jones	1949-1967 E. Watkin Jones
1939-1949 Ifor Oswy Davies		1968-1975 D. Ben Rees

BETHEL
1976-2008 D. Ben Rees

Before 1865 the ordained ministers such as Thomas Edwards, Thomas Hughes, Richard Williams, John Hughes and for a time Henry Rees served all the Welsh Calvinistic churches of Liverpool rather than specific chapels.

ELDERS WHO SERVED IN THE CHAPELS OF WEBSTER ROAD AND HEATHFIELD ROAD

1889	John Jones (Salisbury Road)	resigned 1892
	John Jones (Tennyson Street)	moved to Rock Ferry 1894
	Robert E. Jones	resigned 1890
1892	Hugh Hughes	moved to Llangoed, Anglesey 1895
1893	Edward Owen	resigned 1911
1894	Hugh Griffiths	moved to Birmingham 1901
	Owen Hughes (Salisbury Road)	died 1947
1896	John Jones (Mayfield)	died 1936
1900	William Davies	died 1934
	John Hughes	resigned 1903
	W. Morris Owen	moved to Princes Road 1919
1911	J. W. Jones	died 1945
	Dr Gwilym Owen	moved to New Zealand 1914
	Henry Williams	died 1945
1919	R. J. Evans	died 1925
	David Griffiths	moved to Tremadog 1954
	George Jenkins	died 1946
1925	J. R. Davies	died 1956
	R. J. Jones	died 1956
1931	J. Llewelyn Jenkins	died 1961
	J. R. Jones	died 1955
1939	John Lloyd	died 1966
1946	Evan Edwards	died 1956
1947	John Edward Jones	Bethel
	David Williams	moved to Port Dinorwic 1953
1953	Griffith R Jones	moved to Abergele 1970, died 1979
	R. Glyn Williams	died 1975
1955	Goronwy Davies	moved to Abergele 1972, died 1975
	Ifor Griffiths	Bethel
	R. D. Jones	moved to Penmorfa, near Porthmadog 1959
	Arthur O. Roberts	died 1960

1960	Howell V. Jones	Bethel
	Idris Lloyd Williams	died 1962
1966	Glyn Davies	Bethel
	Owen Evans	Bethel
1971	R. Arthur Hughes	Bethel
	Vincent Roberts	Bethel
1974	D. Hughes Parry	Bethel
	Gwilym J. Roberts	Bethel

Heathfield Road and Bethel chapels were fortunate in having the support and presence of elders who had served other Welsh churches in the city. From Douglas Road Chapel in 1974 came Gwilym Hughes, Greenbank Drive who died in 1985, and from Anfield Road Chapel in 1979 came W. Elwyn Hughes, Calderstones (who died in 2002) and Gwilym Meredydd Jones, Mossley Hill (who died in 1992), from Edge Lane Chapel, Dr Idris Owen, Menlove Avenue, Allerton (died in 1993) and Trefor Williams, Fairfield and later of Llanfairfechan (who died in 1999) from Huyton Quarry, W. T. Jones who died in 1984.

THE ELDERS OF BETHEL WHEN THEY UNITED

1946	D	Pierce S. Roberts, Woolton	moved to Betws-in-Rhos 1977
1947	H	John Edward Jones, Allerton	died 1999
1953	E	E. Emlyn Griffiths, Broadgreen	moved to Bangor 1977, died 1987
1955	H	Ifor Griffiths, Wavertree	died 1980
1960	H	Howell Vaughan Jones, Allerton	died 1978
1962	D	T. R. Williams, Dingle	died in Australia
1966	H	Glyn Davies, Roby	move to Rhuthin 1990
1966	H	Owen Evans, Allerton	died 1978
1966	D	John Medwyn Jones, Aigburth	moved to Colwyn Bay 1983
1966	E	R. Conwy Roberts, Wavertree	died 1976
1967	D	Mrs L. Clement Evans, Toxteth	died 1988
1970	E	Miss N. C. Hughes, Newsham Park	moved to Llandudno 1985
1971	H	R. Arthur Hughes, Calderstones	died 1996
1971	H	Vincent Roberts, Toxteth	moved to Blaenau Ffestiniog, died 1986
1971	D	Miss Mary B. Owen, Mossley Hill	died 1985
1974	H	D. Hughes Parry, Woolton	retired 1982, died 1987
1974	H	Gwilym J. Roberts, Gateacre	moved to Anglesey 1977

a)   The letter which follows the year of ordination stands for the chapel which elected them as a leader:
D – Drindod (Trinity);   H – Heathfield;   E – Edge Lane.

b)   These men were elected elders in other churches.

R. Arthur Hughes	1944	The Jaiaw Church, Shillong, Khasia Hills, India
Owen Evans	1948	Aberfan and in 1950 Pontmorlais, Merthyr
Tudfil		
W. Elwyn Hughes	1947	Anfield, Liverpool
E. Goronwy Owen	1952	Garston

c)   At the union of Heathfield Road, Edge Lane and Drindod chapels all the officers of the three churches became elders of Bethel, except 3 from the Drindod Chapel, namely W. Hywel Williams, who moved to Shrewsbury, T. Glyn Owen and Ellis J. Morris, who became members at Garston Welsh Presbyterian Church.

ELDERS WHO ACCEPTED THE INVITATION OF THE CONGREGATION TO BECOME LEADERS AT BETHEL

1977	E. Goronwy Owen, Calderstones	an elder at Garston from 1952 to 1976
1982	W. Elwyn Hughes, Calderstones	died, 2002. An elder at Anfield Road from 1947 to 1979
	Hugh John Jones	died 1996
	Humphrey Wyn Jones, Allerton	
	Dr John G. Williams	
	Mrs Bronwen Rogers, Calderstones	moved to Deganwy near Conwy 1987
1987	J. Gwyndaf Richards, Smithdown	moved to Llwydiarth, near Llangadfan, Mongomeryshire 1996
1990	Nan Hughes Parry, Woolton	
	W. Meirion Evans, Allerton	resigned 1999
2008	Mair Powell, West Derby	
	Dr Pat Williams, Allerton	

Other Elders from other Churches at Bethel

On the union of Bethel with St Helens Junction in 1988 Idris Jones and Herbert Davies became elders at Bethel. Idris Jones was first elected an elder in Carmel Welsh Chapel, Ashton-in-Makerfield in 1965 within the Liverpool Presbytery. He still remains an Elder. Herbert Davies of Ashton-in-Makerfield was elected an elder at Carmel in 1977. He died in the year 2005.

Then in 1992 the amalgamation of Garston Welsh Chapel and Bethel took place and Trefor W. Griffiths became an elder at Bethel. He had been elected an elder at Garston in 1963. He stll remains an elder.

OTHER OFFICERS

Secretaries of the church at Webster Road and Heathfield Road from 1889-1975

-1889	Robert T. Jones
1890-1892	John Jones (Hartington Road)
1893-1947	Owen Hughes, Salisbury Road
1947-1956	J. R. Davies, Dovedale Road and Calderstones Road
1956-1975	Ifor Griffiths, Charles Berrington Road, Wavertree

Secretaries of Bethel Church from 1976-2008

1976-1977	E. Emlyn Griffiths, Chelwood Avenue, Broadgreen
1978-1985	Dr R. Arthur Hughes, Green Lanes, Calderstones
1985-2008	Humphrey Wyn Jones, Wheatcroft Road, Allerton

Treasurers of Webster Road and Heathfield Road from 1889-1975

1889-1894	John Jones (Albert Park)
-1895	Hugh Hughes
1896-1903	Edward Owen
1904-1919	W. Morris Owen
1919-1936	John Jones (Mayfield)
1936-1945	J. W. Jones
1945-1960	J. Llewelyn Jenkins
1961-1973	Howell V Jones
1974-1975	F. H. Williams

Treasurers of Bethel Heathfield Road Chapel from 1976 to 2008

1976-1977	F. H. Williams
1976-1990	T. M. Owens, FCA
1977-2008	E. Goronwy Owen

A number of individuals acted as Deputy Treasurers or Assistant Secretaries. The Pulpit Secretary in Bethel has been Miss Mary B. Owen, Gwilym M. Jones, J. Gwyndaf Richards, Dr John G. Williams and Miss Mair Powell while Glyn Davies, Dr Glyn Roberts, W. Meirion Evans and Dr John G Williams have been Finance Secretaries.

Chapel Caretakers since 1890

1895-1890	Elias Jones
1896-1902	Williams Hughes
1903-1925	John Jones (Bird Street)
1927-1953	William Owen
1959-1959	John L. Griffiths
1959-1964	W. J. Jones
1965-1981	R. E. Jones
1982-1999	D. Elwyn Jones
2000-2003	Edna Jones
2003-2008	Sam and Blodwen Prowting

Organists since 1887

1887-1892	Lewis Evans
1892-1900	John Evans
1899-1901	Edward Williams
1901-1940	John P. Taylor
1941-1944	Mrs Nansi M. Thomas
1941-1942	Mrs Mary Davies
1941-1951	Miss Margaret G. Owen
1945-1951	Miss Alwena Davies
1945-1950	Miss Gwen Griffiths, LRAM
1952-1959	Elwyn Jones, ARCO
1960-1963	Glyn Jones
-1964	W. Llewelyn Evans, ARCO

Then, Miss Alwena Davies, Glyn and Mrs Gwyneth Rowlands, Miss Mair Powell, Mrs Glenys Arden, David Williams, Mrs Megan Davies, Mrs Eirlys Richards, Ifan Jones and Rhys Williams have assisted. Today, we depend on Arthur Edwards, Mrs Margaret Annwyl Williams and Mrs Rhiannon Liddell as organists.

Precentors from 1887-1972

1887-1892	R. T. Jones
1893-1922	William Davies
1922-1950	R. J. Jones
1922-1925	Henry Owen
1922-1925	W. Penry Williams
1951-1960	Arthur O. Roberts
1960-1971	W. G. Jones
1967-1972	Gwynfryn Evans

Deputy Precentors from 1901-1960

1901-1903	William Jones
1901-1907	William Griffiths
1904-1908	David R. Owen
1909-1912	Jonathan Evans
1928-1947	W. Glyn Jones
1928-1934	Robert Thomas
1934-1951	Arthur O. Roberts
1953-1959	John L. Griffiths
1953-1960	W. G. Jones

Distributors of the community newspaper, *Yr Angor*

1979-1982	Trevor Williams, Whitland Road, Fairfield
1982-1987	Trevor Roberts, Sefton Park
1987-2005	Arthur Edwards, Aigburth
2006-2008	Roderick Owen, Springwood

Appendix H

ORDAINED MINISTERS, WHO HAVE BEEN MEMBERS OF WEBSTER ROAD, HEATHFIELD ROAD AND BETHEL CHAPELS

1887-1889	Edward Lloyd	Freelance Preacher
1896-1900	Owen Jones	Freelance Preacher
1903-1905	Josiah Thomas MA	Retired General Secretary of the Foreign Mission Board operating from Falkner Street
1929-1936	D. E. Jones, Allerton	A retired missionary from North East India
1957-1961	R. Leslie Jones, BA, BD	Home Secretary to the Mission Board
1961-1987	D. Hughes Parry, BA, BD	Comprehensive School Teacher
1962-1970	H. Jones Griffiths, BA	General Secretary of the Mission Board
1963-	R. Wyn Griffiths, BA	School teacher
1964-1970	G. W. Rogers	A retired minister
1965-1970	Alun Williams, LTSC	Home Secretary of the Mission Board
1969-1971	Alun Wyn Owen, MA, MD	Schoolteacher
1970-1975	J. Meirion Lloyd, MTh, BA, BD	A missionary and a secretary of the Bible Society on Merseyside

Between 1920 and 1940 eight members of the chapel were trained and ordained into the Christian ministry, Ivor Platt, David C. Edwards, D. Jones Hughes, John Trevor Jones, H. Godfrey Jones, Alwyn M. Jones, Trefor Davies Jones and R. Aled Davies. In the post War period the Reverend Mair Bowen (neé Davies) of Dovedale Road was ordained for the work of a missionary and minister with the Welsh Baptist Union (See her contribution and her husband, Thomas Irfonwy Bowen (1924-1998) in D. Ben Rees *Vehicles of Grace and Hope: Welsh Missionaries in India: 1800-1970* (Pasadena. 2002), 8. Also the account of another missionary from our community, Nansi Mary Thomas (1910-1998), eldest daughter of Winifred and John Roberts Davies, Dovedale Road, Liverpool, and wife of the Reverend Trebor Mai Thomas of Shillong – see pages 221-222 written by D. Ben Rees).

Appendix I

STATISTICS OF WEBSTER ROAD / HEATHFIELD ROAD / BETHEL

Year	Communicants	Children	Young People accepted into full membership
1890	236	74	7
1895	197	70	13
1900	412	201	0
1905	543	206	7
1910	544	216	10
1915	552	182	29
1920	580	171	11
1925	576	135	11
1930	655	93	21
1935	682	79	10
1940	642	82	0
1945	600	74	6
1950	555	84	7
1955	520	65	8
1960	458	50	5
1965	401	51	0
1970	363	65	6
1975	318	66	6
1980	389	52	7
1985	332	44	0
1990	280	43	0
1995	236	48	0
1999	226	39	0
2005	158	36	4

Year	Baptised	Died	Married	Sunday School
1890	11	4	0	287
1895	5	2	0	230
1900	20	6	0	393
1905	20	5	0	490
1910	19	2	0	517
1915	10	4	0	429
1920	14	5	2	431
1925	2	8	4	372
1930	4	3	4	424
1935	5	12	2	381
1940	5	9	6	320
1945	5	9	6	Rhyfel
1950	7	18	1	213
1955	4	5	1	170
1960	4	15	0	106
1965	5	5	1	100
1970	6	12	5	65
1975	6	10	1	50
1980	4	13	4	38
1985	3	13	1	22
1990	3	8	0	23
1995	0	6	2	27
2000	3	5	0	18
2005	0	6	1	16

The members who came and who left between 1890 and 1959

	From Merseyside	From Wales		
1890-1899	193	184	354	202
1900-1909	336	258	494	377
1910-1919	125	201	371	296
1920-1929	167	162	294	236
1930-1939	132	131	291	234
1940-1949	131	158	62	241
1950-1959	65	63	119	151
TOTAL	**1149**	**1157**	**1985**	**1713**
SUNDAY SCHOOLS				

WEBSTER ROAD RAMILIES ROAD

Year	Adults	Children	Total	Adults	Children		Total
TOTAL							
1904	193	104	297	85	32	118	414
1909	210	119	329	171	51	222	551
1914	132	92	224	138	79	217	441
1919	114	76	190	157	65	222	412
1924	95	53	148	156	75	231	379
1919	114	76	190	157	65	222	412
1924	95	53	148	156	75	231	379

Appendix J

SUBSCRIPTIONS FOR THE LIMITED EDITION OF THIS VOLUME

1. David Armstrong, Wavertree, Liverpool
2. Mr and Mrs J. O. Clitherow, Kensington, Liverpool
3. Mike Chitty, Gateacre, Liverpool
4. Martin Lloyd Chitty, Gateacre, Liverpool
5. Alun Hartley, Allerton, Liverpool
6. Mrs Eva James, Pwllheli, Gwynedd
7. Mrs Cathy Jones, Aigburth, Liverpool
8. Siôn Wyn Morris, Waterloo, Liverpool
9. Miss Nansi Pugh, Aigburth, Liverpool
10. Dr W. T. Rees Pryce, Rhiwbina, Cardiff
11. Dafydd Llywelyn Rees, Maida Vale, London
12. Hefin and Bethan Rees, Harpenden, St Albans
13. Tomos Llywelyn Rees, Harpenden, St Albans
14. Joshua Caradog Rees, Harpenden, St Albans
15. Dr Pat Williams, Calderstones, Liverpool
16 Dr Lowri Williams, Cardiff
17 Miss Carys Williams, Stratford-upon-Avon
18 Mr David Fletcher, Kingsley, Frodsham
19 Rev John Williams MBE, Prescot (in memory of his grandmother Angharad Williams, organist for many years at Penmaenmawr)
20 Modern Welsh Publications (through Dr D. Ben Rees 31 copies)
21 Reverend John G. Morris, Llanddaniel Fab, Anglesey.
22 Gareth James, Aintree, Liverpool.
23 Roderick Owen, Springwood, Liverpool. (2 volumes)
24 Humphrey Wyn Jones, Allerton, Liverpool.
25 Reverend B. Tudor Lloyd, Burry Green, Swansea.
26 Mrs Elizabeth Lloyd and Miss Hilda Lloyd, Rainhill
27 Ieuan Care, Allerton, Liverpool
28 Dr Mallt Care, Allerton, Liverpool
29 Aled Evans, Allerton, Liverpool
30 Wena Evans, Allerton, Liverpool
31 Ted Clement Evans, Liverpool

32   R. Ifor Griffith, Childwall, Liverpool

33   Lisa Hartley, Allerton, Liverpool

34   Sian Hartley, Allerton, Liverpool

35   Cardiff University

36   Dewi Roberts, Allerton, Liverpool

37   Mair Roberts, Allerton, Liverpool

38   Gareth Roberts, Allerton, Liverpool

39   Aimee Johnson, Tuebrook, Liverpool

40   Ben Andrew Thompson, Woolton, Liverpool

41   Lucy Ann Thompson, Woolton, Liverpool

42   Mair Thompson, Woolton, Liverpool

43   Hannah Thompson, Woolton, Liverpool

44   A. W. Owen, Woolton, Liverpool

45   E. Goronwy Owen, Calderstones, Liverpool

46   H. J. Owen, Liverpool

47   R. A. Owen, Liverpool

48   Nan Hughes Parry, Woolton, Liverpool

49   Thomas Samuel See, Woolton, Liverpool

50   Olivia Haf See, Woolton, Liverpool

51   Beryl and Dr John G. Wiliams Allerton, Liverpool

52   Sara Fflur Williams, Allerton, Liverpool

53   Douglas A. S. Higginson, Oldbury, Western Australia (2 volumes)

54   Reverend Dr D. Ben Rees, Liverpool and Meinwen Rees. (2 volumes)

55   Derek Sadler, Liverpool

56   J. J. Moonan on behalf of the Wavertree Society

57   Llyfrgell Genedlaethol Cymru, Aberystwyth

58   Miss Mair Powell, West Derby, Liverpool (2 volumes)

59   Miss Megan Lewis, Broadgreen, Liverpool

60   Mrs Rhiannon Liddell, Wavertree, Loverpool

61   Mrs Olwen Jones, Allerton, Liverpool

62   Mr Trefor Green, Neston, Wirral

63   Mrs Edna Jones, Acton, Wrexham

64   Miss Ann Roberts, Childwall, Liverpool (2 volumes)

65   Mrs Elizabeth Winifred Morris, Llain yr Haf, Llanddaniel fab, Anglesey
      late of 45 Borrowdale Road,Liverpool

Total 100 copies of this limited hardback edition. A softback edition has been prepared for the booksellers.

Appendix K

SELECT BIBLIOGRAPHY IN ENGLISH, WHICH HAS RELEVANCE TO THE VOLUME

Ramsay Muir, *A History of Liverpool* (Wakefield, 1950).

Colin C. Pooley, 'The Residential segregations of migrant communities in mid-Victorian Liverpool', in *Transactions of the Institute of British Geographers*, II. (1977), 367-382.

Nansi Pugh, *The Liverpool Welsh Choral Union: The First 100 Years* (Birkenhead, 2007).

D. Ben Rees (Editor), *The Liverpool Welsh and their Religion* by R. Merfyn Jones and D. Ben Rees (Liverpool and Llanddewibrefi, 1984).

D. Ben Rees, *The Life and Work of Owen Thomas 1812-1891: A Welsh Preacher in Liverpool* (Lewiston, 1991).

D. Ben Rees, *The Welsh of Merseyside, Volume 1* (Liverpool and Llanddewibrefi, 1997).

D.Ben Rees, *The Welsh of Merseyside in the Twentieth Century, Volume 2* (Liverpool, 2001).

D. Ben Rees, 'Welsh Calvinistic Methodists and Independents in Toxteth Park, Liverpool' in *The Journal of Welsh Religious History*, Volume 3: (2003) 78-93.

D. Ben Rees (Editor), *The Call and Contribution of Dr. Robert Arthur Hughes, OBE, FRCS, 1910-1996 and some of his predecessors in North-East India* (Liverpool, 2004).

D. Ben Rees, *Alpha and Omega: Welsh Presbyterian Witness in Laird Street, Birkenhead, 1906-2006* (Liverpool, 2006).

Appendix L

ROLL OF HONOUR OF MEMBERS OF WEBSTER ROAD CHURCH, LIVERPOOL WHO SERVED IN THE FIRST WORLD WAR

BATEMAN, NORMAN, 14 Underley Street, 19th (Service) Batt, KLR
Killed in France 1916

BENNETT, BENJAMIN J., 68 Tunstall Street,
Compounder, Royal Army Medical Corps

BENYON, OSWALD E., 2 Mossley Avenue, 19th (Service) Batt, KLR
Killed in France 1916

BEVAN, RICHARD R., 21 Rose Brae, Mossley Hill,
QM Sergt, 293 Army Field Artillery Brigade

DAVEY, HERBERT P., 13 Earlsfield Road

DAVIES, JOHN IORWERTH, 32 Crawford Avenue,
19th (Service) Batt, KLR

DAVIES, HENRY, 44 Dovedale Road,
Royal Engineers

DAVIES, ROBERT, 22 Olivedale Road,
Royal Engineers

DAVIES, THOMAS C., 44 Dovedale Road,
Camp, Southport

DAVIES, W. PHILIP, 8 Calton Avenue,
Corporal, Army Pay Corps

DAVIES, JOHN L., 44 Dovedale Road,
22nd Batt, Royal Welsh Fusiliers
Killed in France, July 20, 1916

EDWARDS, EDWARD HUGHES, 26 Galloway Street,
54th Training Reserve Battalion

ELLIS, JOHN, 8 Murdoch Street

EVANS, GEORGE, 31 Westdale Road,
7th Indian Division, RFA

EVANS, EDWIN, 25 Deepfield Road,
Royal Engineers

EVANS, D. GARMON, 32 Cantsfield Street,
Steward, Royal Navy

EVANS, JOHN, 9 Bridge Road, Mossley Hill

GRIFFITHS, DAVID JOHN, 29 Empress Road,
Royal Engineers

GRIFFITHS, RICHARD T, 16 Garmoyle Road,
Royal Engineers

GRIFFITHS, W. M. MADOC, 16 Garmoyle Road,
Lance-Corporal, 10th LS

GRIFFITHS, HUGH, 5 Jesmond Street, 5th KLR

GRIFFITHS, ALBERT E., 22 Deepfield Road,
HMS 'Osiris II'

HASLAM, JOHN EDWIN, 19 Ridley Road, Kensington,
Corporal, Army Service Corps

HASLAM, VERNEY H., 19 Ridley Road, Kensington,
HMS 'Talbot'

HUGHES, JOHN THOMAS, 8 Brereton Avenue,
5th KLR

HUGHES, JOSEPH MEREDITH, 8 Brereton Avenue,
5th KLR

HUGHES, JAMES, 8 Brereton Avenue,
Royal Field Artillery

HUGHES, HERBERT LLEW, 8 Brereton Avenue,
Royal Air Force

HUGHES, THOMAS JOHN, 'Moneifion', Green Lane,
British Red Cross Society, Italy

HUGHES, LLEWELYN, 8 Murdock Street,
Marconi Operator
Drowned in the Mediterranean, July 1917

HUGHES, FRED, 94 Brookdale Road
11th Batt, RWF

HUGHES, DANIEL P., 28 Weardale Road,
25th KLR

HUGHES JOSEPH, 5 Patterale Road,
16th Batt, RWF

HUGHES, DAVID, 85 Barndale Road,
Royal Flying Corps

HUGHES, WILLIAM HENRY, 94 Brookdale Road
6th KLR
Killed in France, August 30, 1916

HUGHES, TREVOR, 300 Up Parliament Street,
10th Scottish Reserve, KLR

HUGHES, JOHN, 5 Patterdale Road
530th Battery, RGA

HUGHES, JOHN EMLYN, 41 Hallville Road,
  4th RWF
JENKINS, J. LLEWELYN, 67 Cedar Grove,
  Royal Welsh Fusiliers
JENKINS, E. J., 67 Cedar Grove,
  Royal Engineers
JONES, R. ARTHUR, 23 Harrowby Road, Seaforth,
  Captain, Military Hospital, Seaforth
JONES, THOMAS ARTHUR, 26 Brookdale Road,
  Sergeant, Machine Gun Corps
JOHNES, EVAN, 6 Queensdale Road,
  Lance Corporal, 19th (Service) Batt, KLR
JONES, ROBERT IVOR, 117 Kingsley Road,
  Lient, 1st Manchester Garrison Batt
JONES, JOHN DAVID, Bective St, Royal Welsh Fusiliers
  Killed in the battle of the Mons, September 1914
JONES, GWILYM EMRYS, Jesmond Street,
  Canadian Expeditionary Force
JONES, ERNEST, 22 Karslake Road
  Major, Royal Field Artillery
JONES, COLLIESTER LLOYD, 34 Cranborne Road,
  Royal Engineers
JONES, OWEN, 67 Cedar Grove,
  RAR Engineers
  Killed in France
JONES, RICHARD, 30 Stanmore Road,
  6th Royal Welsh Fusiliers
JONES, JOHN R., 'Cintra', Calderstones Road,
  French Motor Transport
JONES, WILLIAM H., 7 Ensworth Road
  Royal Engineers
JONES, WILLIAM H., 10 Wyndcote Road,
  Liverpoot Scottish
JONES, ROWLAND, 'Hiraethog', Garth Drive,
  Royal Welsh Fusiliers
JONES, GLYN, 'Hiraethog', Garth Drive,
  51st (Grad) Batt KLR
JONES, WILLIAM OWEN, 4 Bird Street,
  10th Scottish Reserve, KLR
JONES, RICHARD JAMES, Cecil Street,
  7th KLR

JONES, RICHARD, 34 Cranborne Road
4th Reserve Regiment, Dragoons

JONES, ROBERT J., 'Eirianfa', Calderstones Road,
7th Battery, RFA

JONES, THOMAS R., 35 Mulliner Street,
4th RWF

JONES, OWEN W., 41 Britannia Avenue,
Machine Gun Corps

JONES, THOMAS G., 42 Lesseps Road

JONES, WILLIAM O., Vandyke Street,
6th Lancashire Fusiliers

MORRIS, STANLEY, 49 Arundel Avenue,
Lieut, 81st Heavy Artillery Group

OWEN, GLYN, 30 Stanmore Road,
Lance-Corporal, 9th KLR

OWEN, JOHN, 92 Blantyre Road,
Lance-Corporal, 5th KLR

OWEN, JOHN RICHARD, 8 Harringay Avenue,
4th Australian Infantry Brigade
Killed in the Galipoli Peninsula, 1915

OWEN, OWEN ROGER, 82 Selborne Street,
188th Machine Gun Corps

OWEN, WILLIAM, 41 Deepfield Road,
Royal Flying Corps

OWEN, WILLIAM, 5 Moss Grove,
Royal Engineers

OWEN, ROBERT JOHN, 22 Hollybank Road,
13th KLR

OWENS, EDWARD, 82 Greenleaf Street,
HMS 'Impregnable'

OWEN, DAVID CHARLES, 88 Ash Grove,
Lance-Corporal, Machine Gun Corps

OWEN, DAVID HUDSON, 8 Harringay Avenue,
53rd Welsh Regiment

OWEN, RICHARD AEL, 26 Cranborne Road,
10th Liverpool Scottish

PARRY, WILLIAM, 46 Tiverton Street,
Lance-Corporal, Royal Engineers

PARRY, HUGH, 178 Alderson Road,
17th (Service) Batt KLR
Killed in France, February 1916

PARRY, ALBERT JOHN, 4 Webb Street,
Royal Engineers

PIERCE, THOMAS J., 262 Upper Parliament Street,
53rd Cheshire Regiment

PRITCHARD, OWEN, 72 Woodcroft Road,
5th KLR

PRITCHARD, WILLIAM, Ingleton Road,
Chief Officer, HMT, 'Calcutta'

PRITCHARD, GEORGE RICHARD, 97 Penny Lane

REES, LESLIE J., 10 Claremont Road,
6th KLR

ROBERTS, SAMUEL, 13 Tiverton Street,
Royal Army Medical Corps

ROBERTS, DAVID G., 12 Stalbridge Avenue,
Lieut – 5th SWB

ROBERTS, JOHN THOMAS, 2 Fallowfield Road,
17th KLR

ROBERTS, HUGH PUGH, 5 Tanat Drive,
Royal Navy Reserve

ROBERTS, ROBERT EDWARD, 4 Edlington Street,
4th Loyal North Lancs

ROBERTS, EDWARD E., 5 Harvey Street,
9th (Service) Batt, KLR

ROBERTS, ROBERT DAVID, 125 Avondale Road,
4th KLR

ROBERTS, DANIEL, 11 Karslake Road,
Lieut, Royal Navy

ROBERTS, EDWARD, 28 Noel Street,
13th KLR

ROBERTS, WILLIAM O. 4 Edington Street,
53rd Batt, KLR

ROOSE, JOHN, 35 Mulliner Street,
5th KLR

ROGERS, DANIEL G., 54 Lichfield Road,
Royal Engineers

THOMAS, JOHN, 1 Picton Grove,
RFA

WILLIAMS, W. PENRY, 'Moneivion', Green Lane,
Lieut 1st RWF

WILLIAMS, JOHN, 54 Eversley Street,
Lance Corporal 17th Batt, RWF

WILLIAMS, JOSEPH, 54 Eversley Street,
  17th Batt RWF
WILLIAMS, W. O., 28 Weardale Road,
  5th DAC
WILLIAMS, DAVID, 48 Crawford Avenue,
  Royal Field Artillery
WILLIAMS, JOHN R., 35 Oakdale Road,
  9th (Reserve) Batt, London Reg
WILLIAMS, GWILYM O., 12 Newborough Avenue,
  3rd Welsh Batt
WILLIAMS, ROBERT, 38 Crawford Avenue,
  7th Black Watch
WILLIAMS, THOMAS LLOYD, 5 Southdale Road,
  Cheshire Regt
WILLIAMS, LESLIE H., 19 Bromley Avenue,
  Royal Navy

Ministering to the wounded –

JONES, Mrs R. ARTHUR, 23 Harrowby Road, Seaforth
  Red Cross Nurse
ROBERTS, Miss GWLADYS, 16 Mayville Road,
  Voluntary Aid Detachment

Index

Beauclair Drive 89

Beaufort Street 242

Beckenham Avenue 63, 77, 83, 93

Bective Street 44

Beddgelert 50, 110

Bedford Street, Liverpool 10, 12, 13, 240

Belhaven Road 62

Belvidere Road 59, 240, 241

Benllech 120

Berbice Road 112, 157, 173

Berrington Road 63, 64, 109, 112, 158, 249

Bethel 3, 4, 6, 7, 9, 41, 92, 141, 143, 145, 146, 150, 151, 152, 153, 154, 155, 156, 159, 160, 163, 165, 167, 168, 169, 170, 171, 172, 173, 174, 175, 176, 177, 181, 182, 183, 184, 186, 187, 189, 190, 191, 192, 193, 194, 195, 196, 198, 199, 200, 201, 202, 203, 206, 207, 208, 210, 212, 213, 215, 216, 218, 219, 220, 223, 226, 227, 228, 229, 230, 232, 233, 234, 235, 239, 240, 241, 245, 246, 247, 248, 249, 250, 252, 253, 284

Beverley Road 92

Bird Street 78, 242, 250, 261

Birkenhead 1906-2006 101

Birth of the *Angor* (Merseyside Community Newspaper) 153

Bishopsgate Street 242

Blaenau Ffestiniog 45, 54, 56, 88, 99, 161, 178, 216, 230, 247

Blenheim Road 57

Bont 91, 113, 135, 153, 154, 155

Bontddu 222

Bootle 9, 19, 23, 24, 60, 85, 89, 91, 105, 106, 110, 116, 139, 148, 189, 195, 213, 226, 240, 241, 242

Bouch, Gwenno 88, 178

Bowen, Mair 174

Bower Road 141

Boyd, Elin 148

Boyle, Mary 184, 185

Bradley, Warren 229

Bray, Billy 18

Breckfield Road North 242

Brendon Road 133

Briardale Road 112

Bristol Road 63, 88, 112, 132

Brodie Avenue 78

Brookdale Road 77, 260, 261

Brothen Jones, W. 108

Brownlow Hill, Liverpool 10, 11

Brynsiencyn (Anglesey) 20, 74

Brython (Weekly paper for the Welsh of Merseyside 1906 – 1939) 91

Buckley (Flintshire) 101

Bundoran Road 173

Bunyan, John 128

Burlington Street 10, 240, 242

C

Calderstones 18

Calderstones Road 39, 50, 77, 85, 103, 165, 181, 183, 186, 249, 261

Caldwell, Idaho 179

Caldwell Road 230

Calvinism 34, 40, 231, 234

Calvinistic Methodism 9
  Activities 40, 57, 60
  Values of the Denomination 23

Calvin, John 163, 234

Cameo Cinema, Webster Road, Liverpool 20

Canada 56, 110, 139

Caneuon Ffydd (The songs of faith) 219

Canterbury Street 242

Cantsfield Street 62, 259

K

L

MORE VALUABLE PICTURES

Young people from Bethel during their Annual weekend at the Bala Youth Centre of the Connexion.

William Owen (Mossley Hill) who came to Bethel at the closure of the Wavertree Welsh Baptist Chapel.

Muriel Edwards of Fallowfield Road, Wavertree.

John and Mair Thompson and Philip and Eirian See with their children after a morning service at Bethel.

An Ecumenical Good Friday procession from Bethel to All Hallows Church.

An Eisteddfodic Chair created by H. John Jones, Bethel for Llangwm Eisteddfod.

Reverend Eleri Edwards, Mrs Nancy Hughes and Reverend D. Andrew Jones of Cardiff at the Memorial Lecture.

Members of Bethel Sunday School after a family service in the sanctuary.

The grave of the builder and elder at Bethel J. W. Jones and his kith and kin at Allerton Cemetery.

Nine members of the Bethel Youth Circle as well as Denis Hartley, Idris and Mair Roberts, Alan and M. Anwyl Williams on a walking tour of Snowdonia.

Rhys Williams of Bethel in Iceland on a mission to raise funds for the British Lung Foundation.

(From left to right) Dr D. B. Rees, Mrs Rhiannon Liddell, the late T. Gwynn Jones, Llanfairfechan(well-known conductor and composer), Mrs Margaret Anwyl Williams and W. Meirion Evans at a Bethel Singing Festival.

Members of the Angor (Community Welsh language newspaper for Merseyside and Manchester Welsh). Executive committee in the 1990s: Back row (left to right), H. Wyn Jones, William Evans (Anfield), E. Goronwy Owen, Ken Williams, Hywel Jones, the late Walter Rees Jones (Birkenhead), Ron Gilford (Cheadle). Front row (left to right), Marian Prys Davies, Anne Jones, Dr D. Ben Rees, Mair Jones and Lois Murphy.

Miss Marian Prys Davies being presented with a gift on leaving Liverpool for Colwyn Bay.

Dr D. Ben Rees, Professor Mari Lloyd-Williams of the University of Liverpool and R. Ifor Griffith at the 2008 Gymanfa Ganu (Singing Festival) on Sunday, 29 June 2008 at Bethel.